THE FALL
of the
ROMAN
EMPIRE

THE FALL
of the
ROMAN
EMPIRE

Michael Grant

COLLIER BOOKS
Macmillan Publishing Company
New York

Maxwell Macmillan International
New York   Oxford   Singapore   Sydney

Collier Books
Macmillan Publishing Company
866 Third Avenue, New York, NY 10022

Collier Macmillan Canada, Inc.
1200 Eglinton Avenue East, Suite 200
Don Mills, Ontario M3C 3N1

Library of Congress Cataloging-in-Publication Data
Grant, Michael, 1914–
The fall of the Roman Empire/Michael Grant.—
1st Collier Books ed.
p. cm.
ISBN 0-02-028560-4
1. Rome—History—Empire, 30 B.C.–476 A.D.
2. Byzantine Empire History—To 527. I. Title.
DG311.G75   1990
937′.09—dc20   90-34330   CIP

Macmillan books are available at special discounts for bulk
purchases for sales promotions, premiums, fund-raising, or
educational use. For details, contact:

Special Sales Director
Macmillan Publishing Company
866 Third Avenue
New York, N.Y. 10022

First Collier Books Edition 1990

10   9   8   7   6

Printed in the United States of America

And if a kingdom be divided against itself,
that kingdom cannot stand.
Gospel according to St Mark 3:24

Then join hand in hand, brave Americans
all: by uniting we stand, by dividing we fall.
*John Dickinson, 'The Liberty Song', Boston
Gazette, July 1768*

Yes, we must, indeed, all hang together, or
most assuredly we shall all hang separately.
*Benjamin Franklin at the American Declara-
tion of Independence, 1776*

We cannot any longer afford the luxury of
tearing ourselves apart.
British politicians, 1973–5

Contents

Contents

List of Maps

Introduction

The fall of the Western Roman Empire was one of the most significant transformations (a favourite word for the whole process, especially in Germany) throughout the whole of human history. A hundred years before it happened, Rome was an immense power, defended by an immense army. A hundred years later, power and army had vanished. There was no longer any Western Empire at all. Its territory was occupied by a group of German kingdoms.

Hundreds of reasons have been suggested for the collapse of the Roman West. Some indication of their variety can be obtained from reading Edward Gibbon's superb and never truly superseded *History of the Decline and Fall of the Roman Empire* (1776–88). He lists at least two dozen supposed causes of that decline and fall – military, political, economical and psychological. Many of these 'causes' will be referred to in the pages that follow. But the historian himself made no attempt to marshal them one against another, or choose between them. That is rather disconcerting for the reader who is searching for quick answers. But it also shows a good deal of prudence. For an enormous, complex institution like the Roman Empire could not have been obliterated by any single, simple cause.

It was brought down by two kinds of destruction: invasions from outside, and weaknesses that arose within. The invasions are easy to identify, and they will be described in the preliminary section of the present volume. However, they were not sufficiently formidable in themselves to have caused the Empire to perish.

It perished because of certain internal flaws which prevented resolute resistance to the invaders: and the greater part of this book will be devoted to discovering those flaws.

I have identified thirteen defects which, in my view, combined to reduce the Roman Empire to final paralysis. They display a unifying thread: the thread of *disunity*. Each defect consists of a specific disunity which split the Empire wide apart, and thereby damaged the capacity of the Romans to meet external aggressions. Heaven forbid that we ourselves should have a monolithic society without any internal disunities at all, or any differences of character or opinion. But there can arrive a time when such differences become so irreconcilably violent that the entire structure of society is imperilled. That is what happened among the ancient Romans. And that is why Rome fell.

This theme has always attracted keen interest, largely because of the guidances and warnings it is supposed to offer to later generations, and this relevance has never seemed more visible than today. Britain thinks of its own vanished empire. The United States of America think of their current leadership, and of how it might be in danger of coming to an end. The Soviet Union seems to be showing at this very moment how smaller peoples break away from empires. France is the country where, in ancient times, this first happened. Germany spans the east-west border, and is very conscious of its ancient role as the destroyer of the Western Roman Empire. Italy is the country where that empire ruled and fell. And so on. I have not, in this revised edition, attempted to flag or discuss every echo, every similarity. But one or another of them, in various parts of the world, readily leaps to the eye.

I want to thank Mr Walter Annenberg, who invited me to write the original version of this book when he was the United States Ambassador in London, for his constant help and encouragement. I am also deeply grateful to the late Mr David H. Appel for his unfailingly constructive and sympathetic aid. I wish to express my profound appreciation to Mr Christopher Falkus for a great deal of stimulating, invaluable assistance. I owe acknowledgments to Mrs Enid Gordon, Mr Peter Quennell, and Miss Susan Reynolds for help that they have given, to the Annenberg School Press for preparing the first edition, and to Miss Jocelyn Burton who has, with constructive suggestions, produced this second, revised edition. And my wife's support has been indispensable.

MICHAEL GRANT Gattaiola 1990

Acknowledgments

I would like to acknowledge the quotation of passages from ancient authors translated by W. B. Anderson, P. Brown, J. B. Bury, O. A. W. Dilke, C. D. Gordon, A. Hawkins, H. Isbell, D. Magie, F. X. Murphy, A. F. Norman, C. Pharr, R. S. Pine-Coffin, J. C. Rolfe, E. M. Sanford, E. A. Thompson, H. G. E. White, F. A. Wright and T. A. Sinclair.

HISTORICAL SURVEY
OF THE ROMAN EMPIRE

The Roman Empire was of enormous dimensions, extending from the Atlantic to the River Euphrates, and from Britain to the Sahara desert. It was the greatest political achievement of ancient times, and one of the very greatest of all ages. Well might one of its own writers, Pliny the elder, speak of the 'immense majesty of the Roman peace'.

The creation of this mighty organism was a slow and gradual process. In the dim, distant days of the semi-legendary past, Rome had been a small Italian city-state under the rule of kings. Then, perhaps at about the turn of the sixth century BC, the kings were overthrown and a Republic came into being. Its sovereign body was an Assembly of Roman citizens, but the real power was concentrated in the hands of a few noble families. These formed the nucleus of the Senate, which, although technically only an advisory body, in fact directed the government for generation after generation.

During the next two hundred years Roman rule was gradually built up over one region after another in Italy itself. Then, in the third century BC, Rome clashed with the sea-power of north-African Carthage and gained control of the western Mediterranean. Thereafter, up to the last years before the Christian era, this Empire was extended to the eastern Mediterranean basin as well. Under the strain of governing these vast and varied territories, the machinery of the Republic broke down, and in the

1

time of Julius Caesar and then Augustus (31 BC–AD 14), founder of the long line of Roman Emperors, the Senate was reduced to a subservient role from which it never emerged again. Its members, the leading men of the state next to the ruler himself, retained an importance that could not be ignored. But the Emperors, however much this was concealed beneath Augustus' constitutional façade, depended for their survival on the army.

That moment when the Republic ceased and the Empire or Principate began also witnessed the breakthrough of Imperial rule to the central and northern portions of the European Continent. Caesar established his northern frontier on the Rhine, and Augustus prolonged this boundary for the whole length of the Danube. On the other side of these barriers, all the way from the Netherlands to Aquincum (Budapest), the peoples who gazed across the rivers at the Roman defences were Germans. As time went on, forcible encounters between Germans and Romans became more and more frequent.

The chief gods worshipped by the German tribes were gods of war. But the tribesmen were also familiar with agriculture and stock-breeding, and what they saw and learned of Rome's settled and prosperous provinces excited their desire for a share of these benefits. Furthermore, they themselves were under pressure from remoter peoples living further north and east. When, therefore, in the second century AD, the Germans near the frontiers began to co-ordinate their activities in larger confederations and coalitions, the Empire – which was also in confrontation with the Parthian kingdom along its eastern borders – was in trouble.

The problem first became grave in the reign of Marcus Aurelius (161–80), who had to face a collusive general onslaught from the north which plunged the Empire into its first major crisis for many years. Septimius Severus (193–211) noted the lesson and increased the size of Rome's army. He also remunerated it better. This meant, in the years ahead, fiercer taxation for the civilian population whose comparatively easy-going, comfortable lives had to be drastically modified in order to pay the 400,000 soldiers of the army.

Nevertheless, for the greater part of the third century AD the Imperial frontiers were broken by repeated and simultaneous hostile incursions, from Germans and others in the north and from Persians (the much more formidable successors of the Parthians) in the east. It seemed as if the Roman world, which was also split into fragments by internal revolts, could not possibly survive. Yet, in one of the most striking reversals in world history, Rome's foes were hurled back by a series of formidable military Emperors.

However, the price the inhabitants of the Empire had to pay was enormous. In order to raise the gigantic contributions in cash and kind that were needed to maintain an army capable of performing such feats, tax requirements continued to rise to unprecedented levels. First Diocletian (284–305), and then Constantine the Great (306–37), radically overhauled and regimented the entire administrative system in order that the necessary payments should be extorted.

Constantine, in common with other Emperors of the time, made extensive use of German soldiers and officers in his own army – at first Franks and Alamanni, later Visigoths and Ostrogoths (the two branches of the Gothic race) and Vandals and Burgundians. Moreover, like some of his predecessors but on a larger scale, he allowed German immigrants to settle under Roman supervision within the frontiers. But the military threat from German tribesmen who were still outside, as well as from the Persians at the other extremity of the border, persisted with undiminished force.

Constantine drew the conclusion that Rome was no longer a suitable capital. Living there, it would be too hard for him to maintain simultaneous control over the two vital frontiers, the Rhine and Danube in the north and the Euphrates in the east. Earlier rulers, already feeling the same, had from time to time established their residences at places more accessible to the defence zones. Mediolanum (Milan) had been a favourite choice, and Constantine himself had dwelt in a number of other centres: Treveri (Trier) in western Germany, Arelate (Arles) in southern France, Ticinum (Pavia) in north Italy, Sirmium (Sremska Mitrovica) on the Illyrian (Yugoslavian) river Savus (Save), and Serdica (Sofia) in Moesia (Bulgaria). But he now decided that the ideal site for simultaneous supervision of the Danube and Euphrates frontiers alike was Byzantium on the Bosphorus; and there he founded his new capital, Constantinople, on the site where Istanbul is today.

Constantine also put into effect a second major revolution by officially converting the Empire from paganism to Christianity – raising a relatively small and uninfluential Christian community to a dominant position in the state. Then he died, and left the Empire divided amongst his three sons, of whom Constantius II (337–61) proved the survivor. In his reign troubles on both the northern and the eastern frontiers revived sharply. Near the Rhine, his cousin Julian won an important victory over the Germans at Argentorate (Strasbourg) in 356; five years later, he came to the throne. Known as 'the Apostate', Julian reverted to official paganism. But in 363, during a Persian campaign, he lost his life, and under his successor, Jovian, the Empire returned to Christianity. However, he died in the following year.

DECLINE AND FALL

The hundred and twelve years beginning from that date, and concluding with the termination of the Western Empire, comprise the period with which this book will be mainly concerned.

The date when the Empire first began to decline and fall has long been disputed. A school of Marxist historians, with the support of Arnold Toynbee, declared that the crisis of classical civilization leading to Rome's collapse started as far back as 431 BC, when the city states of Greece were locked in hostility with one another in the Peloponnesian War – four centuries before the Roman Emperors, whose downfall this event was alleged to foreshadow, even began.

Edward Gibbon had taken a very different view, refusing to see too much wrong with the Empire at a date a full six hundred years later:

> . . . If a man were called to fix the period in the history of the world during which the condition of the human race was most happy and prosperous, he would, without hesitation, name that which elapsed from the death of Domitian to the accession of Commodus [AD 96–180].

Subsequent historians have queried his assertion, pointing out that the slave population, for example, could scarcely be described as 'happy and prosperous', and that many of the things that went manifestly wrong later on were already quietly going wrong behind the scenes as early as Gibbon's supposed golden age. Yet, if we limit the 'human race' to the population of the Empire, and consider how its majority was faring, he was probably not too wide of the mark.

Subsequently, in the third century AD, under the joint pressures of external threats and internal rebellions, the Empire began to fall apart. Yet this was by no means the end, since it was only a good deal later still, as late as the turn of the fifth century AD, that the final downfall really began.

A start, therefore, with the present book will be made in the reign of Valentinian I (364–75), when this downward process was about to start: though in his day Rome still seemed to be at the height of its power.

VALENTINIAN I

In 364 the army acclaimed Valentinian I as Emperor, and he was the last really impressive Emperor Rome ever had. He came from Cibalae (Vinkovci) in Pannonia (Yugoslavia). He was tall and vigorous – a champion wrestler – with fair hair and bluish-grey eyes, regular features, a long face and a large straight nose. Although his enemies sneered at his barbarous origins, he was quite thoroughly educated, and a clever painter and sculptor.

His character was disconcerting: cruel, jealous, evil-tempered and panicky. Nor was he a reliable judge of the civilians he chose to govern the Empire on his behalf. Yet Valentinian was a superb soldier and a conscientious worker, endowed with ferocious energy. He felt a strong duty to the state, and, much more unusual, a strong duty to the poor, an emotion which he combined with a considerable distaste for the Roman upper class. More unusual still, in the age in which he lived, he believed in tolerating differences of religious opinion. For all his faults he would have been an outstanding man in any epoch, and it is only because of the misleading tradition which dismisses the personalities of the later Empire that most people have never heard of him.

Valentinian decided that the needs of national defence required there should not be one single Emperor only, but two. In consequence, he gave his brother Valens the East, and took the West for himself. The Western Empire that he inherited was immense, with a large army to defend it, and after his eleven-year reign he left it stronger than ever.

But this great strength had only been maintained by his own unremitting vigilance and energy. For as soon as he came to the throne, he was plunged immediately into a variety of emergencies. In the words of Ammianus, who wrote a magnificent Latin history of the later Roman Empire, 'at this time, as if trumpets were sounding the war-note throughout the whole Roman world, the most savage peoples raised themselves and poured across the nearest frontiers'. Yet Valentinian and his able generals were a match for them.

The first thing that had happened was that Germans broke across the Rhine, capturing the fortress of Mainz. But they were defeated by the Romans three times, and then the Emperor himself, moving his headquarters from Lutetia (Paris) to the frontier city of Treveri (Trier), marched up the valley of the River Neckar and won a ferocious victory in the Black Forest. He remained in Germany for seven years, constructing an elaborate system of fortifications on the Rhine, building a strongpoint at Basilia (Basel), and moving to Ambiani (formerly Samarobriva, now Amiens) in order to direct operations in Britain, which was overrun by Saxons from across the sea and Picts and Scots from the north.

Valentinian also deliberately stirred up dissensions among the Germans themselves by calling to his aid the Burgundians, hereditary foes of their compatriots the Alamanni who were the enemies of Rome. Meanwhile, many Germans continued to be admitted as settlers within the boundaries of the Empire.

In 374 a more easterly section of the northern border was breached when other Germans, as well as members of the great group of Sarmatian peoples of mainly Iranian stock, erupted across the middle and upper Danube into what are now Hungary and Austria. In the following year Valentinian established his residence at Sirmium, and restored the fortresses on the Danube, which he crossed to ravage the German territory on the other side. Later in the same year the insolent attitude of German envoys who came to see him in Hungary so infuriated him that he broke a blood-vessel and died.

His son Gratian, a somewhat insignificant sixteen-year-old, became his successor, but in his absence on a different part of the frontier the powerful Roman army of the Danube attempted to set up one if its own generals as Western Emperor in his place. To prevent this, German staff officers hastily summoned Valentinian's widow Justina and her four-year-old son, who was proclaimed Emperor as Valentinian II at Aquincum (Budapest). Neither Gratian nor Valens had been consulted. But they accepted the child as joint ruler, and assigned him half of the Western Empire, comprising Italy, north Africa, and most of the Balkans.

The Eastern Empire now suffered a terrible setback, which profoundly affected East and West alike. This was the battle of Adrianople (Hadrianopolis, now Edirne in European Turkey) which had been fought against the Visigoths.

Descriptions of the various, differing Germanic peoples can be found in E. A. Thompson, *Romans and Barbarians: The Decline of the Western Empire* (1982) and J. D. Randers-Pehrson, *Barbarians and Romans: The Birth Struggle of Europe, AD 400–700* (1983). There were two great German states in eastern Europe, the Ostrogoths ('bright Goths') in the Ukraine, and the Visigoths ('wise Goths') centred upon what is now Rumania. But the formidable cavalry of the Huns, a non-German people, had broken into these regions in about 370, destroying the Ostrogothic kingdom and driving 200,000 Visigoths before them across the Danube into the Eastern Roman Empire, where the representatives of Valens allowed them to settle. However, these Visigoths very soon complained, with a good deal of justice, that they were being oppressed and exploited by the Eastern Romans, against whom they consequently rebelled. Led by their chieftain Fritigern, they devastated the Balkans, while at the same time further German tribesmen burst across the Danube in their wake. The Eastern Emperor Valens hurried from Asia to deal with the emergency, and moved to the attack at Adrianople on 9 August 378. But the Visigoths, after a successful flank attack by their horsemen, won an overwhelming victory. The Roman cavalry fled and the Roman infantry was utterly destroyed. Valens perished, but no one ever found his body.

'We might stop here,' declared the nineteenth-century historian Victor Duruy; 'the invasion has begun: Fritigern has come right up to the gates of Constantinople: in a few years Alaric will take Rome.'

THEODOSIUS I

The Western Emperor Gratian, having failed to reach Adrianople in time, moved back again into his own territories. But he also took steps to appoint a new colleague. His choice fell on the thirty-two-year-old Theodosius, the son of a land-owner of the same name from Cauca (North-west Spain) who had at one time (before falling into disgrace) been Valentinian I's most successful general. Proclaimed Emperor at Sirmium, his son ruled for ten years in the Eastern Empire, to which the West now ceded the greater part of the Balkans. Then he became the ruler of the Western Empire as well, so that the two Empires were momentarily reunited before his death.

Theodosius, with his fine aquiline nose and hair as fair as Valentinian's, presented an elegant appearance. But Theodosius was less uniformly energetic, oscillating between passionate activity and indolence, between the simple existence of a soldier and a resplendent court life, diversified by the reading of Roman history. He liked to dole out cruel sentences and penalties, but was quick to revoke them and grant pardons. Greedy and extravagant, he wanted to please, and tried to keep his promises, though he lacked the reputation of a reliable friend or chief.

Theodosius was called 'the Great', because of the uncompromising Christian orthodoxy which characterized his reign. Its other dominant feature was the acceptance of the Visigoths *en bloc* inside the Empire (382), to live under their own laws and ruler on the condition that they provided soldiers and agricultural workers for the Romans – the first of a number of German nations to be granted such allied, 'federate' status.

Theodosius soon lost his Western colleague Gratian, murdered at Lyon in southern France by the troops of a usurper, Magnus Maximus, in 383. Four years later, Maximus suddenly invaded Italy, but Theodosius I defeated him in two battles, and beheaded him at Aquileia. However, in about 389, he had to yield to severe external pressure, and ceded to the Germans the western extremity of the upper Danube line north of Lake Brigantinus (Constance), near the modern border between Germany and Switzerland.

When Theodosius returned to Constantinople, he left behind, as the real ruler of the West, his Master of Soldiers or commander-in-chief, Arbogast; and in 392 it was he, in all probability, who was responsible for the death of Valentinian II at Vienna (Vienne) in southern France. Arbogast then endeavoured to assert his independence from Theodosius. Being a German, he did not aspire to the purple himself, since men of his race, however great their practical power, were not acceptable as Emperors. Instead he set up a puppet, the rhetorician Eugenius, in whose name he assumed control of Italy and the Spanish provinces.

But Theodosius defeated Eugenius at the River Frigidus (Vipava) and put him to death. He was again ruler of the entire Empire, East and West alike. Yet he only reigned over it for five months, since in January 395 he died.

STILICHO AND ALARIC

Theodosius' elder son Arcadius, aged eighteen, now took the East, while his brother Honorius, aged eleven, became the titular lord of the West; and the reunification of the Empire came to a permanent end. They remained Emperors for thirteen and twenty-eight years respectively. Arcadius was undersized, somnolent, and slow of speech. Honorius was pious and gentle, but incompetent and mulishly obstinate. The eighteenth-century Scottish historian William Robertson decided that the hundred-and-fifty-year perid during which the condition of the human race had been most calamitous 'began with the joint accession of this uninspiring pair'.

Obviously the task of governing the two Empires devolved upon others. The effective ruler of the West, and the outstanding military and political personality of his time, was the enigmatic Stilicho, half-Roman and half-German, who had become Theodosius I's Master of Soldiers, and was married to his favourite niece Serena.

Stilicho was an army commander of exceptional talent and energy. Yet a career that might have brought a prolonged respite to Rome was darkened by two clouds. The first overshadowed his attitude to the Eastern Roman Empire, and the second his relations with the Visigothic 'federates' who were now settled within the Imperial borders.

Towards the Eastern authorities, Stilicho behaved in a cool and

9

finally hostile manner, because he wanted to prise the Balkan region out of their hands once again – and this alienation created a disastrous disunity between the two Empires. To the Visigoths on the other hand, and particularly their very able ruler Alaric I (395–410), Stilicho was not as hostile as he might usefully have been. On the death of Theodosius I, Alaric had broken into rebellion, complaining that subsidies promised to his people had not been paid. Later, Stilicho fought a number of battles against him – and could have broken him, but never did so, because he believed that his fellow-German might prove a useful counterweight against the Eastern Empire. Yet Alaric, although initially aiming at a peaceful settlement with the Imperial authorities, had as time went on become their enemy, and it was perilous to let him be.

The trouble began because Stilicho, left by Theodosius as Honorius' regent in the West, resented the fact that another man, Rufinus, was given the guardianship of the young Eastern Emperor Arcadius. When, therefore, Alaric rebelled and marched towards Constantinople, and Stilicho was requested by the East to stop him, he deliberately intervened with insufficient determination to produce decisive results – and then in 395 arranged for Rufinus, whom he suspected of sabotaging his plans, to be murdered.

Two years later, Stilicho appeared in the Balkans with another army, and surrounded the Visigoths in Greece. But once again, to the indignation of the Eastern government, he did not compel them to capitulate.

In 401 Alaric, in spite of Stilicho's forbearance towards him, turned against the Western Empire, and launched an invasion of Italy. Stilicho, whose daughter Maria was married to the Emperor Honorius, summoned troops from the Rhine and Britain, and defeated the invaders in north Italy in the successive years 402 and 403. Yet once again Alaric got away, and was allowed to leave the country.

But meanwhile a different group of German tribes, the Ostrogoths, had been eroding Imperial territories on the middle Danube; and a large part of the Roman population had fled from the Hungarian plain, thus depriving the Western Empire of one of its finest recruiting grounds. Now, in 405, these Ostrogoths and others, led by a certain Radagaisus, poured southwards into

Italy. Stilicho overwhelmed and massacred them at Faesulae (Fiesole) near Florence. He then made overtures to Alaric with a view to a coordinated military offensive – not against an external foe, but against the Eastern Empire. But his plans were interrupted by the gravest and most decisive of all the German invasions of the West.

This took place on the last day of 406, when a mixed host of various German tribesmen – Vandals, Suevi, Alans, Burgundians – crossed the ice of the frozen Rhine, and in the face of only a feeble resistance fanned out into the adjacent territories and into Gaul beyond, spreading devastation everywhere they went. Moguntiacum (Mainz), near their crossing point, was plundered, and so was Treveri (Trier), and many other cities in what are now Belgium and northern France suffered a similar fate.

On marched the raiders and infiltrators until some of them had crossed the entire country and reached the Pyrenees. On the way, only a very few towns, notably Tolosa (Toulouse), put up a fight. 'Innumerable and most ferocious people', declared St Jerome, 'now occupy the whole of Gaul. . . . All but a few cities have been ravaged either from without by the sword or from within by starvation.' This was rather too gloomy a picture, but in discerning that the breakthrough was a landmark, Jerome was perfectly right.

. . . The memorable passage across the Rhine [observed Gibbon with hindsight] may be considered as the fall of the Roman Empire in the countries beyond the Alps; and the barriers, which had so long separated the savage and the civilized nations of the earth, were from that fatal moment levelled with the ground.

Stilicho did nothing effective to help, because he was so preoccupied with his plans for invading the East. But meanwhile the shock-waves of these German onslaughts stimulated several attempted usurpations of the Western throne by ambitious Roman generals. One of these usurpers, Constantine III, was declared Emperor by the troops in Britain, whereupon he crossed the English Channel, leaving the country wide open to subsequent Saxon incursions, against which the Britons were told to organize their own defences as best they could. Then, fighting the Germans in Gaul and extorting temporary recognition from the Imperial government, Constantine moved on into Spain; but he could not prevent many of the German invaders from following him, and reaching that country in their turn.

Meanwhile Alaric had demanded four thousand pounds of gold from the Roman authorities, and Stilicho compelled a highly reluctant Senate to give him what he asked. However, Stilicho's influence was on the wane, and soon afterwards he found himself accused of conspiring with Alaric to place his own son on the Imperial throne. In consequence, a mutiny against Stilicho was fomented among the garrison at Ticinum (Pavia), which then proceeded to massacre his supporters, including many of the highest military and civil officials. He himself went to Ravenna, which was now the capital of the West, and there, after refusing to allow his German bodyguard to come to his protection, he surrendered to the Emperor Honorius and was executed. An Imperial edict pronounced him a brigand who had worked to enrich and incite the barbarian nations. For half a century to come, no German was able to assume the position of the Western commander-in-chief again.

In the wave of anti-German feeling that accompanied Stilicho's death, the Roman troops massacred the wives and children of their German federate fellow-soldiers, who consequently went over *en masse* to the Visigoths. Alaric, lacking the helpful contacts he had hitherto maintained with Stilicho, demanded money and land for his men, and when these were refused, marched on Rome and cut off its food supply, only raising the siege and withdrawing when the Senate paid him large quantities of gold, silver and copper. In the next year, after the government had again refused to grant his demands, he descended once more upon Rome, where he established a transient Emperor, Priscus Attalus.

In 410, in the face of continued intransigence from the imperial authorities, Alaric besieged the city for the third time. The gates were treacherously opened to admit him, whereupon, to the horror of the Roman world, his soldiers moved in and occupied the ancient capital, which had not been taken by a foreign foe for nearly eight hundred years. Much wealth was plundered, and some buildings were burnt – but not very many. For this was not quite final downfall of the Roman Empire which Renaissance historians subsequently pronounced it to be, since the Visigothic troops only stayed for three days.

Evacuating Rome, and taking the Emperor's twenty-year-old half-sister Galla Placidia with him, Alaric marched on to the southern tip of Italy. From there, he planned to invade north Africa. But his ships were wrecked, and he turned back. When he reached Consentia, the modern Cosenza, he died. His body, adorned with many spoils, was buried deep in the bed of the River Basentus (Busento), so that it should never be found, and might remain free of desecration for evermore.

CONSTANTIUS III

The dominant Roman military leader of the next decade was Constantius, a general from Naissus (Niş) in what had formerly been Upper Moesia and was now the province of Dacia Mediterranea (Yugoslavia). Entrusted with the supreme command by Honorius, he later, for a few months, became the Emperor Constantius III. We know all too little about the details of his remarkable career, but a description of his personal appearance and habits has come down from a contemporary Greek historian, Olympiodorus.

> . . . On his progresses Constantius went with downcast eyes and sullen countenance. He was a man with large eyes, long neck and broad head, who bent far over toward the neck of the horse carrying him, and glanced here and there out of the corners of his eyes so that he showed to all, as the saying goes, 'an appearance worthy of an autocrat'.
>
> At banquets and parties, however, he was so pleasant and witty that he even contended with the clowns who often played before his table.

In the year after the sack of Rome, Constantius invaded Gaul, where he put down no less than three usurpers, including Constantine III whose earlier recognition Honorius had by this time withdrawn. Constantius then established himself at the defeated man's former headquarters of Arelate (or Constantia, now Arles), which now replaced the ravaged Treveri (Trier) as capital of the Western provinces. In 413, he granted one of the invading German tribes, the Burgundians, the status of allies or federates. They were allowed to dwell on the west bank of the middle Rhine, where they established their capital at Borbetomagus (Worms).

13

Meanwhile, Ataulf, successor of his brother-in-law Alaric as leader of the Visigoths, had marched northwards out of Italy and occupied south-western Gaul, where his people settled in the fertile lands between Narbo (Narbonne) and Burdigala (Bordeaux). Ataulf declared that his greatest wish was now no longer a Gothic Empire – which he admitted he had wanted before – but partnership with the Romans inside the Roman Empire itself. At Narbo, in 414, he married Honorius' half-sister Placidia. But the Emperor had not given his consent to the marriage, and in the following year Ataulf was forced by Constantius to retreat from Gaul into Spain, where soon afterwards, at Barcino (Barcelona), he was murdered.

His brother Wallia (Vallia) gave up Placidia to the Romans and helped them, in return for liberal grain supplies, by fighting his fellow-Germans in Spain. He and his Visigoths were then allowed to return to their former lands in south-western France where, in 418, they were granted federate status, with Tolosa as their capital. In the same year, Honorius proclaimed a measure decentralizing his authority in Gaul to a regional administration at Arelate (Arles), in which Romans and Visigoths were intended to collaborate. But the project never became really effective.

Constantius, who was now all-powerful, had married Placidia – against her will – in the previous year, and early in 421 Honorius proclaimed him joint Emperor of the West, the third Constantius to occupy the throne. However, after a reign of less than seven months, Constantius III prematurely died. Had he lived, he might have postponed the downfall of the West – but only at the cost of damaging his Eastern partners, who had angered him by refusing to recognize his accession.

PLACIDIA, AETIUS, GAISERIC, ATTILA

Honorius now proceeded to quarrel with the dead man's widow Placidia, so that she was obliged to take refuge at Constantinople. She took with her Valentinian, her four-year-old son by Constantius. But when Honorius died of dropsy in 423, an Eastern army helped her to return to the West and dispose of a usurper, and Valentinian was proclaimed Emperor (425–55) as Valentinian III. During the first years of his minority, the West was ruled by Placidia. Though she could not improve her son's idle, irresponsible character, and commanders and ministers continued to jostle for power, she, 'the most pious, everlasting mother of the Emperors', stayed firmly, for a long time, at the summit.

Her varied life, which had seen so many dramatic ups and downs, did not come to an end until 450. But long before then she had yielded the central position to another. This was the general Aetius, a Roman from the country that is now Rumania. A fifth-century historian, Renatus Frigeridus, is full of praise for his manliness and incorruptible courage. And indeed Aetius must have been a man of extraordinary distinction. He assumed the leadership of the Western Roman world, relegating Placidia to second place, at a time when this Empire was at a very low ebb. Thereafter, for more than twenty years, he laboured to keep the destructive elements in check. For a time he even partially succeeded. Had it not been for him, the disintegration would have come quicker. But more than that he could not achieve, since he came too late upon the scene.

Before rising to the heights of power, Aetius experienced many vicissitudes. As a youth he had spent some time as a hostage of the Visigoths, and then of the Huns as well, acquiring valuable insight into the leading non-Roman peoples of his day. With the Huns he remained friendly for a long time. In 423–5, he brought a large force of them to oppose Placidia's successful attempt to set Valentinian III on the throne, but then he succeeded in making his peace with Placidia's new government.

During the transitional period the vital region of North Africa, on which Rome depended for its grain, had been under the semi-independent control of the Roman general Bonifatius (Boniface). A curious blend of saint and medieval knight and freebooter, he was described by an eminent sixth-century Byzantine historian, Procopius, as 'the last of the Romans'. In this connexion Procopius bracketed him with Aetius, and it was right to consider the two men together, since their rivalry proved momentous. In 427 Placidia was persuaded to recall Boniface from Africa. But he refused to obey her summons and, in 429, after defeating her troops, called in the aid of one of the German nations which had invaded Gaul and then Spain two decades earlier, the Vandals, led by Gaiseric. But Boniface soon found it impossible to keep his new allies within bounds, and returned to Italy.

15

There he became reconciled with Placidia, and their friendship inspired in her the hope that he would suppress Aetius, whom she was beginning to find excessively powerful. And so the two Roman commanders clashed in civil war. In 432, Boniface was wounded, and later died. According to a legend giving a foretaste of medieval chivalry, the rivals had decided to struggle by single combat, and Boniface, with his dying breath, commended his wife to his victorious enemy as the only man worthy of her love.

His death meant that Aetius, with the help of his Hunnish soldiers, was at last in a position to exercise decisive influence on Placidia and the court. Before long, he was appointed commander-in-chief. It was said that envoys from the provinces no longer reported to the Emperor, a youth in his early teens, but were granted their Imperial audiences by Aetius himself.

It was a task of the most urgent priority to limit the Vandal Gaiseric's power. However, a joint army of the Western and Eastern Empires which was sent against him failed dismally, and serious alarm was felt at Rome.

Gaiseric was a leader of single-minded, ruthless will, whose enormous ability presented the Romans with a more intractable problem than any previous German had posed. We have a description of this man, whose mother had been a slave, from Jordanes, the sixth-century historian of the Goths.

> . . . Of medium height, lame from a fall off his horse, he had a deep mind and was sparing of speech. Luxury he despised, but his anger was uncontrollable and he was covetous.
>
> He was far-sighted in inducing foreign peoples to act in his interests, and resourceful in sowing seeds of discord and stirring up hatred.

Since peasant revolts inside Gaul were leaving its frontiers perilously vulnerable to the Germans, the Western government felt obliged to come to terms with Gaiseric. A treaty was therefore concluded by which the Vandals were granted federate status in large areas of what are now Morocco and western Algeria. But, this time, it was a federate status which was not far removed from complete independence.

Moreover, four years later, Gaiseric struck a new and devastating blow by invading Tunisia and north-eastern Algeria, the very

16

centres of Rome's essential grain supply. Gaiseric also captured the African capital Carthage itself. It was the second city of the Western Roman world: and its loss made the dissolution of the Empire lamentably apparent. Three years later, the Western government signed a fresh treaty with Gaiseric. Under its terms, he kept the regions he had lately seized, while ostensibly (though not permanently) returning to Rome the more westerly regions of Morocco and Algeria that he had occupied earlier.

Gaiseric now ruled openly over his own sovereign state, which was torn away from the Empire altogether. He was unique among the 'barbarian' rulers in two other respects as well. He had established an authentic, unquestioning kingship; and he possessed the only German fleet – which terrorized the central Mediterranean and threatened Italy. Gaiseric contributed more to the downfall of the Western Empire than any other single man.

Aetius was powerless to stop him. Elsewhere, however, he scored certain successes. The Germans were temporarily forced back beyond the westernmost upper Danube. The peasant resistance movements in Gaul were suppressed. And when, in about 437, the Burgundians tried to penetrate Gaul from the Rhineland, Aetius defeated them utterly (an event prominent in German saga, where it figures in the *Nibelungenlied*). Then, in 443, he transplanted the entire Burgundian federated state to an area centred on Sapaudia, which is now Savoy in south-eastern France.

The Roman hold on Britain, on the other hand, never recovered from its usurpers, who had left for the continent with all their troops, abandoning the province to its fate; and finally, in spite of appeals to Aetius, its population found itself left to the mercy of Celtic neighbours and German invaders, the Angles, Saxons and Jutes.

These were also the years when the Huns, who had hitherto provided Aetius with many of his troops, began to be the enemies of the Romans – fighting first against the Eastern Empire, and then against the West. The historian Ammianus had seen them as deceitful, fickle, hot-tempered and greedy – savages of an exceedingly disagreeable kind.

. . . The people of the Huns exceed every degree of savagery
. . . They all have compact, strong limbs and thick necks, and

are monstrously ugly and misshapen. They eat roots of wild
plants and the half-raw flesh of any kind of animal whatever,
which they put between their thighs and the backs of their
horses, and thus warm it a little.

Not even a hut thatched with reed can be found among them
. . . They dress in linen cloth or in the skins of field-mice sewn
together, and they wear the same clothing indoors and out
until it has been reduced to rags and fallen from them bit by bit.
They cover their heads with round caps and protect their hairy
legs with goatskins.

They are almost glued to their horses, which are hardy, it is
true, but ugly, and sometimes they sit them woman-fashion
and relieve themselves in that position . . .

By the 430s these Huns had built up a huge Empire in eastern
and central Europe, extending all the way from south Russia to
the Baltic and the Danube. In 434 this entire territory was
inherited by Attila and his elder brother. Known as the 'Scourge
of God', Attila murdered his brother, and played an outstanding
part in the events of the Roman world during his nineteen-year-
reign. Blustering, irritable, arrogant, indefatigable in negotiation,
he became the most powerful man in Europe. The Gothic
historian Jordanes described his appearance and manner.

. . . A large head, a swarthy complexion, small, deep-seated
eyes, a flat nose, a few hairs in the place of a beard, broad
shoulders, and a short square body of nervous strength though
of disproportioned form. The haughty step and demeanour of
the king of the Huns expressed the consciousness of his
superiority above the rest of mankind, and he had the custom
of fiercely rolling his eyes as if he wished to enjoy the terror
which he inspired.

During the 440s, Attila remained on friendly terms with
Aetius, but ruthlessly ravaged the Eastern Empire, and forced it
to conclude two treaties in increasingly unfavourable terms.
Then, however, a new ruler of the Easter, Marcian (450–57),
refused to pay his subsidies any longer, and Attila turned against
the Western provinces in order to replace these sums by plunder.

He was given a pretext for intervening when the sister of
Valentinian III, Honoria, resenting an Imperial order to marry a
Roman she disliked, sent her signet ring to the Hunnish

monarch, urging him to come to her rescue. Professing to interpret this as an offer of marriage, Attila demanded half the Western Empire as her dowry; and when this suggestion was turned down, he marched westwards into Gaul. There he was confronted by a combined force of Aetius' Roman army and the Visigoths, together with other federate Germans who had been persuaded by Imperial envoys that Attila was the common enemy of all mankind. And so in 451, as Gibbon declared, 'the nations from the Volga to the Atlantic were assembled'.

The battle that followed, fought on the Catalaunian plains west of Troyes in Champagne, was included by Sir Edward Creasy among the fifteen decisive battles of the world. The Visigothic king, Theodoric I, was one of the many who fell. Yet Attila was defeated and withdrew from Gaul. This was the one and only defeat of his lifetime, and the greatest success of Aetius' career.

But Gaul's gain meant terror for Italy, which the Huns invaded in the following year, sacking Milan and other major cities. This time, Aetius had no Imperial army to send against him. But as Attila was about to cross the River Mincio, a tributary of the Po, Pope Leo I arrived from Rome and persuaded him to withdraw – a scene perpetuated in a picture by Raphael in the Vatican. Presumably the Pope gave a warning that there was famine and pestilence in Italy, so that Attila would not be able to feed his army off the land. At all events, the Huns abandoned their onward march, turned back, and left the country.

In 453 Attila, after his marriage banquet, burst a blood-vessel and died during the night. Thereupon, the Hunnish Empire fell abruptly apart. Attila's numerous sons, who had divided it up, began to quarrel violently among themselves. This encouraged their German subjects to band together and fight them.

In the ensuing engagement at the unidentified River Medao south of the Danube, the Huns were overwhelmingly defeated. From this time onwards, they were never a great power again. Yet the Romans, too, were still losing ground in central Europe, where Germans had pressed forward once more in the neighbourhood of Lake Constance.

But meanwhile Aetius had died. He had recently strengthened his position at court, when his son became engaged to the daughter of Valentinian III. Yet courtiers were now whispering to the Emperor that he would perish at the hands of his minister unless he himself struck first. One day, therefore, while Aetius was presenting a financial statement at the palace, Valentinian suddenly leapt from his throne and accused him of treason. He then drew a sword and rushed upon the defenceless man, who was simultaneously attacked by one of the Imperial chamberlains and fell lifeless at their feet.

As one of the Emperor's advisers subsequently warned him, 'you have cut off your right hand with your left'. For the sixth-century Byzantine chronicler Marcellinus had good reason to call Aetius 'the great safety of the Western Empire' – in so far as it still had any safety at all. With his murder its terminal crisis had begun.

THE END

Only six months after Aetius' death, two of his barbarian retainers avenged him on the Field of Mars at Rome by striking down his Imperial assassin, Valentinian III. In spite of that Emperor's personal insignificance, his death was, in its way, an event no less decisive than the murder of Aetius. For Valentinian possessed no male offspring, so that his stable dynasty, which had lasted for so long, was now at an end.

The West now had just twenty-one more years to live. And during that period there were as many as nine more or less legitimate Western Emperors, each from a different family. Most of them could claim only a minimum of power and six came to violent ends.

The death of Valentinian III was followed at once by a major catastrophe. The fleet of the Vandal Gaiseric had extended the range of his influence far beyond northern Africa; and now the King disembarked at Ostia, the port of Rome, and captured the city itself. He remained for fourteen days, extracting plunder far beyond Alaric's casual looting, and when he finally departed, the many thousands of prisoners whom he took away included the widow of Valentinian III and her two daughters.

Within the Imperial government itself, the pre-eminent figure was now the commander-in-chief Ricimer, who made and unmade Emperors continually during the next fifteen years. At last a German had become the supreme commander again. True, his German birth was still felt to disqualify him from occupying the Imperial throne in person. Yet, in so far as anyone was able to maintain control, it was himself. It was he who had to grapple with the problems of the rapidly dissolving Empire.

His most able protégé was the Emperor Majorian (457–61), who momentarily checked German encroachments in both Gaul and Spain. But a campaign which he launched against Gaiseric failed disastrously since, off the Spanish harbour of Carthago Nova (Cartagena), Majorian's fleet of 300 ships was taken by surprise and totally destroyed.

Returning to Italy without an army, he was placed under arrest by Ricimer and put to death. Ricimer's successive estrangement from each of his Imperial appointees in turn was yet another of the many disruptive factors that made any return to stability impossible, and after Majorian's fall the process of collapse accelerated still further.

In 467, Ricimer accepted a candidate of the Eastern court, Anthemius, as Emperor, and a year later Gaiseric, who had been continually raiding Italy and Sicily, found himself under attack, as on earlier occasions, from a large joint expedition of Eastern and Western Imperial forces.

But the assault proved as great a fiasco as all the others, and Anthemius and Ricimer plunged into mutual recriminations which soon turned into civil war. In 472 Anthemius was defeated, and to escape arrest disguised himself as one of the beggars outside a Roman church; but he was detected and put to death. Almost immediately afterwards, however, Ricimer himself died as well, and his latest nominee for the post of Emperor scarcely survived him.

After an unsuccessful attempt by Ricimer's nephew Gundobad (who had followed him as commander-in-chief) to set up a Western ruler on his own account, the Eastern Emperor sent a relative by marriage, Julius Nepos, the commander in Dalmatia, to become the ruler of the West. But in the same year, 474, Nepos had to surrender the loyalist city of Arverna (formerly Augustonemetum, now Clermont-Ferrand), capital of the Auvergne region of Gaul, to the rising power of the Visigothic ruler Euric. The Visigoth controlled the greater part of Spain as well and had followed Gaiseric's pattern by declaring himself wholly independent.

In the following year, Nepos fled back to his Dalmatian base, having been deposed by a new military commander. This was Orestes, a Roman who had once been Attila's secretary. And now Orestes gave the vacant Imperial throne at Ravenna to his own young son Romulus Augustus, known by the diminutive form Augustulus.

The final scene of the tragedy was now beginning. For the last of all Roman armies in Italy, which consisted almost entirely of Danubian Germans and was under the command of a German named Odoacer, decided at this juncture to claim the federate status and grants of land which other German groups had gained over the past century, in the Balkans and Gaul and elsewhere. When their demand met with rejection, Odoacer was acclaimed by his soldiers as king. Seizing Ravenna, he declared Romulus to be deposed, and sent him off into retirement with a pension.

The soldiers duly got their land. But in this year 476, the Western throne ceased to have an occupant at Ravenna for Odoacer, reflecting on Ricimer's difficulties, concluded that it would be wiser not to keep an Emperor in his own neighbourhood any longer. The Senate was accordingly prevailed upon to send a deputation to the Eastern ruler Zeno. The envoys transferred the Imperial insignia into his hands, as the sole remaining ruler of the 'one and indivisible Empire'; and at the same time he was invited to entrust the administration of Italy to Odoacer. Zeno demurred, since Nepos, who had been the nominee of the East, was still alive in Dalmatia. Nevertheless, Odoacer continued to rule in Italy until 493, unrecognized by Constantinople but left undisturbed.

From a formal point of view, the absence of a Western Emperor meant that the division of the Empire into two parts had lapsed; so that, as the Senate suggested, Zeno was now titular ruler of the West as well as the East. But in reality Odoacer had become an independent German monarch in Italy, just like Gaiseric in North Africa, and Euric in Gaul and Spain.

And so, looking back, Byzantine historians of the sixth century canonized this year 476 as the epoch-making final moment of the long decline and fall. The Byzantine Emperor Justin I, who ruled in the East from 518 to 527, recognized the German kingdom of Italy under Theodoric the Ostrogoth, who overcame Odoacer; so that by that time 476, in retrospect, already seemed to represent something more than a purely temporary phenomenon. Scholars of the Italian Renaissance, and of later times, agreed that it was a major turning point.

Since then, there has been a tendency to minimize the importance of the date, because, after all, it was only one more in a long series of disintegrations, and a somewhat unspectacular happening at that. Nevertheless the expulsion of the Emperor in 476 did signify that the last important territory of the West, and indeed its metropolitan territory, had become, for good or evil, just another German kingdom. The Western Empire was no more. That long drawn-out withdrawal from the vast Imperial spaces, which reached its end in 476, 'will ever be remembered', as Gibbon declared, 'and is still felt by the nations of the earth'.

The French historian André Piganiol, writing in 1947, likened the world of the Romans to a man who has been subjected to a violent attack. Rome succumbed, he believed, because of fatal wounds from its external enemies.

'Roman civilization,' he declared, 'did not die a natural death. It was murdered.' Yet people attacked by would-be murderers sometimes survive if they are strong enough to fight back. And the Romans could have survived, if they had possessed sufficient strength. But when the murderous blows were delivered, they could no longer muster the force to parry them.

This was because Italy and the entire Western world were hopelessly disunited. Rome did not fall only because of attacks from outside. The attacks were certainly formidable. Yet had they been the only trouble, the Empire might still have survived, as it had survived other ferocious onslaughts in the past. But by this time it had become paralysed by its internal disunities.

The endeavour will now be made to detect and define these disunities, in their multiple and various shapes and forms. Each one of them was damaging. In accumulation they proved fatal. By making resistance to the external onslaughts impossible, they swept the Western Roman Empire out of existence.

I

THE
FAILURE OF
THE ARMY

1

The Generals against the State

Professor Arther Ferrill, in *Fall of the Roman Empire: The Military Explanation* (1983), has analysed the defects in the later Roman army which caused it to fail against the Germans. Another of the main reasons for the Empire's failure to resist its invaders was the total autocratic authority concentrated in the person of the Emperor. Besides cutting him off disastrously from his subjects, this absolute power created another special and perilous form of disunity. For it was a standing temptation to generals to make a violent bid for the same high stakes.

Autocracy produces a notoriously unstable situation. Some thinking persons during the later Roman Empire were well aware of the peril. For example, the pagan writer Eunapius went out of his way to deplore this total monopoly of power in a single person. One of the Emperors of later Rome, in a legal pronouncement, refers feelingly to 'the agitations and anxieties of his Serene Mind'. Every ruler was honorifically described as His Serenity. Yet there was a bitter, unconscious irony about this choice of title, since an Emperor's agitations and anxieties were ever-present and harrowing. He has been described as the man most to be pitied in the entire Roman world.

Moreover, very few of the monarchs during this last troubled century were impressive enough personalities to live up to these gigantic responsibilities. Leaving aside more or less transient usurpers, the last hundred and twelve years of the Western

Empire produced a total of sixteen rulers, among whom the only outstanding personality was the first, Valentinian I. Theodosius I, too, was a man to be reckoned with, though some of his policies, notably his religious intolerance, were divisive and disastrous. Majorian was gifted, but came too late.

The others were mostly insignificant, so that the actual exercise of their autocratic power fell to their generals. Two of the most insignificant Emperors of all, Honorius and Valentinian III, reigned, between them, for more than half of the total period of nearly a century and a quarter. The unworthiness of these later rulers was just one more handicap that the failing Empire had to bear. But even if they did not effectively rule, even if they were just cloistered, pampered weaklings, they were useful merely because they were there – like a constitutional monarch, however incompetent, today.

The Roman dynastic monarchy was particularly beneficial because of a grave defect that had always weakened the roots of the Imperial system. This was the absence of a satisfactory method of ensuring the peaceful transition from one Emperor to another. When Augustus had founded the system in 31 BC, his ill-defined job had comprised an agglomeration of powers, not one of which, formally speaking, could be passed on to any heir or successor.

That was why the greatest of all Roman historians, Tacitus, began his *Annals* with a detailed account of the critical tensions which arose immediately after Augustus' death. For although Augustus had *in practice* taken the necessary measures, over a number of previous years, to ensure a smooth succession after his death, the historian wanted to stress the potentially catastrophic perils of such moments of transition, since time after time throughout the Imperial epoch they brought crisis, revolution and civil war. 'In elective monarchies', as Gibbon pointed out, 'the vacancy of the throne is a moment big with danger and mischief.' Indeed, Machiavelli plausibly argued, without too much exaggeration, that the faulty constitutional arrangements responsible for this situation were what eventually brought the Empire down.

It was understood that, in theory, each new ruler must be selected by the Senate. But from the very outset this proved to be a fiction. The hard fact of the matter was that *all* Emperors continued to owe their position to the loyalty of the army. And it was therefore the army which appointed each successive occupant of the Caesars' throne.

In the first century AD, the Emperor-makers were often the praetorian guard – the military unit at Rome which was supposed to protect the person of the ruler, but which also possessed the opportunity to strike him down. It was an opportunity the officers of the guard all too often used. And subsequently other army units and garrisons as well, stationed in the provinces, took their turn in the making and unmaking of their supposed masters.

The views held by the Senate and army about who the next Emperor ought to be frequently failed to coincide. This was because the Senators liked to maintain the idea that they themselves had an unrestricted initiative and choice, so that, whenever a ruler died, it was they who would be free to appoint the best man available, not necessarily from the previous Imperial house. In opposition to this desire, successive Emperors continually did their best to bequeath their powers within their own house by bringing forward a son or other relative: partly because rulers are apt to feel it safest to rely upon their families, but partly also since, in ancient Rome, there were times when this nepotism genuinely seemed to provide the best hope of a stable and non-violent hand-over.

Furthermore, whatever constitutionalists might be saying, hereditary transmission was very often strongly favoured by the soldiers. For their loyalty to their commander-in-chief, the Emperor, was a personal sentiment which could easily be transferred to his son or other members of his family. Moreover, the Emperor was their paymaster: any break in Imperial continuity might jeopardize their wages.

From AD 97 onwards, throughout the greater part of the second century, a new formula was tried, according to which Emperors 'adopted' and virtually nominated their successors, men from outside their own families, chosen for their suitability alone. But after that, successive rulers returned to the practice of seeking to establish their own dynasties.

Yet each dynasty in turn, if it ever got off the ground at all, almost immediately collapsed. For, although the army favoured dynasties in theory, it very rapidly became tired of them in practice, owing to recurring discontent with the qualities of individual Emperors. And it was the army, during this entire period, which still continued to place one monarch after another on the throne.

In 364, Valentinian I became yet another of these army nominees. And even Symmachus, an old-fashioned conservative aristocrat, believed, or professed to believe, that this was reasonable enough. For the army, he observed in 369, is better qualified to appoint Emperors than anyone else, since 'the Senate and political institutions are slothful and disused'. The historian Ammianus also supported the army's Emperor-making role, though he liked to think, somewhat over-optimistically, that its decisions were normally preceded by a process of due deliberation among leading men.

The unidentifiable groups of biographers who compiled the *Historia Augusta* disagreed, vociferously praising those rulers from the past whom they believed to have been nominated by the Senate. In consequence, these writers revived and repeated the ancient concept that Imperial rule could not be hereditary, and denied that birth should play any part whatever in determining the succession.

Valentinian I, like many an earlier Emperor, held the opposite view, and wanted to establish his own dynasty. Moreover, although he did not come from an Imperial family himself, he felt in a strong enough position to turn the army's preference for heredity to his own advantage. For when, in 367, he promoted his son Gratian to be co-Emperor, he was careful to stage a wholly military ceremony, at which he commended the youth to the soldiers. At this ceremony, after they had acclaimed their new ruler with loud shouts and clashing weapons, Valentinian invested him with the Imperial robes, and declared: 'Behold, my dear Gratian, you now wear, as we had all hoped, the Imperial robes, bestowed upon you under favourable auspices *by my will and that of our fellow-soldiers.*'

Valentinian's attempt to found a new ruling house, with military support, proved extraordinarily successful. For this dynasty, strengthened by the inclusion of Theodosius I through a marriage alliance, lasted for no less than ninety-one years – one of the longest durations in Imperial history, and a remarkable example of continuity at such a disturbed period.

By way of contrast, the death of the last representative of this house, Valentinian III, although he personally had been little better than a cypher, was followed by a period of unprecedented instability, during which, as we have seen, there was a rapid succession of transient Emperors. Indeed, the instability was final and fatal, for with the last of them the Western Empire came to an end.

In the ancient Roman experience, the most perilous phenomenon was the constant succession of military figures who engineered revolts and *coups d'état* in order to set themselves up in place of the established ruler of the day. Their uprisings produced dangerous fragmentations and breakaways of provinces. The men who at different periods and in different regions were declared Emperors by some part of the army, even if they did not usually succeed in maintaining themselves for any appreciable length of time, were lamentably numerous, continuing to erupt one after another for generation after generation. And the rivalry between these usurpers and their 'legitimate' competitors (a distinction that is not, incidentally, always easy to make) was one of the principal causes of the debilitation of Rome's authority.

For the civil wars which resulted from such usurpations decisively undermined the internal security of the Roman world. Furthermore, on many demonstrable occasions these struggles served as an irresistible invitation to Germans and other enemies to break into the distracted provinces. From the first century AD up to the very end of the Roman Empire more than four hundred years later, scarcely a single decade passed when there was not, at some juncture, a rival Emperor in the field, and often there were more than one simultaneously.

This state of affairs was the product of an insoluble dilemma. The army had to be strong enough to protect the frontiers. But if it was strong enough to do that, then it was also strong enough to turn against the Emperor whenever one of its generals prompted it to revolt. True, it was only due to the army that the Empire continued in existence at all. But it was also the fault of the army, and the men who commanded it, that internal peace was never achieved for very many years at a time. And because of this fatally weakening disunity, the Romans sustained huge and continuing dislocations, casualties and wastages.

At times, the anarchy produced by this situation amounted virtually to national paralysis. For example, during the period of only a century and a half leading up to Constantine the Great (306–37), very nearly eighty generals, either in the capital or in some other part of the Empire, were hailed by the Imperial title. Between 247 and 270 alone no less than thirty such men were acclaimed. Some were too afraid to refuse the offer.

These usurpers provide a paradise for modern numismatists, who come into their own as purveyors of historical information. For, as soon as a man declared himself Emperor, he promptly issued the money that was needed to shore up his soldiers' loyalty – and at the same time it served the purpose of spreading abroad the knowledge of his name and image. And specimens of these coins, ranging from tens of thousands in some cases to one single surviving specimen in others, have come down to us and can be seen today.

In the last epoch of the Empire, the same destructive process went on and on, and the succession remained as turbulent and rapidly changing as before. In the time of Valentinian I's dynasty, there were still numerous generals and others who decided to attempt these violent grasps at the throne. At least ten men made these lunges, all unsuccessfully in the end, but with varying degrees of initial acceptance. The number rises to thirteen if we include three North African troublemakers with ambiguous intentions. And perhaps there were more.

It is evident what an additional drain the struggles to put down all these usurpers must have imposed on the already hopelessly strained resources of imperial manpower and revenue. And it becomes clearer, too, not only why Valentinian I was determined to guarantee a peaceful dynastic succession, but why the army and Empire as a whole still persevered with this policy of heredity throughout the long reigns of the incompetent last members of his house.

Moreover, on the question of usurpers, if not on anything else, the Western and Eastern Emperors, who had a common interest in maintaining the dynasty to which both alike belonged, generally managed to work together – it being understood that as long as one lawful Emperor survived in any part of the Roman world, no other could be created without his agreement. This understanding was not, it is true, invariably observed. Nevertheless, as long as Valentinian I's dynasty still occupied the thrones in West and East, not one of its rivals ever succeeded in ousting its representatives from either one of the two Empires.

All the same, the diversion of Imperial resources necessitated by such civil wars was disastrous. And during the very last years of the West, after the dynasty of the Valentinians had finally vanished, the chaos deepened. By now most of the ostensible rulers were mere figureheads depending on powerful generals, among whom the German Ricimer (456–72) was pre-eminent. Yet these war-lords still did not venture to seize the monarchical title itself – until 476, when the last Western Emperor was removed from Ravenna, and Odoacer became King of Italy.

Contemporary writers, throughout the entire duration of the Empire, were very well aware of the exceptional damage caused by all these rebellions. Ammianus, in particular, declared military rebels the supreme evil. He had a clear and definite sense of the mutual obligations which linked the lawful Emperor to his people, and was profoundly conscious that, if the ruler was not loyally obeyed by his subjects, the entire safety of the Roman world would collapse.

Augustine, too, demanded 'what fury of foreign peoples, what barbarian cruelty, can be compared with the harm done by civil wars?'. And two of the most prominent among the many insurgents, Magnus Maximus (383–8) whose generals killed Gratian, and Eugenius (392–4) whose Master of Soldiers probably murdered Valentinian II, are bracketed by the poet Claudian as a pair of truly guilty men:

> Two tyrants burst upon the western climes,
> Their savage bosoms stored with various crimes;
> Fierce Britain was to one the native earth:
> The other owed to Germany his birth,
> A banished, servile wretch: both soiled with guilt:
> Alike their hands a master's blood had split.

Yet such a perpetrator or figurehead of a military revolt, while his tenure of power lasted, sometimes controlled a territory of great size. And, very often, there was no lack of people ready to flock to his colours. As the anonymous treatise *On Matters of Warfare* points out, the discontented poor saw no reason at all why they should not change masters and rally to such rebellions.

The disastrous character of those movements was clearly seen by Gibbon, and by the French historian Montesquieu before him. Montesquieu identified this whole process of traitorous usurpations as one of the principal reasons for the downfall of Rome, tracing how, when once the Empire had grown to such vast dimensions, political differences that had earlier been nothing worse than healthy arguments became transformed into deadly civil wars.

2

The People against the Army

We now come to the second cause of the collapse of the Western Roman Empire: the general failure of its armies to perform the tasks that were required of them. For the Roman armies collapsed, in what at first sight seems an unaccountable fashion, before foreign forces which were, in theory, much their inferiors both in numbers and equipment: the sort of enemies that Rome had often encountered before, and had defeated. In fact, faced with recalcitrant public opinion, and an almost total failure of understanding between the army and the people, Rome had allowed its armies to become fatally weakened.

Our chief source of information about the late Roman army is the Record of Official Posts, *Notitia Dignitatum*. This record gives a list of the principal official posts in the Western and Eastern Empires as they existed in the year 395. Moreover, in so far as the military commanders are concerned, it adds particulars of the units which these officers commanded.

This Record of Official Posts is at one and the same time vitally important and thoroughly misleading. According to its statistics, the troops of the combined Empires numbered between 500,000 and 600,000, twice the size of the forces that had efficiently defended the Roman world two centuries earlier. Of this total number of soldiers, the Western Empire possessed slightly less than half – perhaps a little under 250,000, of whom the majority was stationed on or near the Rhine and Danube borders.

Such numbers, by all precedents, should have been far more than enough for the defence of these frontiers against barbarian incursions. For the armies of Rome's barbarian foes were not, for the most part, numerically very large – no larger than those which had been successfully routed in previous epochs. That is to say, the Visigoth Alaric I and the Vandal Gaiseric may have commanded 40,000 and 20,000 warriors respectively, and the Alamannic host in the 360s had perhaps fallen considerably short of 10,000 fighting men.

But when we look more closely into the forces pitted against these invaders, the picture that emerges becomes strangely different. The Roman armies of the epoch were divided into a high-grade field force and a frontier force. The latter was the less mobile of the two, and harder to free for specific military tasks, being concentrated upon local garrison duties and internal security functions. Besides, as we can detect from a law of 428, it was regarded with less respect and esteem than the field force.

Now an inspection of the Record and other sources of information reveals that no less than two-thirds of the entire army of the Western Empire consisted of such frontier troops, units of second-rate quality. Moreover, the field force suffered such heavy casualties in external and civil wars that it had to take over more and more men – perhaps eventually two-thirds of its total strength – from these frontier armies, particularly in the critical areas of North Africa and Gaul, thus gravely diminishing the frontier defences.

Indeed, the pagan historian Zosimus concluded that Constantine the Great, whom he held principally to blame for this weakening of the frontier force, was thereby largely responsible for the downfall of the Roman Empire. Nor did this situation leave the field force in a satisfactory condition, since it had been obliged to fill up its numbers by so many former frontier troops of lesser calibre. Moreover, the field force had other problems too. For example, its formations in North Africa became, in effect, untransferable to other war-zones, even in an emergency, owing to the need to ensure that the grain from the region should not be lost to Rome.

When we turn to the actual numbers of men commanded in battle by the Roman generals of that time, the position looks graver still. Zosimus remarks that a force of 65,000 put into the field by Julian the Apostate was one of the largest of the age. That seems surprising enough. Yet in the next generation, the most numerous body of soldiers ever mustered by Rome's greatest general of the age, Stilicho – against the Ostrogothic invader Radagaisus in 405 – amounted to no more than 30,000 and was perhaps not much above 20,000. A high figure for any Roman fighting army at this time is 15,000, and expeditionary forces were often only a third as large even as that. This is an enormously far cry from the theoretical figures of the Record of Official Posts, and brings us much closer to the realities of the later Roman Empire. The apparent numerical superiority over the German invaders scarcely existed after all.

The fourth-century writer *On Matters of Warfare* expressed anxiety about this situation. He also offered his Emperors, who are probably Valentinian I and his brother, proposals for putting it right – and they are unusually positive proposals at that. What this author wants the rulers to do, among other things, is to save army manpower by increased mechanization. He therefore suggests a whole series of new types of siege-engines and other equipment. His suggestions went unnoticed, having probably been intercepted and pigeon-holed before they reached the Imperial eyes at all. But their anonymous proposer is important, not merely because he believed, unlike most of his contemporaries, that something practical could be done to improve the world, but because he understood clearly that the recruiting situation of the army was disastrous, and that action would have to be taken to remedy this.

But why was the position so disastrous? The terrific attacks on the frontiers were nothing new. But they were, certainly, becoming more and more frequent – largely because of the weakness within, which invited external encroachments.

There can be little doubt that the weaknesses of the late Roman army were largely due to the eventual failure of the Imperial authorities to enforce regular conscription. Since the beginning of the fourth century AD, it had been the main source of recruitment. Valentinian I, the most effective military leader of the age, conscripted strenuously every year, and Theodosius I also, at the beginning of his reign, attempted recruitment on a national scale.

But the exempted categories were cripplingly numerous. Hosts of Senators, bureaucrats and clergymen were entitled to avoid the draft; and among other groups who escaped were cooks, bakers and slaves. To draw the rest of the population into the levy, the combing-out process was intensive. Even the men on the Emperor's own very extensive estates found themselves called up. Yet other great landlords proved far less co-operative. They were supposed to furnish army recruits in proportion to the size of their lands. But on many occasions they resisted firmly. Moreover, even if they gave way, they exhibited a strong tendency only to send the men they wanted to get rid of. They objected that the levies were a heavy strain on the rural population, which were depleted both in numbers and morale. And indeed there was much truth in this. For, since the inhabitants of the cities were virtually useless as soldiers, that was where the burden fell – on the small farmers and peasants, between the ages of nineteen and thirty-five.

In view of such resistance to the draft, it very soon became clear that ordinary measures of recruitment were not stringent enough. Regimentation became the order of the day – and that included compulsion to remain in one's father's profession, so that there was a rapidly increasing tendency to force the sons of soldiers or ex-soldiers to become soldiers in their turn.

This doctrine was already enunciated, though not necessarily obeyed, in the early 300s AD; and by the fifth century it had become obligatory, as in civilian jobs. Moreover, the obligation was sternly insisted upon, in so far as the government possessed the power to have its wishes carried out. But the results were still very far from satisfactory.

The Christian philosopher Synesius of Cyrene (Shahhat) declared that what was needed to save the Empire was *a nation in arms*. As before, the writer *On Matters of Warfare* takes a look at the problem, in so far as it affected the Romans. Complaining that there was no sizeable reserve either of recruits or of veterans, he suggested that it might be easier to track down the reluctant and elusive conscripts if shorter terms of service were introduced. Yet his proposal, even if accepted, would only have been a minor palliative at best. For in the Western Empire, where, as we shall see, the social structure manifested strains which almost annihilated patriotic feeling, there seemed no escape from St

Ambrose's conclusion that military service had already ceased to be regarded as a common obligation at all, and was considered merely a servitude – which everyone tried to evade. Universal liability to service could no longer be enforced.

As the frontiers drew in, the provision of soldiers fell more and more upon Italy itself. But the Italians were not able to bear the burden, and had not the slightest intention of doing so. A law of 403 implies that an annual levy still existed at that time. But two enactments of 440 and 443 suggest that, by then, call-ups of recruits in the West were already restricted to emergency occasions only. Indeed, Valentinian III, the author of these edicts, pronounced that 'no Roman citizen shall be compelled to serve', except for the defence of his own town if its safety is endangered. And after the death of the vigorous Aetius, we hear no more of Western citizen recruitment at all.

The senatorial aristocracy, who in this final period dominated the civil administration, was most unlikely to support any such drain on its diminishing agricultural labour. The government, however, had long since drawn one conclusion from this critical state of affairs. If it could not extract recruits from the land-owners, then it would extort money from them instead.

Throughout the latter part of the fourth century, therefore, steps were already being taken to explore this alternative. Finally, Senators were formally given the option of paying 25 gold coins in lieu of each missing recruit for whom they were liable. Similarly, individuals could pay cash to escape their own call-ups. The historian Ammianus had already condemned such commuting of service. But, although acceptance of failure, it made a sort of sense once that failure was inevitable. For it proved so hopelessly difficult to secure an adequate number of citizen recruits, even by conscription, that the money would at least ensure that the services of German soldiers could be purchased in their place. And indeed it was to secure their services as fighters that one Emperor after another had permitted them to settle in the provinces as federates and allies. If the West could not have a Roman army, it would have a German force instead. And meanwhile the *Roman* army faded away completely, so that by the time of the Western Empire's final eclipse there was nothing left of it at all.

Ambrose's remark that by his time soldiering had come to be

regarded as a slavery to be shunned had been proved patently true. Yet strangely enough, the pages of Roman historians, for the past two hundred years, had been full of complaints that the soldiery were being given *too favourable* terms: one Roman Emperor after another was accused of just pampering and spoiling them.

The complaints had already been heard, loud and clear, under Septimius Severus (AD 193–211) – and Gibbon was sufficiently impressed to pronounce him, for this reason, the principal author of the Empire's decline. From his time onwards, the soldiers received more and more payments in kind, in the form of foodstuffs, clothing and other goods. The generosity of Constantine, also, towards his troops was condemned as altogether excessive.

However, it was Valentinian I, according to Ammianus, who 'was the first to enhance the importance of the soldiers by raising them in rank and property, to the detriment of the common interest'. Theodosius I, too, was charged with treating them much too indulgently. For example there was anger because they were given agricultural equipment and seeds and stock, since the Emperors allowed them, in their spare time, to double as farmers and land-workers – as these jobs likewise were in short supply. But throughout all such censorious observations runs the traditional viewpoint of the senatorial classes, which had always nostalgically wanted to control the state themselves and had resented their eclipse by the army.

In fact, the soldiers, for all their political ebullience on many occasions, had never been excessively paid or rewarded, and reforms like those of Severus and Valentinian I served merely to bring their emoluments up to a reasonable level. By the fifth century, this situation did not seem much changed, except that nowadays their remuneration, such as it was, did not even reach them any too regularly, because communications were dislocated so often.

For such reasons the results of every endeavour to please the soldiery proved unsatisfactory. For one thing, a principal incentive of military service in the past, the Roman citizenship that went to legionaries on recruitment and to auxiliaries on discharge, was now defunct, because since 212 citizenship had become virtually universal among all the inhabitants of the Empire other than slaves. Moreover, one way and another, the soldiers suffered their share of the hardships of this exacting age. No inducements that could be offered them were sufficient to counterbalance all the factors that undermined their zeal.

And so the young men of the later Roman Empire did their best to avoid military service. Their recalcitrance took bizarre forms. This is evident from the laws of the time, which reveal some of the desperate steps taken to escape the Imperial call-up. Many youths, it is recorded, would even amputate their thumbs in order to make themselves ineligible. For such actions, it was decreed that they should be burnt alive. Theodosius I, however, ruled that offenders should no longer suffer this fate, but must instead, in spite of their self-mutilation, serve in the army after all. And landowners who had to offer their tenants as conscripts must provide two of these damaged persons in lieu of every whole recruit for whom they were responsible. The landowners were also vigorously discouraged from hiding men where the recruiting officer could not find them. Indeed, in 440, such concealment of recruits was made punishable by death.

This was also the fate of those who harboured deserters – an intensification of earlier penalties, which had condemned them to the mines if they were poor, or to the confiscation of half their property if they were rich. The rich, as a class, were constantly blamed for sponsoring such evasions, and sheltering the fugitives in order to swell their own agricultural labour force. Severe official criticism also descended upon landowners' agents and bailiffs, who, in some provinces, were even forbidden the use of horses in the hope that they would thus be prevented from abetting desertions.

Yet another indication of the widespread gravity of the deserter problem was supplied by regulations enacting that new recruits should have their skins branded, just as slaves were branded in their barrack-prisons. The ever-increasing toughness of such legal measures suggested how difficult the government was finding it to enforce its regulations. Moreover, an additional danger was the banding together of these deserters into gangs of brigands, who are denounced specifically in a further series of laws.

Another enactment startlingly reveals the effects of this state of affairs upon the frontier fortifications: for it becomes clear from a law of 409 that their hereditary defenders were just melting away. This was the completion of a process that had long been under way: since the years immediately following the disaster at Adrianople in 378 had witnessed a whole wave of such desertions, abandoning defences to their decay and leaving garrisons seriously undermanned.

Thus when the Germans continued to burst across the Rhine and the Danube there seems to have been a widespread failure to make effective use of towns and strongpoints. According to Salvian, the presbyter of Massilia (Marseille) who painted such a gloomy picture of contemporary disasters, the cities were still left unguarded even when the barbarians were almost in sight. One would have thought, he declared, that the defenders and inhabitants had no desire to die; and yet none of them made the slightest positive move to save themselves from death. Often, it is true, Roman soldiers, for all their initial lack of enthusiasm, continued to fight well if they had able and inspiring commanders. For example, Stilicho several times defeated armies of considerably great size than his own. But on many other occasions the Imperial troops were beaten men before they even glimpsed a German warrior. Many centuries later, this caused no surprise to Karl Marx, who pointed out that there was no reason whatever why such drafted serfs should fight well, since they had been given no encouragement to feel a concern for the state.

On the other hand, as a contemporary observer, Synesius of Cyrene (Shahhat) unkindly noted, if the army was not terrible to its enemies it was terrible enough to the provincial populations.

The rhetorician Libanius of Antioch (Antakya), a contemporary of Constantine, has shown why. He tells of tattered soldiers hanging round wine shops far behind the front line, and spending their time in debauchery at the expense of the local peasants.

Ammianus paints an equally gloomy picture. Before he turned to the writing of history, he had been an officer himself, and when he stresses the vicious savagery and treacherous fickleness of the troops he must to some extent be telling of what he knew. What the soldiers really enjoyed, said the sixth-century Bishop Ennodius of Ticinum (Pavia), was bullying a local farmer. Camp

duties they declared to be a bore. And they complained that their
superiors were impossibly oppressive. If there was any move to
transfer them from places they had grown to like, they became
insubordinate at once. They were, it was said, more like a foreign
occupation force than an army of Roman citizens. As a result,
they were greatly hated and feared. In North Africa, for example,
Augustine criticized the governor's personal bodyguard for the
outrageous way in which it behaved. And the congregation of his
church disliked the army so much that they lynched its local
commander. 'The principal cities on the frontiers', wrote Gibbon,
'were filled with soldiers who considered their countrymen as
their most implacable enemies.'

Is this picture exaggerated? Perhaps to some slight extent,
since it is largely taken from writers who, because of political and
social biases of their own, tend to single out the worst incidents
they can find. Nevertheless, all these reports, combined with the
glum phrases in Imperial laws, indicate unmistakably that
something was wrong with the army.

The military expert Vegetius declared that the solution was a
reversion to ancient discipline. There are always conservatives
who say that. However, it was impossible just to put the clock
back so simply. Valentinian I did what he could, for he set out to
be a ruthless disciplinarian. But he did not venture to carry the
process to its logical conclusion. For although he was so strict to
the soldiers, he felt he had to be lenient with the officers, in order
to make sure that they stayed loyal.

The Roman officer corps still contained many good men. But it
also frequently fell below the splendid traditions of its past. The
troops of the frontier garrisons, particularly, were at the mercy of
their officers, who exploited them shamelessly by grabbing the
payments in cash and in kind that they ought to have passed on
to them, while offering lax discipline as a compensation. There
were also stories of officers deliberately allowing units to fall
below strength, so that they could pocket the remunerations of
non-existent men.

A Greek at the court of Attila told Priscus of Panium (Barbaros)
in Thrace, an envoy of the Eastern Empire, how low his personal
opinion of the Roman officers was. And Attila's description of
war against the Western Empire as 'more bitter' than war against
the East was a good deal less of a compliment to the might of the

West than it sounded, because he did not mean that he found its soldiers formidable: what he meant was that he appreciated the warlike qualities of the Goths, who by now formed such an important part of the Western army.

For that was why the Emperors were glad to commute the military obligations of Roman provincials for gold: they could buy German recruits to fill their places. This recruitment, in itself, was nothing new. In the earlier days of the Empire, the auxiliary units had already included many Germans, mainly serving under Roman officers. Then, early in the fourth century, Constantine greatly increased the enrolment of such men, mostly recruited under contract on an individual basis, and officered by Romans. In the light of this development, Porphyrius, who wrote a bad poem in praise of Constantine, could justifiably declare to him: 'Your Rhine furnishes you with armies.' Apart from certain prisoners of war who had been compulsorily mobilized, these Germans were not in the slightest degree enemies of Rome, but were only too eager to enlist in its service. They saw the Roman Empire not as an enemy but as a career.

Julian the Apostate (361–3) expressed disgust for Constantine's 'pro-barbarism'. Yet he had no time, during his short reign, to reverse this trend, and probably he could never have done so, since the German soldiers had already become indispensable.

When Valens, before the disastrous defeat at Adrianople, invited Visigoths into the Imperial provinces, his major justification for this move was the prospect of enlarging the army – and increasing the revenue as well, since the sum which provincials would contribute in order to escape their military service amounted to more than he would need to pay the Germans. But then, in 382, it was Theodosius I who took the fateful, decisive measure. For the German 'allies' or federates whom he enrolled as soldiers were not merely individual recruits any longer, but whole tribes enlisting under their own chieftains, who received from the Roman Emperor an annual sum, in cash and kind, to pay the troops they thus continued to command. These men joined the army as volunteers on very easy terms, and were allowed to withdraw from it if they provided a substitute.

In 388, Ambrose emphasized the decisive role of the Germans in Theodosius' army – and he might have added the non-German

Huns as well, since they too provided Rome with many soldiers at this time. Once introduced, the new federate participation in the army grew apace. And it grew with particular speed because the battles between Theodosius I and rival contestants for the throne were fought between a great many German and other non-Roman troops on either side.

Although the flatterers of Emperors praised their wisdom in mobilizing such men, the process was widely denounced by other Romans and Greeks. Synesius declared it futile to entrust the defence of the flock to the very wolves who ravened against it, men of the same race as the Romans' slaves. Jerome, too, pronounced that the Romans were now the weakest people on earth, since they depended wholly on barbarians to fight for them. And the fifth-century pagan historian Zosimus, who agreed with Jerome about little else, likewise deplored that Theodosius had reduced the truly Roman army to nothing at all. That was still not yet quite true. But it was only a slight anticipation of the truth: for the Roman army, apart from the Germans, was approaching extinction.

Since the problem of obtaining other recruits had become so desperate, Theodosius' action in replacing the Roman soldiers by Germans was probably the best practical remedy that was available to him. It also offered remarkable opportunities for racial partnership, although, owing to a blend of Roman prejudice and German turbulence, these were not effectively seized, and in consequence the federate units became disillusioned and unreliable.

In order to supplement their dubious services, the central government made occasional endeavours to mobilize local defence groups against the recurrent invasions. There were precedents for such measures, for example the defence of Treveri (Trier) from a usurper in the 350s. But then in 391 the right of using arms against 'brigands' was granted, contrary to the usual practice, to all indiscriminately, on the principle, enunciated by the *Historia Augusta*, that men will fight best when they are defending their own property.

Around the turn of the century, again, there were occasional sporadic instances of local defence, but they were neither numerous nor very effective. In the desperate crisis of the invasion of Italy in 405, the state appealed to provincials to join up as temporary volunteers 'for love of peace and country' – but without any conspicuous success. Movements towards autonomy, three years later, in Britain and Brittany may have been exercises in concerted self-help. It was soon afterwards, in 410, that Honorius wrote to Britain instructing the authorities there to arrange their own protection; and the British once again received a similar message thirty years later. In Italy, when Gaiseric and his Vandals threatened the country, its citizens were authorized to carry arms. In Gaul, too, in 471–5, the people of the Arverni (Auvergne), inspired by their bishop Sidonius, defended their capital Arverna (formerly Augustonemetum, now Clermont-Ferrand) against the Visigoths.

Yet such efforts at local self-defence are only worth mentioning because they were so exceptional. They played no substantial part in military events. And as for the Roman army itself, apart from the unruly federates, its end was indeed now at hand. A legal pronouncement of Valentinian III in 444 scarcely contrived or attempted to conceal the desperate situation, since the Emperor openly admitted that his military plans had been totally frustrated.

There was collapse on every side. Britain, despite all exhortations, was completely lost. Along extensive stretches of the Danube, the troops had already been disbanded at the beginning of the century, while the frontier crumbled around them and no one paid their wages any more. Only the strip of the river that lay closest to Italy remained in Roman hands until the end.

A certain Eugippius, in his biography of a local monk, wrote about this Danube garrison's last days in about 482. He told how the frontier forces and the frontier itself finally disintegrated, and recorded how the ultimate surviving unit at Castra Batava (Passau) sent some men back to Italy to draw the last instalment of pay that they would ever receive. Meanwhile in Italy itself there were no longer any Roman troops whatever. The country's ultimate Roman army, the army of Odoacer which forced the last Western Emperor to resign, consisted entirely of federates.

If the Romans *had* been able to maintain an army, they might well have saved themselves from destruction. Their failure to raise the troops any longer was one of the principal causes of their downfall. In later Rome too, there had been a total lack of mutual sympathy between army and civilians; and this discrepancy between defence needs and the people's willingness to fulfil them contributed materially to the downfall of the Roman West.

But *why* did such a discrepancy ever reach these catastrophic proportions? The answer lies a little below the surface, in the deep cleavages which shattered the structure of late Roman society. And it is these cleavages which must now be investigated.

II

THE GULFS BETWEEN THE CLASSES

3

The Poor against the State

The principal reason why the civil population would not maintain the army and fill its ranks was the massive burden of taxation demanded for this purpose – a gigantic imposition which alienated the poor from the states for ever, in a disunity of fatal proportions. The perilous situation into which oppressive tax policy had plunged the Western Roman world was correctly analysed by the unknown writer *On Matters of Warfare*. As he expressed the matter, in the cautious terms appropriate to a memorandum designed for the Imperial bureau, 'the vast expenditure on the army must be checked, for that is what has thrown the entire system of tax payments into difficulties'.

In one sense, this was unfair; or at least it only dealt with part of the problem. For huge expenditure on the army was necessary, if the Empire was going to be able to survive at all. The expense of defending the frontiers had become truly colossal. In 360, when the state treasurer Ursulus happened to visit the ruined site of Amida, now Diyarbakir in southern Turkey – which the Romans had been forced to abandon – his bitter comment concentrated on the financial aspect: 'Behold with what courage the cities are defended by our soldiers, for whose abundance of pay the wealth of the Empire is already becoming insufficient.'

The remark later cost Ursulus his life, at the hands of the soliders he had criticized. And, indeed, even if his censure of the fall of Amida was justified, and even if wastages of money were not uncommon, it still remained true that the army had to be maintained, so that the money for its upkeep simply had to be found. But it did not prove possible to find it. When Valentinian III confessed that his plans for the army had failed, he blamed the failure upon lack of funds. There was not enough money, he said, for his existing forces, let alone for new recruits.

The writer *On Matters of Warfare*, not content with pointing to the general problem, has a number of specific suggestions to make: though, unfortunately, they are not always very useful. One such proposal – which he recognizes to be a perilous point to make to his masters – is that the government should cut down or abolish the bonuses it habitually paid to soldiers and civil servants alike, since he regards these payments as the principal cause of the Empire's decline. But earlier rulers, too, had found it a political necessity to distribute whatever gifts they could, whether the proceeds of taxation or of plunder, among their troops and their henchmen.

Certainly the unknown author was justified in saying that the bonuses heavily burdened the taxpayer. But the only trouble was that it might be suicidal to cut them. He also suggested demobilizations at a younger age, in order to save higher salaries. But this too was probably not a practical possibility, owing to the absence of manpower to replace those who were discharged.

Another anonymous author of the same period, one of the biographers of the *Historia Augusta*, refers with enthusiasm to an alleged statement by the Emperor Marcus Aurelius Probus (276–82) that since things, under his rule, were going so well, there would soon be no need for a Roman army any longer.

> . . . What great bliss would then have shone forth, if under his rule there had ceased to be soldiers! No rations would now be furnished by any provincial, no pay for the troops taken out of the public largesses, the commonwealth of Rome would keep its treasures forever, no payments would be made by the prince, no tax required of the holder of land!
> It was in very truth a golden age that he promised.

It was indeed, and the golden age never arrived. What happened, instead, was exactly the reverse: the army became larger and larger. The *Historia Augusta*, however, was entirely correct in identifying the army as the principal cause and recipient of taxation. When, therefore, Valentinian I and Theodosius I both made gigantic efforts, in their different ways, to strengthen the military forces, heavy taxes were the inevitable result. Owing to the absence of floating capital, the government could not, in the modern fashion, throw part of its burdens on posterity by creating a public debt.

As far as Valentinian, at least, was concerned, this taxation was imposed with considerable reluctance, since Ammianus specifically informs us of that Emperor's desire to grant the provincials financial relief. But whatever his personal wishes, he felt obliged to allow Petronius Probus, his praetorian prefect in Italy, Illyricum (Yugoslavia) and North Africa, to resort to very severe extortions, and towards the end of the reign taxation rose steeply.

As for Theodosius I, his laws show a passionate desire to increase the influx of revenue by every possible means. 'No man', he pronounced in 383, 'shall possess *any* property that is tax exempt.' And he set out by a whole spate of regulations to enforce this principle, with ever-increasing harshness.

He did so at the cost of unprecedentedly ruthless methods. The employment of such methods for the collection of taxes was no novelty. It had been practised for more than a hundred years past. The third century AD, crammed with critical foreign and civil wars, had witnessed an almost total breakdown of the political structure and of national defence. This was a crisis from which the Empire was only rescued by fantastic military efforts. But the price of maintaining the recovery had been a huge, permanent increase in taxation, and an intensification of all the numerous totalitarian kinds of pressure needed to rake its proceeds into the treasury.

And now the pressure had become more exacting still. Successive Emperors each tried to turn the screw a little tighter, and a torrent of laws and edicts of Theodosius I shows that he, in particular, tightened it almost to breaking point. It was no use the poet Claudian patriotically denying that the provinces were hard hit by taxes, or the envoy Priscus of Panium (Barbaros) in Thrace, half a century later, assuring an expatriate Greek that all was for the best in the Imperial arrangements.

Valentinian III openly admitted the savagery of his own system, and even remitted arrears of taxation – at least for the rich. When Majorian came to the throne shortly afterwards, and

Sidonius welcomed his accession with a congratulatory address, he managed to insert a reference to the tax burden which oppressed his native Gaul. And the new Emperor himself issued a legal pronouncement deploring these severities with a vivid frankness that left nothing to the imagination.

During the emergencies of the third century, the custom had grown of demanding tax-payments in goods rather than cash – a reversion (like the payment of soldiers by the same means) towards the barter systems of primitive times. Towards the end of the Empire, this taxation policy began to be reversed, and levies in kind were increasingly commuted to gold once again – first of all, the provision of horses, oxen and uniforms for the army, and then the regular land-tax previously payable in grain, wine, oil and meat. This was a sort of recovery, in terms of general, long-term concepts of progress. Yet it did not help the men and women who were hardest hit by taxation.

And to make matters worse, the population was gravely inconvenienced by the inadequacies of the currency, which was far inferior to the well-planned coinages of earlier Imperial times. It was true that, after a period of unreliable gold issues, Constantine had done well to reintroduce a stable unit in this metal, the *solidus*. But that was of little use to the vast majority of the inhabitants of the Empire, who rarely if ever possessed a gold coin at all (although payment in gold was required for certain taxes); and even Theodosius' new gold denomination, one-third of the *solidus* in size, did not seriously help to bridge the gulf. He and his colleagues also issued a small silver coin, but it did not last for any length of time. Most people never saw anything but a coinage of bronze or lightly silvered bronze, and this, moreover, as time went on, was able to buy less and less.

This inflation was largely caused by increases in the face-value of the *solidus*. This ostensible value, in terms of its bronze fractions, was no less than forty-five times larger in 400 than it had been one hundred years previously. That meant that the government issued more and more of the bronze pieces – without withdrawing many in the form of taxation, so often paid in gold – so that they cluttered the market and became worth progressively less and less in terms of goods. The authorities remained unconcerned about this unfortunate result, since the bronze, being a token currency, could be issued at quite arbitrary face-values, bringing a large profit to themselves. And in any case, like everyone else in the ancient world, they were unaware of the economic law insisting that if the number of coins increases and the goods available remain the same, then prices are bound to rise.

The resulting hardship was colossal, as it had already been during successive inflations throughout the previous century. The tradespeople of the Western provinces, who were mainly Greeks and Jews, must have found life almost intolerable, especially as the government's choice of mints, which were distributed to suit the needs of the army, showed not the slightest concern for their convenience. Money-changers, too, are seen complaining to the Roman city-prefect Symmachus that they could scarcely carry on. And another difficulty which caused hardship to everyone was that unofficial forgery of the coinage was rampant.

This unfavourable currency situation became harder still for the population to bear when, early in the fifth century, the Western government virtually gave up any attempt to provide small change at all, only producing restricted issues of the minutest bronze denomination. It is true that this reduction of the number of new bronze coins probably brought the inflationary process to a belated end. But the absence of any other token coinage at all, and the extreme scarcity of silver currency too, must have made all transactions of every kind – except for the few who possessed a large supply of gold pieces – a good deal more laborious and hazardous even than they had been before.

This inconvenience, however, was merely a side-issue compared to the main horror: which was the crushing taxation. Besides, the payment of these huge taxes was only part of the contribution a citizen had to make to the state. There was also widespread requisitioning of his personal services. For example, he was compelled to provide wood and coal, especially for the use of state arsenals and mints; to boil lime; to supply expert labour of various kinds, if he possessed the qualifications; and to help maintain roads, bridges and buildings. One Emperor alone, Honorius, pronounced no less than ten edicts on the condition of the major roads, of which the decay had caused the Imperial postal service, operated by a system of requisitions, to fall into serious disorder.

To remedy this crisis, the recruiting of compulsory labour grew tougher. 'The service of one's country', it has been said of late Rome, 'had become something very like a forced loan.' And yet there were far too many exemptions: notably the clergy (to some extent), lessees of Imperial properties, and the upper class in general – though they would have been by far the best equipped to bear the burden.

There was also a terrifying amount of corruption involved in applying all these compulsions. The fraudulent oppressiveness of the bureaucrats showed itself particularly in the collection of taxes. Emperors were well aware of this, and assailed these officials with menaces. Valentinian III complained that 'those responsible put out a smoke-screen of minute calculations involved in impenetrable obscurity'. Behind the smoke-screen very much was rotten. The mass of treasury officials pursued their corrupt bullying with an arrogance and impunity scarcely disturbed by the distant sound of unenforceable Imperial threats.

The fourth-century rhetorician Libanius told of the harrowing scenes when the tax-collectors arrived at a town or village.

. . . While merchants can recoup themselves by speculations, those for whom the work of their hands scarcely furnishes a livelihood are crushed beneath the burden. The lowest cobbler cannot escape from it. I have seen some who, raising their hands to heaven and holding up their shoe-knife, swore that they would pay nothing more. But their protests did not abate the greed of their cruel oppressors, who pursued them with shouts and seemed quite ready to devour them.

From the time of Constantine onwards, there had been similar reports, referring to the extraction of taxes by violence and torture, and of the methods adopted such as the forcing of children to testify against their parents, and the compulsion of wives to betray their husbands.

It was no use offering relief from land-tax, as Honorius did on several occasions, since the districts he exempted had already been so severely ravaged that they could not have paid anyway. In such cases, as one Imperial edict frankly admits, official insistence would only have meant even graver ruin for the taxpayer, without any compensatory benefit for the state. Cancellations of arrears, of which the most comprehensive came in an edict of Majorian, were not much use either, since they did little more than write off bad debts. And in any case, the debts were mainly those incurred not by the poor but by the rich, who made a fine art of delaying their repayments, bringing down, once again, the vain wrath of Imperial legislators.

A terrible dilemma had arisen. There was no doubt whatever that the state had to have the revenue if it was to survive; and indeed the insufficiency of such revenue was one of the reasons why Rome fell – because the Romans could no longer maintain their army. Yet the collection of this utterly necessary national income imposed frightful miseries.

Was that because the sums and contributions required were entirely beyond the capacity of the population to pay? If so, the equation was a hopeless one, and it was no use the Western Empire even attempting to defend itself, for there was no possibility of raising the funds needed to do so. But it appears more likely that the necessary sums *could* have been paid if the system for collecting them had been less oppressive – and, because less oppressive, less inefficient. As it was, the collectors were guilty of the gravest abuses, and in consequence tax-dodging was rampant.

When critics of the system pointed out that by far the worst sufferers were the rustic poor, what they said was no more than the truth. The state drew over ninety per cent of its revenue from tax levied upon the land, that is to say upon the agricultural population. And this tax was not progressive in its operation, so that it hit the poor proportionately much harder than it hit the rich – additional unfairness being caused by its failure to take quality of soil and size of yield into account. By 350, the sums exacted from this principal source had multiplied threefold within living memory, and thereafter, too, the land tax continued to weigh its victims down with ever increasing severity.

Furthermore, the most important tax in kind, utilized for many years to pay government employees, was once again agricultural: for it had to be paid in the form of grain, the principal food crop of the Roman Empire. But the supply of grain was often inadequate to fulfil the tax collectors' vast demands. This was scarcely surprising, since transportation was still primitive, and labour-saving devices were deficient. A slave economy did nothing to remedy this. Nor did the new Christian state, in which men like Eusebius and Ambrose pronounced science a vain labour – since it did not help a man to be saved.

Besides, manpower was short. The American historian A. E. R. Boak considered population decline a fatal cause of the fall of Rome. His detailed arguments have been contested, but some decrease there arguably was. Invasion, devastation and poverty had all made their dreadful contributions, for after rent and tax payments had been extorted there was often no money left to rear enough children to counter-balance the high death-rate. Another reason why the supply of free-born children diminished was because the poor sold their newborn infants into slavery. This had formerly been forbidden by Roman law, but from about 300 onwards the practice was officially tolerated; and in a terrible famine of 450 it became widespread. In vain had Valentinian III, ten years earlier, decreed tax remissions to stop rural depopulation. It had gone much too far to be reversed.

Lack of manpower meant the abandonment of cultivated soil; and the crushing load of taxation drove small farmers off their farms. The average shrinkage of utilized land, taking into account soil denudation and regional climatic changes, has been estimated at ten to fifteen per cent of the total area. Admittedly this abandoned soil was mainly marginal, so that the diminution of produce was percentually less. Nevertheless, it meant that the tax burden, which was based so overwhelmingly upon agriculture, became all the heavier for those whose fields still remained under cultivation.

When successive Emperors invited Germans into the provinces, it was the intention that these immigrants, like Roman frontier garrisons in their spare time, should serve not only as soldiers but as cultivators. But the continual, ineffective, remedial laws about abandoned lands show that the problem of reclamation was never solved, and was indeed scarcely touched. For a tax system which bore down so heavily and unfairly provided no incentive to get back on to the soil. The weak and badly handled Imperial economy had proved wholly insufficient to meet the demands that were being made on it.

In certain regions, such as Mauretania and the Middle Danube territories, slaves were numerous enough to provide a substantial contribution to the labour force. However, this did not have the desired effect of increasing the total number of workers available. For its only effect was to depress the 'free' poor still further, since they could not compete with this unpaid labour, and dropped out of the market altogether.

In most areas, however, there were at this epoch not enough slaves to make any appreciable difference. It is true that captures of prisoners of war, as well as the sale of infants and the downgrading of destitute citizens to servile status, may have made the supply of slaves slightly more abundant than it had been during the immediately preceding period. But since many of the war prisoners, instead of being relegated to slavery, were now taken on as Roman soldiers, too few of them became available on the land to counterbalance the shortage of agricultural labour.

During the military crises in the years just after 400, the Roman government took the desperate step of calling slaves to arms, for the first time for centuries. But the danger was that, instead of accepting such patriotic suggestions, they would prefer to side with the invaders, who were often their compatriots. Indeed, Marxist historians once argued that slavery collapsed at the end of the Roman Empire – thus inaugurating a new epoch in world history – because slaves and peasants alike made common cause with the foreign invaders.

This, however, was to overstate the case. There were, certainly, instances in which slaves helped the enemy. This happened, for example, before the Battle of Adrianople against the Visigoths, and when Alaric was at the gates of Rome. In about 415, too, certain slaves under the leadership of youthful noblemen were plundering round Bordeaux. But such instances were few and far between. The slaves occupied a relatively unimportant role in the history of this period.

So did the free poor of Rome. Ammianus says they divided their days among wine-bars, cook-shops, dice-tables, chariot-races and gladiatorial combats. But Ammianus was probably exaggerating, since he felt such a special contempt for the urban lower classes.

Nevertheless, it is true that a hundred and seventy-five days of the year were given up to public shows, as opposed to a mere hundred and thirty-five two centuries earlier; moreover the fabric of the Colosseum was restored as late as 438. It is also true that in the mid-fourth century 300,000 Romans held bread tickets which entitled them to draw free rations from the government; and even a century later, when the population of the city had greatly diminished, there were still 120,000 recipients of these free supplies. Certainly the population of Rome was largely parasitic. However, this city proletariat played little active part in guiding the course of events which brought the later Roman Empire to a halt.

It was, on the other hand, the 'free' poor of the rural countryside upon whom the government, struggling to raise money for the army, imposed the full rigours and terrors of taxation. Although technically still distinguishable from slaves, they were no better off and perhaps even worse off, since they often found themselves driven into total destitution. Between these rustic poor and the government, the relationship was that of oppressed and oppressor, of foe and foe.

This is perhaps the gravest of all the disunities that afflicted the Western Empire. The state and the unprivileged bulk of its rural subjects were set against each other in a destructive and suicidal disharmony, which played a very large and direct part in the downfall that followed. It was because of this rift that the taxes which were needed to pay for the army could not be raised. And because they could not be raised, the Empire failed to find defenders, and collapsed.

When the small farmers and agricultural labourers of the later Roman Empire were so overwhelmed by the weight of taxation that they could not make both ends meet any longer, they sought protection where they could best find it.

Whole villages, for example, formally declared local army officers to be their 'patrons'. Since such military men, for a consideration, were prepared to drive the Imperial tax officials away, this practice was at first declared illegal. In 415, however, in some provinces at least, it was allowed official tolerance, provided that the patron assumed responsibility for the total tax-collection from the villages in question.

More numerous villages – and this was particularly true in the West – chose local landowners rather than soldiers as their patrons. And not only villages did this, but countless individuals as well: small farmers for the most part, men reduced to destitution who abandoned their plots of land and fled within the walls of the nearest great estate, where they stayed for the rest of their lives. This massive transference of populations, brought about by the impossible demands of the state, became one of the most important social developments of the age.

Now these magnates were glad to have the displaced persons, since agricultural labour was so hard to get. That was why, declared Salvian, 'the poor surrender unconditionally to the rich'. And indeed, unconditional surrender it virtually was. The men may have already been heavily in debt to their new landlord before they arrived within his walls. In any case, they henceforward paid him a cash rent, or made a fixed payment in kind, or contributed a proportion of the crop they were permitted to grow on his land, or sometimes served him in person as labourers. Of security, stability, guarantee against arbitrary action they enjoyed less than the barest minimum. Worst of all, after their flight from their own holdings, the government actually insisted that they should pay the taxes on the plot they had left for ever.

Here their protective landlords were once again necessary, since, like the military patrons, these great men were often prepared to chase the tax-collector away from their gates – in exchange for total submission by the men who had put themselves at their mercy. But then the landlords came to an understanding with the government, and a deal was done: so that the refugees found themselves re-inscribed on the tax rolls in their new locations.

Diocletian, in order to simplify the collection of the vast taxes he needed, had tied all inhabitants of rural areas compulsorily to the places where they were registered, and from those places they were never intended to move again. And in keeping with this principle, what the landlords agreed to now was that they should not repel the tax-gatherer any longer, on the condition that the state enforced this same compulsion upon their tenants, including the families who had fled into their hands.

Thus Valentinian i duly forbade the tenants to uproot

themselves without their landlords' consent; and Theodosius I was even more explicit:

> . . . In order that it may not appear that licence has been given to tenants to be free from the tie of taxation and to wander and go off where they wish, they shall be bound by the rule of origin, and though they appear to be free-born by condition, shall nevertheless be considered like slaves of the land itself to which they are born, and shall have no right of going off where they like or of changing their place: but the landowner shall enjoy his right over them with the care of a parent and the power of a master.

Moreover, further edicts made it clear that any one of them who left the place he belonged to was considered to be committing a serious crime, an act of theft: 'he is stealing his own person'.

The laws frequently note tenants' acts of defiance against such regulations and their attempts to flee from the estates where they were tied down, followed by the concerted efforts of landlords and tax officials to bring them back. By the fifth century, they were not even allowed to go and join the army. The bonds were not yet quite those which linked ancient master and slave, or medieval master and serf: yet slaves or serfs were what, in fact, they had become. They were not even allowed to bring civil actions against their masters; and the compulsions to which they were subject were, like so many compulsions of the age, hereditary.

Their only consolation was that the laws – as their repetitive tone reveals – were inefficiently enforced, so that loopholes of escape were not lacking. Besides, some small properties still managed to endure. But, on the whole, the picture of thousands of free farmers gradually sinking into total dependence represents the grim reality.

One Emperor at least made an attempt to help the poor. This was Valentinian I. Such a conclusion may seem surprising, since he had played such a large part in binding tenants firmly to the estates of the rich. But perhaps he had been acting from motives of plain realism: for there was one thing worse, he may well have reflected, than being frozen into one's occupation, and that was being frozen out of it – and had it not been for the landowners, these farmers and peasants would have been without jobs and food altogether.

For Valentinian I showed clearly, by other measures, that he felt a profound concern for the welfare of the humbler classes, to which he himself had belonged. In one edict he applies to their pursuits the high-flown phrase 'innocent and peaceful rusticity'. Another of his proclamations appeals specifically for social justice on the part of his own tax officials, demanding that special concessions to favoured persons should be eliminated – since such concessions operated at the cost of the ordinary inhabitants of the Empire.

Most important of all, during the years 368–70, Valentinian appointed officials described as Defenders of the People, or Defenders of the Community. These functionaries somewhat resembled the Ombudsmen of modern countries, whose duty it is to remedy the abuses suffered by individuals. But Valentinian's Defenders were explicitly designed to assist the underprivileged classes. In a letter to his praetorian prefect Petronius Probus he writes, 'we are taking a very necessary measure to ensure that the people shall have patrons to protect them against the iniquities of the powerful'.

In every town, therefore, the prefect was to appoint a Defender of the People, and the Emperor himself required to know personally the names of all the men who were selected for these posts. The appointees would have power to deal with every minor grievance themselves, and it was their duty to make justice more accessible to the poor in every way. Earlier Emperors had experimented on similar lines, but it was Valentinian I who elevated their experiments into a comprehensive scheme.

However, it was ominous that his first instruction on the subject had to go to Petronius Probus, who was a noted oppressor himself. And then, once Valentinian died, the institution of the Defenders was so thoroughly watered down that it ceased to retain very much value any longer. For Theodosius I transferred the task of selecting them to the city councillors – the very men responsible for the collection of the taxes.

Next, Honorius reallocated these appointments once again to a committee on which the landowners were fully represented. Valentinian's original aim had been to rescue the poor from the landlords' arbitrary power. But now the Defenders and magnates were bound together in an unholy alliance.

And so there had, for a time, been a serious, positive effort to improve the lot of the oppressed. But it had failed. The extent of its failure becomes apparent from the ancient literature. Most authors of the time, it is true, were pretty insensitive to the plight of the oppressed. Yet there were remarkable exceptions. One of them was John Chrysostom, bishop of Constantinople, who was profoundly conscious of the gulf between rich and poor. Although motivated by theological at least as much as by social considerations, he found the difference between the two ways of living so painful that the historian J. B. Bury, writing in 1923, declared him to be 'almost a socialist'.

As for Salvian of Massilia (Marseille), he has no programme other than moral regeneration. Nevertheless the sins for which he sees the world chastised by God are unerringly diagnosed as the sins of material oppression. The age he lived in, like the nineteenth century, was one in which poverty was almost regarded as infamous. Salvian loathed and detested that stigma. He is so profoundly radical that no class whatever finds favour with him except the destitute, whose fate he deplores with unrelieved gloom.

. . . Taxation, however harsh and brutal, would still be less severe and brutal, if all shared equally in the common lot. But the situation is made more shameful and disastrous by the fact that all do not bear the burden together. The tributes due from the rich are extorted from the poor, and the weaker bear the burdens of the stronger. The only reason why they do not bear the whole burden is that the exactions are greater than their resources. . . .

As the poor are the first to receive the burden, they are the last to obtain relief. For whenever, as happened lately, the ruling powers have thought best to take measures to help the bankrupt cities to lessen their taxes in some measure, at once we see the rich alone dividing with one another the remedy granted to all alike. Who then remembers the poor? . . . What more can I say? Only that the poor are not reckoned as taxpayers at all, except when the weight of taxation is being imposed on them. They are outside the number when the remedies are being distributed.

Under such circumstances can we think ourselves undeserving of God's severe punishment when we ourselves continually so punish the poor?

An expert rhetorician, Salvian paints the picture in the blackest colours he can find. But there is ample evidence that the situation was scarcely better than he reports. For example Sidonius, too, when he became bishop of Arverna (Clermont-Ferrand), was besieged by crowds of destitute petitioners who opened his eyes to the social distress of his age. And an obscure writer of Christmas sermons, Gaudentius, wrote that the peasants who had died of hunger, or had been forced to take refuge with the charity of the church, were so numerous that he felt too ashamed to disclose their number.

The consequence was that thousands of men despaired of making an honest living at all, and went underground to form travelling gangs of robbers and bandits. These guerilla groups, the equivalents of today's drop-out terrorists – likewise thrown up and thrown out by social systems they find unacceptable – were swollen not only by deserters from the army, but by hordes of destitute civilians as well. This had happened before, but now the problem assumed truly formidable dimensions.

Banditry on a considerable scale was reported from Italy, North Africa, Spain and the Danube. But it was in Gaul that the gravest disorders occurred. In the third century this had already been one of the worst trouble-spots, and now there were major outbreaks once again. These Gallic bands assumed, at some stage or other, the old name of Bacaudae or Bagaudae, meaning 'rebels'. This designation, like their whole quasi-military movement, may have had certain nationalist overtones. For this was an epoch when the decay of central control meant a revival of regional sub-cultures, particularly in countries such as Gaul where the people had still, in some areas, retained their own language.

And so Ammianus reports a serious Gallic upheaval in 369. Later, for a number of yeas between 401 and 406, gangs of marauders were active in the Alps. Next, during the decade that followed, armed men in Brittany turned out to be not so much the local defence-groups for which the Emperor Honorius was hoping, as brigands operating almost on the scale of a nationwide uprising, in which tenants and slaves rebelled in unison against their landlords.

In 435, a further large-scale Gallic disturbance of the same kind arose under a certain Tibatto, who once again appealed to the slaves, and held out against the Romans for two years. The 440s witnessed a serious revival of similar troubles, under the leadership of a physician named Eudoxius, who eventually fled to the Huns. In Spain too, not for the first time, disorders continued to break out, until a Visigothic army sent by Aetius finally crushed the militants in 454.

A curious verse play called *The Protester* (*Querolus*), which appears to be attributable to the early fifth century, tells how the Bagaudae formed rudimentary political structures, holding their own People's Courts, 'where capital sentences are posted up on an oak branch or marked on a man's bones'. Such was the disorder reigning over wide areas of the provinces that these desperate characters, runaways from government and landlords alike, had been forced, as best they could, to take matters into their own hands.

In vain the Imperial officials uttered their menaces. In the later years of the fourth century it was enacted that anyone giving aid or comfort to brigands would be flogged, or even burnt alive. The right of using arms against all such men was granted to every member of the public in self-defence: a law of 409 suggests that 'shepherd' and 'bandit' had virtually come to be regarded as synonymous terms.

Seven years later, however, owing to the 'overwhelming calamities of the times', it was decided to declare an amnesty, in the hope that more lenient policies, for a change, might bring these warlike gangs to reason. Yet none of these measures, whether stringent or conciliatory, availed to restore public order.

And can you wonder, asks Salvian? Unlike most of his contemporaries, he was extremely hostile to the measures taken by Aetius against the bandit gangs, whose flights from society and disorders he blames entirely upon the Roman rulers and their upper-class supporters. The brigandage, he admits, is universal, and no one is safe from it. But in his opinion the so-called brigands themselves are not in the least guilty. Once again, their actions are wholly due to the deeds of their wicked and bloodthirsty oppressors.

. . . The poor are being robbed, widows groan, orphans are trodden down, so that many, even persons of good birth who have enjoyed a liberal education, seek refuge with the enemy to escape death under the trials of the general persecution. They seek among the barbarians the Roman mercy, since they cannot endure the barbarous mercilessness they find among the Romans. . . .

We transform their misfortunes into crime, we brand them with a name that recalls their losses, with a name that we ourselves have contrived for their shame. We call those men rebels and utterly abandoned, whom we ourselves have forced into crime. For by what other cause were they made Bagaudae save by our unjust acts, the wicked decisions of the officials, the proscription and extortion of those who have turned the public exactions to the increase of their private fortunes and made the tax indictions their opportunity for plunder?

Like wild beasts, instead of governing those put under their power, the officials have devoured them, feeding not only on their belongings as ordinary brigands would do, but even on their torn flesh and their blood. Thus it has come to pass that men who were strangled and half killed by brutal exactions began to be really barbarians, since they were not permitted to be Romans. They were satisfied to become what they were not, since they were no longer allowed to be what they had been; and they were compelled to defend their lives as best they could, since they saw that they had already completely lost their liberty.

How does our present situation differ from theirs? Those who have not before joined the Bagaudae are now being compelled to join them. The overwhelming injuries poor men suffer compel them to wish to become Bagaudae, but their weakness prevents them. So they are like captives oppressed by the yoke of an enemy, enduring their torture of necessity, not of their own choice; in their hearts they long for freedom, while they suffer the extremes of slavery. Such is the case among almost all the lower classes.

Far distant, whole aeons past it seemed, was that earlier Imperial golden age when, as Ammianus believed, 'high and low alike with united ardour and in agreement had hastened to a noble death for their country, as if to some quiet and peaceful haven'. Those days were indeed gone and had been succeeded by a fundamental, self-destructive *lack* of any such united ardour. 'Men fight not as they fought in the brave days of old,' Macaulay makes an earlier Roman say in his poem *Horatius*. But equally serious, in these later days, was their failure to contribute the sums which were necessary if the army was to exist and fight at all.

This conflict between the authorities and the mass of the people was one of the principal causes of the downfall of the Empire. Karl Marx used this situation to illustrate his point that the classes have no common interests at all, their struggle against one another being essentially illimitable. But Marx also claimed that the specific reason why the Roman Empire fell was because its social pattern, founded on slavery, gave way to a feudal system, which broke down the Imperial structure. It would perhaps be more exact to say that one of the main reasons why the collapse occurred was because the 'free' population, which had to provide most of the Imperial revenue, was so severely ravaged by these tax demands that it could not pay up any longer and, in consequence, ceased to be free at all, so that scarcely a trace of any viable commonwealth survived; and the empty husk of a community which alone remained could no longer resist the invaders.

Such was the appalling disunity between the government and the vast bulk of its subjects: and indeed between the rich and the poor in general.

4

The Rich against the State

The last chapter discussed the tragic circumstances which set the Roman government on a course of direct conflict with the impoverished majority of its subjects. An equally unhappy outcome awaits a state, when its governmental authorities are in conflict with its upper class. This situation, too, arose violently in ancient Rome – despite all the privileges which that class possessed – and was another of the disunities which contributed to its collapse.

In the declining Roman Empire the topmost layer of the population mainly consisted of the men entitled to describe themselves as Senators. Under the earlier Emperors the Senate, that advisory council which formerly guided the decisions of the state, had already become a subordinate and somewhat pitiable body. Yet in these days of Imperial decay, there had been a change: and as far as the Senators were concerned it was a change for the better. For even if the Senate itself, as a body, still did not count for very much, its individual members were now more powerful than they had ever been before.

Those of them who habitually sat in the Senate-house at Rome did not see a great deal of the Emperor, who generally resided in Mediolanum (Milan), and later in Ravenna. The repercussions of his absence were partly unfavourable to senatorial authority – and partly favourable. The doctrine 'where Caesar is, there Rome is', and the fact that Rome itself was usually where he was not, might have seemed to reduce the Senate to little more than a city council; and this was sometimes rather how things looked. On the other hand the removal of Emperor and court to other cities gave the conscript Fathers, in some ways, a new degree of independence. Moreover, Constantine, whose conversion to Christianity made it essential to placate the pagan aristocracy, had increased the important posts available for Senators.

True, he still excluded them from the army; they had been excluded for a good many years. But the annual pair of consulships which still stood at the summit of their career was raised to loftier heights than in earlier Imperial times, since the office was now completely reserved for the Emperor's most prominent supporters, the close friends whom he described as his Companions. They did not have a great deal to do during their consular year. As Gibbon remarked, a consul of late Imperial times 'enjoyed the undisturbed contemplation of his own dignity'. But his mere tenure of the post ennobled for ever all the members of his whole line to come, and usually enriched them as well.

So, although Rome itself was no longer the centre of events, the city's leading residents regained a degree of personal influence that they had not possessed for four hundred years. Class consciousness was immense. Symmachus, himself a leading nobleman, remarked, 'good blood tells and never fails to recognize itself'. Yet the aristocratic structure was not altogether closed at the base. The poet Ausonius, for example, won his way into its privileged ranks, and, while displaying a depressing servility towards men of superior pedigree, succeeding in gaining jobs for all his relations.

However, his fellow-author Claudian echoes the widespread indignation felt among Senators when a eunuch, Eutropius, became consul in the East; and Jerome writes of their fury whenever men of humble birth, or 'rustics', took away from them the consulships they felt ought to have been theirs. Moreover, most writers take it for granted that the lower classes will regard a consul and a Senator with immeasurable respect.

But the term 'Senator' had broadened its meaning since the early days of the Empire. For by this time such personages were by no means only the comparatively few individuals who actually sat in the Senate. Their meeting place during the later Western Empire, the Curia, is still standing beside the Roman Forum today. It could scarcely have held even the 600 members which the Senate had possessed at the time when the Empire began. And now there were as many as 2000 members, in addition to another 2000 belonging to its counterpart in Constantinople.

These 4000 Senators were divided into three groups according to property qualifications, each with its own grade of privileges. By the year 450, the two lower grades were excused from attending Senate meetings. Earlier, there had been a regulation that Western Senators must live in Rome. But this rule became obsolete and indeed had to be formally relaxed, since large numbers of Senators, including many belonging to the highest of the three grades in the hierarchy, preferred to live outside the capital and even outside Italy altogether, in the midst of their vast estates. Yet, scattered geographically though they were, these major aristocratic families enjoyed intimate connexions with one another, forming a closely interlocking, self-perpetuating pattern throughout the territories of the West, and dominating the landscape all around them.

Although the lower grades of Senators tended to sink downwards and join their inferiors in the general impoverishment of the times, the richest noblemen became a very great deal richer still. We hear of people whose leases earned them an annual income of four thousand pounds of gold, with the addition of all the revenue they derived from grain and wine and produce of other kinds. Such men may have been five times wealthier, on an average, than their counterparts in the early days of the Empire.

In Rome and Constantinople, Senators appointed to consulships were under a legal obligation to celebrate their appointment by paying for lavish public entertainments or games. Augustine preached critically against rich men who were prepared to ruin themselves in order to give displays. A certain Petronius Maximus, who subsequently became Emperor for a few weeks in 455, expended 4000 pounds of gold on such games. Symmachus, when his son attained office, spent 2000 pounds. Although classed by a contemporary as a man of only medium wealth, Symmachus possessed three houses at Rome and at least thirteen more in various parts of Italy, as well as others in Sicily and Africa.

One of the ascetic ladies in whom Jerome took an interest, Saint Melania the younger, owned estates in Italy, Africa, Spain, Sicily and Britain. Her Sicilian property was maintained out of the revenue of sixty farms, and cultivated by 400 slaves. At one juncture, she emancipated 8000 slaves by a single act. Nevertheless, she was a shrewd financier. In the words of her biographer, 'blessed are those who perceived, and sold their property before the coming of the barbarians'. And she and her family also perceived the sound sense of transferring the proceeds to the East in good time.

As the possessions of people like Symmachus and Melania reveal, anyone who wanted to make a fortune would do well to invest his or her money not in industry but in land. Christian moralists such as Ambrose and John Chrysostom attacked the wealthy figures who bought house after house and field after field, ejecting the former owners and absorbing entire hamlets into their own insatiable hands. As the poet Rutilius Namatianus sailed up past the Etruscan coast in 416, he saw these enormous properties along the shore.

> We sailed north past Alsium, and Pyrgi
> Was soon behind us. Today these are large estates;
> At one time they were little villages.

Many of the great houses presiding over these lands were fortified like castles; this was the almost impregnable security to which so many destitute and displaced persons fled for shelter. The estates were whole little kingdoms in themselves, self-contained economic and social units full of farm-workers, slaves, artisans, guards, bailiffs, and hangers-on.

The mosaic of a certain Julius at Carthage shows one of these battlemented country palaces; and the families of Mauretanian chieftains such as Firmus and Gildo, who felt powerful enough to rise against the government in 373 and 397, lived on the same sort of scale.

Sidonius gives a description of another great château, the Gallic Burgus of Leontius at the confluence of the rivers Duranus (Dordogne) and Garumna (Garonne). Indeed, in Gaul there was a particularly massive concentration of powerful landowners, who lived more and more in the country and rarely came to Rome – a vigorous senatorial aristocracy of about a hundred families,

who handed down their hereditary power and kept their own
armed retainers.

Many a village near their homes still keeps their names today –
Juilly (Julius), Vitry (Victor), Savigny (Sabinus), Lezigny
(Licinius). So powerful were these Romano-Gallic lords that the
Emperor Honorius, in time of crisis, virtually decentralized the
control of the country into their hands. In 455, meeting at Arelate
(Arles), they even proclaimed one of their own number, Avitus,
as Emperor.

This act was a triumph of the Gallic nobles over the Roman
aristocracy itself, though only a momentary one, since Avitus
was deposed and died very soon afterwards. His son Ecdicius,
however, was still wealthy enough to support 4000 starving poor
in time of famine – a charity which by no means all his fellow
landowners would have performed.

A glance at the clothing of one of these noblemen would have
shown how times had changed. The plain white robes of earlier
Roman dignitaries have gone. A fourth-century Senator wore a
linen tunic (*camisia*), with a woollen robe (*dalmatica*) thrown over
it. On top of the *dalmatica* was a stiff-hooded cloak, or a
diaphanous mantle, floating lightly behind him. These clothes
were brilliantly coloured with patterns, and further adorned by
handkerchiefs and scarves. Women liked silk dresses,
emblazoned with gold thread. Jerome offered many a malicious
portrait of extravagantly bejewelled matrons, and Ammianus,
too, deploys a whole battery of savage attacks upon the outrageous luxury of the rich. So, of course, does the radical Salvian.

No doubt opulent Romans and Gallo-Romans lived very
grandly indeed. But Ammianus' picture is to some extent a
deliberate literary echo of a traditional satirical theme; and in any
case he was an Easterner who felt embittered because he had not
quite made the social grade at Rome. In fact, there is no reason to
suppose that Roman Senators were much more extravagant than
they had been in earlier times. It is true that the Greek historian
Olympiodorus declared that 'each of the great houses of Rome
had in itself everything that a moderate-sized town would be
likely to possess – a hippodrome, forums, temples, fountains and
numerous baths'. But another writer of the day who was in a
position to know, Macrobius, congratulates the men of his

generation on being *less* luxurious in their personal style of living
than their ancestors. In the eighteenth century, Montesquieu
partially attributed Rome's collapse to the excessive luxury of the
rich; and he has been followed by countless painters and film-
makers who depict orgiastic scenes with the puritanical implications that this was the sort of self-indulgence that brought the
Empire down. But the same or greater luxury had existed for
centuries, without any such lethal results.

Much more serious is another accusation that can be brought
against these senatorial noblemen of later Rome. 'There is in the
city', reported a visitor from the East, 'a Senate of wealthy men.
. . . Every one of them is fit to hold high office. *But they prefer not
to.* They stand aloof, preferring to enjoy their property at leisure.'
Like many people today, they felt that politics was a dirty
business, which they preferred to avoid. And this, in the later
300s and earlier 400s, was how the rich betrayed the Empire and
contributed to its fall. In Rome and the provinces alike, they failed
to pull their weight in public life. Exempted from service as city
councillors, they tended only to consider the interests of their
estates, or the advancement of their own friends. Towards the
very end of the Western Empire there was a change, because by
then the landowners had become more powerful than the
Emperor himself, and successfully invaded his councils. But
many still remained apart even then, and oblivious of any wider
claims upon their time.
Up to a point, this attitude was scarcely a novelty. For some
degree of leisure and alienation from public events had long been
regarded as essential for the well-rounded life a Roman gentle-
man should lead. Nevertheless the later Imperial aristocracy
fiddled with noteworthy insouciance while Rome burned.
Salvian felt this deeply, and declared that the higher a man's
status might be, the greater was his obligation, and the greater his
guilt if he fell short. Sidonius, too, called his fellow Gallo-Romans
to task for this failure, and wrote to one of them, a certain
Syagrius, urging a more public-spirited attitude.

. . . Why guide the plough-handle, and yet forgo all ambition
for the consul's robe? Do not bring a slur on the nobility by
staying so constantly in the country. . . . I would not indeed

say that a wise man should fail to concern himself with his private affairs, but he should act on the even principle of considering not only what he should *have* but what he should *be*.

Moreover, for a brief and gallant period, Sidonius practised what he preached. That was mainly during the years 471–5 when, as bishop of Arverna (Clermont-Ferrand), he helped Ecdicius in the local defence against the Visigoths – until the Imperial government let him down by making the territory over to them. During the remainder of his life, too, Sidonius made a few brief interventions in public affairs.

Nevertheless, the nine books of his literary letters, addressed to many friends and relations, remain a vivid advertisement for the very same ivory-towered seclusion he deplored to Syagrius. Ardent patriot though Sidonius felt himself to be, his letters perfectly depict an aristocracy which, although living under the very shadow of the Germans, was content to bask in the last feeble rays of the Imperial sun, largely indifferent to the encroaching darkness. At Rome, too, the ten books of epistles composed by Symmachus, two generations earlier, had revealed that the elegant metropolitan nobility of his time could scarcely spare a thought for public affairs, or worry about the menacing storm.

When the writer *On Matters of Warfare* suggested that provincial landowners living near areas threatened by German invasion should help to build up the Imperial defences, he may have been attempting a sardonic joke. As he must have known, there was no chance that this would happen. They were quite content with keeping the fortifications of their own palaces in good trim. In spite of frequent lip-service to the romantic concept of Eternal Rome, many noblemen were not prepared to lift a finger to save it. Indeed Orosius and Salvian accused a number of aristocrats of decamping to the barbarians, whom they even bribed, added Orosius, to escort them and carry their baggage.

It is true that, though they did not know it, these landowners, with their scribes and libraries and literary tastes, were playing a historic role in transmitting the culture of the past through and beyond the downfall of the Western Empire to future generations. But their escape from the practical tasks of patriotic service and defence was one of the reasons why the Empire fell at all.

One such landowner, the poet Ausonius, objecting strongly because his fellow-magnate Paulinus wanted to withdraw from his lands and become a churchman, could point to the chaos that would ensue if Paulinus' estates were broken up. It could equally have been argued, however, that the proprietors were centrifugal forces of destruction. Nor was that merely because of their passive failure to associate themselves with the Empire's needs. They also undermined the state in a very active fashion. For of all the obstacles to efficient and honest administration, they were the worst. They forcibly ejected collectors of taxes, harboured deserters and brigands, and repeatedly took the law into their own hands.

Symmachus declared it to be perfectly right that any provincial governor, when performing his duties as a judge, should favour nobles and gentry against the proletariat. They possessed their own private prisons: Theodosius I, receiving complaints about their arrogant behaviour, forbade them to maintain such establishments, but he spoke in vain. Ammianus told of local potentates whose 'private properties were enlarged by public disasters'. When the Germans broke into the Empire in 410, the selfish egotism of some of the landowners – especially a great lady named Proba – was reported to be making the appalling task of the government a good deal harder than it had been already.

Emperors and their advisers were well aware that an oligarchy of Senators in every province created a barrier between the average man and the government, and that the patronage which landlords exerted over their tenants and the surrounding population was destructive of the powers and rights of the Imperial authorities.

Indeed, rulers repeatedly passed laws seeking to restrict and limit such patronage; and in the end they 'abolished the name of patron altogether'. But this was meaningless verbiage, since nothing whatever happened. In fact, successive Emperors virtually had to give in. The Senators attained such power that those of them who wished to were finally able to infiltrate into the government itself, and into the top strata of the Imperial civil service; and in spite of forlorn attempts by Valentinian III to re-establish regular stages of promotion, the high offices became automatically theirs.

Moreover, 'patrons' though the rich were, some of them were

also the most brutal oppressors of the poor. Symmachus' father Avianius declared, in a time of wine shortage, that 'he would rather mix lime with his wines than sell them to the mob'. That was, perhaps, unimportant; but it was symbolic of a basically cruel social attitude.

It was bad enough when the landowners gained a say in the appointments of the Defenders of the People, whose specific duty had been to protect the poor. But, besides, these prosperous property-owners themselves were exempt, not only from all municipal responsibilities, but also from a wide range of taxes; and as for the taxes they were expected to pay, it was they who had perfected the facilities for evasion or postponement. This meant that the burden imposed on the poor became correspondingly greater. And, once again, when tax rebates were declared, it was the rich, not the poor, who secured them.

A series of Imperial decrees, however ineffectual, show that the government was uncomfortably aware of all this. Salvian is scarcely overstating it when he declared that the rich were guilty of slaying the poor.

> . . . Who can find words to describe the enormity of our present situation? Now when the Roman commonwealth, already extinct or at least drawing its last breath in that one corner where it still seems to retain some life, is dying, strangled by the cords of taxation as if by the hands of brigands, still a great number of wealthy men are found, the burden of whose taxes is borne by the poor; that is, very many rich men are found whose taxes are murdering the poor. Very many, I said: I am afraid I might more truly say all. . . .
>
> The rich have thus become wealthier by the decrease of the burdens that they bore easily: while the poor are dying of the increase in taxes that they already found too great for endurance. So the vaunted remedy most unjustly exalted the one group and most unjustly killed the other. To one class it was a most accursed reward and to the other a most accursed poison.

Indeed, the leading men had the whip-hand in every way. It was even they who themselves levied the taxes payable by their tenants. This was part of their deal with the government, the deal which eventually placed most of the official posts at their disposal. And yet Valentinian III, in 450, still found it diplomatically advisable to express sympathy with the alleged hardships of the wealthy class as taxpayers.

Even so, however, they did not move into patriotic obedience. On the contrary, they often remained hostile to the Emperor, and estranged from his advisers. For a long time many were pagans while their ruler was Christian. And their relations with the armed forces, in which they themselves were not allowed to play a part, were particularly bad. Their resistance to every attempt to recruit their labourers remained just as determined and became even more successful than before.

A postscript may be added about a brief interlude in this political and financial advance of the rich landowners and Senators. For their progress had been momentarily halted by Valentinian I, a Danubian soldier from quite outside the magic circle, who very much disliked them and their influence. Indeed, they suffered severely at his hands, and for a short time something like a total rift developed between the government and the aristocracy. Yet his appointment to the praetorian prefecture of the highly aristocratic and oppressive Petronius Probus was an attempt to conciliate the most significant noble families, and helped them to bow before the storm until this period was over – as it soon was.

And meanwhile there were writers imbued with their tradition who could hit back and damn Valentinian I, if not to his face, at least after his death. One such man was Ammianus who, although snubbed by the nobility, was steeped in its cultural values. Ammianus admits that Valentinian I could not be described as a 'semi-rustic' like his brother. But he could feel no real sympathy or identification with a family brought up to drink the wretched barley-wine of its native Danubian frontier province.

This snobbery about the people who did not socially belong was one of the most tedious phenomena of the ancient world, and proved perilous at a time when the welfare of the Empire, and even its survival, depended upon such men – men like Valentinian I and his Danubian fellow-countrymen, who had been saving Rome now for more than a hundred years, supplying almost all its best Emperors and soldiers.

Yet prejudice dies hard. The historian Dio Cassius, early in the third century, had already depicted such Danubians as rough, wild, primitive brawlers, and Galerius, an Emperor from a village near Florentiana (Dacia Ripensis, formerly Upper Moesia) who ruled from 305 to 311, was declared to have passed laws that were 'rude and boorish, corresponding to his origin as a cowherd'. One of his successors, Julian, was obliged to listen to orators mocking the uncouth, countrified entourages of these Danubian Emperors. Many a writer, too, expressed horror of barbarian careerists in general. The fastidious Symmachus, predictably, nagged at the 'outlandish ways' of Valentinian 1's friends and compatriots. It was all very negative: and when the same spirit of rejection was extended to the entire German element in the government and the army, it became mortally dangerous. By adopting this attitude, the Senators made yet another of their contributions to the downfall of the Empire.

When on the other hand the West had fallen, the nobles at once, somewhat ironically, established excellent relations with the German Odoacer who had brought it to an end, and became his collaborators throughout Italy. In Gaul, too, the landed aristocracy survived exposure to German rule without important material or cultural damage – handing on their incipient feudalism to the kingdoms of the Germans, whose flexible class structure made it possible for them to receive and absorb it.

Yet, gravely blameworthy though the Roman senatorial class was, the fault cannot be placed entirely at its door. For one of the reasons why it increasingly took matters into its own hands was because of the growing incapacity of the authorities to defend the persons or possessions of that class, or indeed of any other class either. A government must be master of its own house; and this the late Roman government was not. For all its passionate desire to regiment everybody in order to raise money, it failed in the last resort to do so, and because of its failure it collapsed.

5

The Middle Class against the State

The controllers of the later Roman Empire in the West had succeeded in totally alienating the rich and ruining the poor. And they also first alienated, and then ruined, the solid nucleus of those who lived between those two extremes – the middle class.

The middle class had always been the backbone of the Roman Empire, as it had been in the Greek city states that had come before. The reason why it fulfilled such a central role in the Roman world was because the Empire was made up of cities, more or less autonomous city-states, dating back in many cases to the period before the Romans took over. Under the general suzerainty of the Roman provincial governors, each of the cities retained a piece of land of its own, quite a large tract in some cases. The provinces, and especially those covering the more highly developed areas, were little more than the aggregates of these cities and their territories. It was, and had been for centuries, an urban civilization, in which the middle class who ran the cities comprised the central and vital element. The interests of the rural populations were not taken very much into account.

But in the third century AD these cities received a terrible blow. External invasions and internal rebellions gravely damaged them and their local leaders, and monetary inflation caused their endowments and lands to vanish into thin air. Nor were the military Emperors of the time particularly sorry; many of them were out of sympathy with the urban Greco-Roman culture, and felt closer to the rustic populations which the representatives of that culture had always ignored.

So when, shortly before 300, by grim and authoritarian measures of reorganization, Emperors of this military stamp managed to consolidate the Imperial regime once again, the cities received little encouragement to recover. Constantine the Great and his sons confiscated their tax-revenues and annexed much of their remaining territory, and then, after a momentary relaxation under Julian, similar measures were repeated by Valentinian I. Later, the towns were allowed just enough money to repair their public buildings, but new construction work of any kind still remained severely restricted.

These cities began to look thoroughly dilapidated, and the whole of the old middle-class civilization fell rapidly apart and into economic decline. The historian Zosimus attributed its collapse primarily to Theodosius I. This was partly because the author, a pagan, deplored the Emperor's strict Christianity. But there is truth, all the same, in his general estimate that the age of Theodosius was a period of continued and intensified urban decay.

And the depressing process still continued after that. Such glimpses as we are given of later city life are far from encouraging. When the Imperial envoy Priscus of Panium (Barbaros) in Thrace visited Attila, a businessman from the Empire whom he found at the Hun court complained that the Roman citizens he had left at home no longer felt the smallest hope. Moreover, in addition to the attitude of the Imperial authorities, the cities had destruction by German invaders to contend with. Although some ancient authors overstated the devastating effects of invasion, these effects were quite grave enough to strike further crippling blows at city life.

In such circumstances, the townsmen became inert. Their one object was to prevent their buildings and property from being sacked by invaders, and once this was guaranteed they were usually prepared to surrender. But they often suffered serious damage from the Germans all the same. Thus Sidonius pays a poetic tribute to the city of Narbo (Narbonne) in southern Gaul, which was half destroyed: 'such glorious ruins make you precious in our sight.'

The moralist Salvian, on the other hand, deplored the continued enthusiasm of the people of Treveri (Trier) for their games, which they still continued to hold even though the place had been sacked and plundered on no less than three occasions. 'The Roman people', he declared, 'are dying and laughing.' Dying they certainly were; or at least the cities, their traditional social units, were dying, and had already become the merest shadows of their former vigorous selves.

The essential element in the urban middle class consisted of the *curiales*, the members of the city councils or *curiae*; and the title was extended to their sons and descendants. These councillors had tended to become a hereditary group, because only the solid citizens, those who had some property to hand down from father to son, could endure the financial burden involved. But wealthy men had long since become increasingly unwilling to enrol as councillors. In due course, Imperial compulsion was exerted upon them to serve.

However, various ways of evading this compulsion were found. There was also a considerable list of exempted categories, including not only professional men, clergy, and lessees of state farms, but all Senators too, and the 'knights' who came next to the Senators in financial qualifications. This unwillingness of the rich to join the town councils meant that the membership of these bodies devolved upon the upper sections of the middle class. That is to say, all possessors of land below the Senators and knights were eligible to join – or rather, forced to join – if, within the city's territorial boundaries, they owned twenty-five Roman acres (fifteen by modern measurements).

And their offspring, when their turn came, were likewise enrolled under compulsion. (In this respect they were on a par with the commercial corporations, which had become an essential feature of the life of the later Roman Empire, and may also be regarded as representatives of the middle class. For the food-supplying and shipowning corporations provided such vital services to the state that they too were harnessed to their jobs by inherited compulsion, which is the subject of a stringent law of Valentinian I.)

The functions of the city councillors were very different from what they had been at earlier epochs. At a time when the growing loss of their cities' autonomy had caused their actual municipal duties to become minimal, they instead found themselves virtually transformed into agents of the central authorities. For far and away their most important duty nowadays was to carry out work for the government, and, above all, to collect its revenues. It was incumbent upon councillors, and their sons when their turn came, to induce their fellow-citizens to disgorge the money taxes demanded by the state, as well as the required levies in kind: foodstuffs, clothing and the like. Moreover, the councillors were even required to assist in the management of Imperial mines and estates and to help call up recruits for the army.

Since these were their tasks, it was inevitable that, regarded from below, they should look like oppressors. The Emperor Julian, too, agreed with this view, and did his utmost to curb what he regarded as their exploitation of the people – though Ammianus, usually his admirer, gave him no credit for this, being himself of the city-councillor class.

To Salvian, the councillors' behaviour towards the poor seemed horribly brutal: he saw them as rapacious persecutors of widows, orphans and monks. 'What cities are there,' he cried, 'and not only cities but even towns and villages, in which they are not so many tyrants?' For people who felt as Salvian did, it had not been comforting when Theodosius I let the appointment of the Defenders of the People, who were supposed to protect the poor from oppression, get into the hands of these members of the councils.

One can scarcely blame the overtaxed destitute populations for taking this view. Yet it was too one-sided all the same, since the situation of the councillors, also, was appallingly difficult. From the beginning of the fourth century onwards, the government redoubled its strenuous, almost neurotic, efforts to ensure that they did not abandon their posts and their hereditary duties. Julian's efforts to prevent them from acting heavy-handedly were paradoxically accompanied by particularly vigorous attempts to round them up and keep them at their jobs; and subsequently the Code of Theodosius II contains no less than 192 edicts threatening and brow-beating them with every sort of menace.

For example, they were not allowed to sell their properties without permission. And they must not even travel abroad, for to do so was declared to be 'an injury to their city'. If they ignored this injunction, they found, after five years' absence, that their possessions had been confiscated. They were denied the asylum provided by churches – sharing this disqualification with insolvent debtors, Moreover, any landowner's bailiff who connived at their flight from their duties was liable to be burnt at the stake. There was unconscious black humour in an edict of 365 which forbade the imposition of a councillor's status on any man as a punishment.

To describe this state of affairs as disunity was putting it mildly: the councillors and the government were perpetually at war. The anonymous writer *On Matters of Warfare* was shocked by their sufferings at the hands of the authorities – and, although probably of council rank himself, he seems to have been a reasonably objective man.

According to the rhetorician Libanius, the official intimidation of councillors who remained recalcitrant actually went as far as brutal physical violence.

> . . . It is that which has chiefly emptied the council chambers. There are perhaps other causes, but this especially, lashes and subjection to such corporal injuries as not even the most criminal slaves endure.
>
> In many cities, your Majesty, after these floggings, this is what the few surviving town councillors say: 'Goodbye house, goodbye lands! Let one and the other be sold, and with their price let us buy liberty!'

What destroyed these men, the orator goes on to say, and degraded them to such a slavish condition, was their enforced personal liability for their whole region's tax deficits, which they were often quite unable either to prevent or make good.

In the conflict between the government and the taxpayer, they were hopelessly caught in the middle. Yet it was a remarkable situation that *any* man who occupied the supposedly dignified office of city councillor should be flogged by agents of the central government. Nor can the testimony of Libanius easily be dismissed as mere rhetorical fiction. For when Theodosius I exempts councillors from blows of a whip loaded with lead, it is evident from what he says that this is the treatment they had been receiving.

A further edict of the same ruler declares in preposterous language that 'like men dedicated with religious headbands, the council members must guard the perpetual mysteries'. For while always ready enough to employ pressure and force to keep these functionaries at their posts, Emperors sometimes remember to show a tardy consideration for their feelings of dignity. They are urged not to be 'forgetful of the splendour of their birth'. Valentinian III frankly admits their overwhelming burden, and Majorian declares them to be 'the sinews of the commonwealth and the hearts of the cities'. But it was much too late for such poetic compliments to have any effect.

A. H. M. Jones, in *The Later Roman Empire* (1964), doubted whether the lives of this Roman middle class of the fourth and fifth centuries were really as grim as has been made out. But if his great work has a fault, it is that he tends occasionally to minimize the hardships of the age, which were painfully real. He was right, however, to point out that (as in the case of the oppressions of the agricultural labourer) there was at least a saving grace of governmental inefficiency – the very repetitiveness of the Imperial pronouncements, and their strident tone, are sure signs that they were not being fully enforced. In consequence, many city-councillors contrived to escape to honorary senatorial rank, or to Imperial service, or to the army, or to the clergy, and others just somehow disappeared from view.

Nevertheless, the lives of councillors had become little less than unendurable. By this time, except for merchants, they are almost the only representatives of the once resplendent middle class about whom we hear anything at all. And they were in almost total decline – mere harassed agents of the central government. Such distress was almost universal. Crushed between the upper and lower millstones, the middle class had virtually been squeezed out of existence.

Obviously, in a society which had always so largely depended on this class, its destruction contributed very substantially to the Empire's downfall. For it left a vacuum which nothing could fill, and meant that from now onwards the population mainly consisted of very rich and very poor. No doubt, the traditional urban culture had always exhibited a disequilibrium, since the towns were parasites upon an agrarian economy. Nevertheless, that was the culture which had held the ancient world together, so that the obliteration of its middle-class nucleus meant that this world could not remain in existence any longer.

III

THE CREDIBILITY GAP

6

The People against the Bureaucrats

So throughout the last two centuries of the Roman world there was a fearful and ever-increasing loss of personal freedom for all, except the very rich and powerful. Ever since the arch-regimenter Diocletian declared that 'uncontrolled activity is an invention of the godless', each of the leading rulers in turn hammered the nails in more fiercely. The Roman Empire had become a prison: or a military camp in a perpetual state of siege, where each man was assigned a place he must not desert. And his descendants must not desert it either.

And so the whole of the population was in conflict with the government: there was disunity, or rather a whole series of disunities, on a colossal scale. The authorities desired and enforced the very greatest degree of regimentation that it was possible to obtain – even if this meant servitude for almost everybody – since this seemed the only way to raise the money needed to save the Empire.

And yet the result was just the opposite to what was intended. Paradoxically, this regimentation did not halt the disintegration of the Roman world, but accelerated its destructive progress. The individual spirit of initiative that alone could have kept the commonwealth alive was stifled and stamped out by the widespread deprivation of personal freedom, which thus became one of the most potent reasons for Rome's collapse.

The downward process was also precipitated by the vast size and deteriorating quality of the civil service employed to extort this greatly needed revenue. It was, moreover, a self-perpetuating body – because in common with so many other elements in late Roman society its membership assumed a hereditary character. Civil servants were at first *allowed* to enrol their sons in the same posts as they themselves held, and then, in the time of Valentinian I and Theodosius I, they found themselves compelled to do so. Yet even Theodosius, in 394, declared a further practice by prudent parents to be preposterous – their enrolment of their children, when they were still infants, in the same ministries to which they themselves belonged.

Since the beginning of the fourth century there had been a new Imperial aristocracy of service, so that successive Emperors of that period did not have to enlist the aid of a hostile hereditary nobility but could make use of a more docile body of helpers. Later, however, the civil servants of this new brand gained confidence, and felt able to exhibit a serene defiance of the Emperors. And they for their part, although they confusingly intervened in the administration at any level they pleased, failed to prevent the bureaucracy from encroaching gradually on their power, which its representatives finally reduced to paralysis.

Valentinian I found on one occasion that he had been granting pardons to murderers without his knowledge, or even the knowledge of his personal staff. This distressed him, since he was eager to check up on everything he could. It was in order to impose this firm hand and make sure that the process of supervision was as thoroughgoing as possible that he initiated a major expansion of the whole machinery of government, importing professional administrators, often from his own Danubian territories. Senators hated and feared this element, and in the course of the fifth century they took their revenge by permeating the senior ranks of the administration until it virtually became an appendix of the Italian and Gallo-Roman nobility.

Valentinian I had disciplined his bureaucrats strictly, equating their duties with military service. Nevertheless, their relations with army officers were frequently strained, owing to jealousies on both sides. Yet it remained the principal duty of the civilian officials to serve the army, by keeping it supplied with manpower and money, and as these military demands became more and more pressing the number of functionaries rose to correspondingly vast dimensions. The governor of Africa, now northern Tunisia, employed 400 subordinates; the Director of Imperial Largesses was assisted by 834.

There were also whole armies of spies, to round up political suspects. They were particularly concentrated in the Imperial postal service, where they doubled as dispatch-carriers and kept the government informed of any suspicious movement they noticed. Certain Emperors, notably Julian, tried to cut down the espionage service to a more modest size. But it was too characteristic of the times to be checked, and all attempts to keep its dimensions and activities within reasonable bounds proved unsuccessful.

And so the later Roman Empire was essentially a bureaucratic state. It would be too simple, however, to regard these bureaucrats as wholly bad. For one thing, the Roman government possessed no police force, and had to rely on its civil service to enforce law and order. And so, for a time at least, these officials, whatever their faults, played a substantial part in holding things together. Indeed, had it not been for them, the Empire would have collapsed long before it did. But ultimately their numbers became altogether excessive; and so did their capacity to dominate the state.

The laws of Theodosius I reveal that this had become alarmingly apparent to the Emperor himself. But a perusal of these Imperial pronouncements also shows us something much worse – thus confirming the evidence of many an ancient author. For it becomes clear that the bureaucracy of the later Roman Empire was not only rigid, over-conservative and slavish, but also desperately corrupt. The writer *On Matters of Warfare* does not, like some thinkers of the age, blame everything on the landowners. Instead, he concentrates on the faults of the Imperial bureaucrats – which he sees as a still more sinister pressure group. And he does not seem to be overstating his case, because the works of his contemporaries, too, confirm that efficient public servants had become so rare that they are singled out in astonished tones for exceptional praise.

The best type of man just did not go into such jobs at all. This was partly because promotion was so narrowly hereditary, and partly also because many of the most competent people had been diverted to the Christian clergy, leaving the service of the state to less gifted, less reliable, and above all less scrupulous careerists. Besides, the Western Empire was too poor to pay its ministerial staffs decently – and this made them ready to grab whatever they could. Even retired officials still remained rapacious. 'An office once held,' remarked Salvian, 'gave them the privilege of a perpetual right to rob others.'

It was the easiest thing in the world for civil servants and ex-civil servants to evade orders from governors and demands from tax-collectors. And what counted, when you wanted these functionaries to come to a decision, was all too often influence and graft – known as 'the selling of smoke'. It has been declared that moral corruption was one of the causes of Rome's downfall, and when we look at the civil service this claim seems conspicuously justified. Nor, unfortunately, were even the few competent Emperors good judges of the integrity of their subordinates. For example, Valentinian I and his brother were notorious for the selection of men described by Ammianus as detestable.

The outcome of this wildly uncontrollable proliferation of dishonest bureaucracy was shocking. Administration was paralysed. Remedies, if applied at all, proved ludicrously ineffective. Ten years after the death of Valentinian I, public criticism of these defects had become so loud that the authorities, in an absurd act of self-defence, pronounced it an act of sacrilege even to discuss the merits of anyone chosen by an Emperor to serve him. For the government was all too clearly aware of the bureaucrats' corruption, as well as of their power. It sought to combat such practices by frequent and strident edicts, regulations and warnings. Successive rulers threatened their officials with fines, banishment and torture and even death. In 450 Valentinian III specifically denounced tax collectors and a wide range of other financial officials. Then Majorian, too, assailed them in menacing and even insulting terms. But all this was clearly not of the slightest avail.

Nor did the principal administrative remedy to which Emperors resorted prove any more helpful. This was ever intenser *centralization*, which not only slashed personal freedom still further but harnessed the government with increasing responsibilities which it was quite unable to carry.

The organization of the Empire was much more complicated

than it had been in earlier times. Since the beginning of the fourth century AD, the West and East together comprised one hundred provinces, just twice as many as there had been before. The increase had been intended to guarantee that no minutiae of administration were over-looked by the provincial governors. And it was also designed to ensure that no governor should feel himself strong enough to try to grab the throne for himself.

In neither of those aims was the reorganization successful. Fearing that this might prove the case, and realizing that it was beyond their capacity to supervise every governor personally, Emperors employed no less than two sets of intermediary officials to help them with the task.

First, there were the heads (vicars) of thirteen 'dioceses', among which the hundred provinces were divided. Second, these thirteen dioceses were distributed among three, later four, praetorian prefectures, each under a separate prefect.

In the days of the earlier Empire, the praetorian prefect had been the commander of the Emperor's military bodyguard and, at times, his chief of staff as well. But now there was a complete change. For although the prefectures were still of enormous importance, they had assumed, for the most part, a civilian character. The prefects of the later Empire were the magnificent personages who, under the immediate direction of the ruler himself and in constant touch with his inner cabinet or Consistory, controlled the government of the Imperial territories. 'To their wisdom', as Gibbon observed, 'was committed the supreme administration of justice and of the finances, the two objects which, in a state of peace, comprehend almost all the respective duties of the sovereign and of the people.'

Two of these prefects belonged to the West. One was in control of Italy, North Africa, and Illyricum (central Europe as far as the Danube, and, for a period, the Balkans as far as the Black Sea hinterland). His colleague was the prefect of the Gauls, who controlled Gaul, the Rhine provinces, Britain and Spain. Mauretania, in north-western Africa, was divided between these two Western prefectures.

As in any vast state, the standard of efficiency and integrity maintained by these various grades of officials was neither uniformly good nor bad. For example the legislation of successive Emperors reflects the strenuous efforts of at least a number of

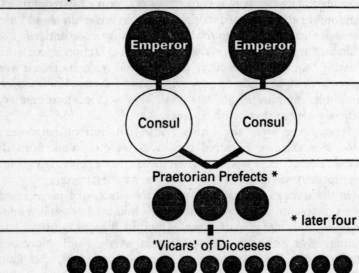

Administrative Structure of the later Roman Empire	Western Roman Empire *Milan* and *later Ravenna*	Eastern Roman Empire *Constantinople*

Emperor　**Emperor**

Consul　Consul

Praetorian Prefects *

* later four

'Vicars' of Dioceses

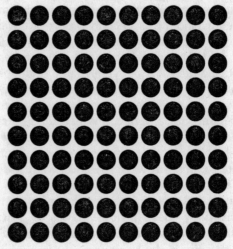

Governors of Provinces

praetorian prefects to check the rapidly accelerating slide into chaos. Yet it was unfortunate that Valentinian I's prefect of Italy, Africa and Illyricum – who occupied the post no less than four times, under three successive rulers – was Petronius Probus. For it is impossible to ignore Ammianus' account of Petronius as a person who, although careful never to order an illegal act, nevertheless was a suspicious, merciless and sinister hypocrite, eaten up by anxiety and jealousy.

Moreover, there is evidence that provincial governors, too, had fallen below the high levels of early Imperial times. It was hardly to be expected, in such a difficult and exacting age, that every one of the hundred governors at any one time should be entirely respectable characters; and the weakness of city councils was a positive encouragement to these officials to interfere right and left. The writer *On Matters of Warfare* paints a deeply depressing picture. 'The appalling greed of the provincial governors', he asserts, 'is ruinous to the taxpayers' interests. . . . The buying of recruits, the purchase of horses and grain, the monies intended for city walls – all these are regular sources of profit for them, and are the pillage for which they long.' It was the brutal cynicism of governors and their henchmen that caused the Visigoths the hardships which impelled them, in desperation, to attack the Romans in 378. Orators declared in the presence of Emperors that the conduct of such administrators made the provincials actually long for barbarians to occupy their territories.

Salvian found governors venal and cruel – men who subjected the poorer communities to virtual devastation. A severe judgment from so censorious a writer was only to be expected, but the much more conservative Sidonius, too, felt that the abuses committed by Roman functionaries in Gaul had gone to intolerable lengths. One fifth-century official, Seronatus, behaved with such brutality that he drove many of the population into the woods.

After all this, it would be funny, if it was not sad, to read an Imperial edict which declares it better for a governor not to frequent fascinating houses of ill-repute (*non deverticula deliciosa sectetur*).

A special word of condemnation must be reserved for the lawyers of the later Empire. One of our outstanding documents for the period is the Theodosian Code which was drawn up in 438 on the orders of the Eastern monarch Theodosius II, and was accepted by the West. The Code consists of sixteen books, containing a collection of Imperial enactments extending back for a hundred years and more.

It was intended to eliminate the many notorious ambiguities, inconsistencies and contradictions of which the existing laws were full. Although exercising an influence upon subsequent German legislation, it was largely superseded in the sixth century by the Code of Justinian I.

As a source of historical information, however, it remains highly significant. The measures it records tell us a tremendous amount about conditions in the two Empires, Eastern and Western alike. And equally informative are certain further edicts by Western Emperors of the same period and later, notably Valentinian III and Majorian.

But these regulations are particularly instructive for reasons which it would not have pleased their compilers to hear. For many of the documents in question, especially as the Western Empire drew towards its end, display an almost hysterical violence, revealing emotional confusions between sin and crime that would have been quite alien to the classical Roman law of earlier times. Sir Samuel Dill, who wrote feelingly on the hardships suffered by these later Romans, was convinced, with some justice, that this prolonged repressive legislation was not only a symptom of the Roman collapse, but helped decisively to bring it about.

Above all else, the Imperial pronouncements are intensely, monotonously repetitive. Such constant repetitions suggest that these successive measures, emerging in a continuous torrent, were circumvented, disobeyed and ignored with equally continuous impunity. Their endless reiteration shows that the government, while alive to what it ought to be doing, was overwhelmed by the situation, and quite impotent to improve it. Never has there been such a futile spate of over-legislation. And its futility seems to be underlined by a curiously baroque and wordy style of drafting, with many flowery references to the potency of evil and the need to remould those citizens who were ignorant and liable to be deceived by depraved persuasion.

Some legislation, it is true, was both humane and enlightened.

There were laws, for instance, alleviating the lot of slaves, and granting assistance to needy debtors and forbidding infanticide. However, there was also a terrifying amount of bloodthirsty judicial inhumanity. Besides, there was not even a pretence of equality before the law. Not only were noblemen entitled to have their lawsuits heard in a specially constituted court, but, with the explicit approval of Symmachus, the privileges and punishments of rich and poor were entirely different. 'If a man be poor,' declared the theologian Theodoret, 'his terror of the judge and law-courts is doubled.'

Certainly, there were brief moments when this trend was reversed, for example under Valentinian I, who dealt sternly with the upper class. All the same, Valentinian himself was a poor advertisement for judicial balance. For even if we do not believe Ammianus' assurance that he fed victims to pet bears, he was evidently liable to terrible fits of anger, one of which caused his death. And the ferocity with which he ordered summary executions was notorious. 'Shift his block!' he would cry. And Theodosius I, too, for all his religious principles, often behaved with the grimmest cynicism and brutality.

Such were the character defects of hard-pressed Emperors. But worse still was the savagery with which, throughout the Empire, the law was administered and enforced by the courts. True, they were only reflecting the Codes which continually menaced floggings and burnings alive – or perhaps the Codes were reflecting the practice of the courts. When landowners, too, took matters into their own hands and dispensed justice themselves (as a Carthage mosaic shows one of them doing) the results were no less harsh. The veto of Theodosius I on their private prisons proved ineffective. And even the cultured Sidonius, after coffin-bearers had inadvertently left their tools on the ground covering his grandfather's grave, tells us how he acted on his own responsibility to have them flogged or tortured on the site of their offence.

But by far the most serious problem affecting the operation of the laws was the defect already noted in the civil service as well. For the administration of justice, like the operations of the bureaucracy, was riddled through and through with corruption. Many lawyers behaved quite abominably. The writer *On Matters of Warfare* selects this particular theme as the culmination and climax of his essay.

. . . Most Sacred Emperor, when the defences of the state have
been properly provided both at home and abroad through the
operation of divine Providence, one remedy designed to cure
our civilian woes awaits Your Serene Majesty. Throw light
upon the confused and contradictory rulings of the laws by a
pronouncement of Your August Dignity. And put a stop to
dishonest litigation!

The Code of Theodosius II was intended to tidy up the
contradictory rulings. But for the dishonest litigation it did not
begin to find a remedy. An anxious awareness that there was
corruption in the very centre of the legal scene was openly voiced
at a curious ceremony in the Emperor's presence, when the
Senators chanted a series of ritual incantations, one of which,
repeated no less than twenty-five times in succession, took the
form of an appeal 'that, to prevent the edicts being interpolated,
all the Codes should be written in longhand'. Dishonest inter-
polations, that is to say, were not only feared, but fully expected.

The envoy Priscus of Panium (Barbaros) in Thrace, visiting
Attila's court, tried to persuade the disaffected Greek merchant
he met there, in an oration which even in his own account sounds
wooden and unconvincing, that Roman justice was still a fine
thing. The Greek replied that the system might be all right, but
that the men in charge of it were appalling.

But much the most damning indictment of the lawyers comes
from Ammianus. Not content, he says, with promoting utterly
useless legislation, they employed their audacious, windy
eloquence for criminal frauds, procrastinated by creating hopeless legal tangles, deliberately raised deadly hatreds between one
member of a family and another, and 'laid siege to the doors of
the widows and childless'. The coarse-mouthed offensiveness of
their speeches, he added, was only equalled by their lamentable
ignorance of the law.

Perhaps Ammianus was indulging in some rhetorical over-
statement, in the spirit of the satirists of old. But he is a
responsible historian, and much of what he says must have been
true. Indeed, the Imperial edicts themselves stress the existence
of precisely such abuses. The lawyers, almost as much as the civil
servants, caused Rome's administration to grind gradually to its
paralysed halt. Between them, the jurists and bureaucrats

bequeathed to the barbarians an Empire which, in the words of the German philosopher Johann von Herder, was 'already dead, an exhausted body, a corpse stretched out in its own blood'.

7

The People against the Emperor

The rulers who poured forth these constant torrents of ineffectual edicts often lived very cloistered lives. Isolated among their advisors and courtiers, they lost contact with the rest of their subjects. And this was another of the fatal disunities that brought the Empire down.

The Emperor's position was exceedingly elevated and withdrawn. A fourth-century philosopher and rhetorician, Themistius, put the matter succinctly: 'you are the living law, and superior to the written law.' It is true that rulers reserved the right to depart from any individual measure which in a special case seemed to be operating unjustly. Yet great ecclesiastics such as Ambrose would have wished to qualify Themistius' statement, owing to their insistence on the independent rights of the church. And others, too, disliked the situation. So Valentinian III considered it advisable to declare publicly that he considered himself bound by the laws.

Nevertheless, the formal powers of an Emperor were virtually unlimited. And they were ostentatiously symbolized by a portentous solemnity, befitting his role as God's regent upon earth. Since this was his unutterably august status, everything relating to him was pronounced sacred. A series of successive edicts even restricted the numbers of those who were entitled to touch his purple robes, and who were permitted to perform their obeisances before His Serenity in person. Those unqualified to obtain such access prostrated themselves before his holy images and portraits instead. His edicts, written in gold on purple parchment and received by his ministers with reverently covered hands, were formally 'adored'. Since they were heavenly and consecrated, breaches of their provisions were sacrilegious, and could be punished accordingly.

Ceremonial reached fantastic levels of elaboration. Particularly grandiose were Imperial Arrivals and Entries into cities. As the carriage of Constantius II drew him into Rome in 357, Ammianus describes his hieratic, icon-like posture.

> . . . For he both stooped when passing through lofty gates (although he was very short), and as if his neck were in a clamp he kept the gaze of his eyes straight ahead, and turned his face neither to right nor to left, but (as if he were a lay figure) neither did he nod when the wheel jolted nor was he ever seen to spit, or to wipe or rub his face or nose, or move his hands about.

The immobile grandeur is a far cry from the relative accessibility with which rulers in earlier days had felt obliged to humour their subjects.

Moreover, an Emperor of these later times was surrounded and cut off from the outside world by a far more extensive court than hitherto. Julian tried to cut down the numbers of his courtiers to reasonable limits, but soon afterwards they became even more numerous than before, especially under Theodosius I. Obviously, their proximity to the Emperor's person gave them enormous influence. They showed their strength at its greatest when they prompted Valentinian III to bring down the virtual master of the Western world, Aetius. But they often immobilized both themselves and the Emperor by quarrels within their own ranks.

This Imperial court, with the cabinet or council (Consistory) at its centre, was inevitably the focus of violent criticism from outside. The historian Olympiodorus attacked it for bribery and embezzlement. Anti-Germans deplored the large number of courtiers who were Germans. And the aristocracy felt implacable hostility against the influence of the ruler's personal chamberlains.

Many of these chamberlains were eunuchs, a class which had often been favoured by ancient monarchs because of its freedom from any sexual loyalties and hereditary ambitions that might weaken its fidelity to the throne. Under Theodosius I, the eunuchs were the people from whom promotion had to be purchased. But attacks against eunuch power were traditional; and under Valentinian III they reached their crescendo. The lofty eminence of these personages, and their influence over Emperors, deepened the rift between the court and the world. It was considered particularly scandalous when one such eunuch, Eutropius, became the chief adviser and general of Arcadius in the East. The poet Claudian lavished ferocious abuse on this development, declaring that not even a nation of barbarians would have tolerated a eunuch as consul and commander-in-chief.

The court was wherever the Emperors were. Until the death of Theodosius I, they still took the field in major wars and spent their lives travelling from one end of the Empire to the other. They often dwelt at Treveri (Trier) close to the German border, or at Sirmium not far from the Danubian front. When they were in Italy they did not usually live at Rome, which was insufficiently central to deal with urgent frontier needs, but established their headquarters at Mediolanum (Milan).

In 402, however, Honorius, while residing at that city, received a severe shock. For during Alaric's invasion of Italy in that year, the young Emperor was besieged for a while within its walls and came within measurable distance of capture by the barbarian enemy. He therefore decided, soon afterwards, to move the government of the Western Empire to Ravenna on the east coast of Italy. He selected Ravenna because it was practically inaccessible to invaders by land, being almost completely surrounded by stretches of water and marsh. On the other hand, it was beside the Adriatic (which has now receded a number of miles), so that communications could be kept open.

The advantages of Ravenna were purely strategic. There were no natural amenities, and not even any water that was drinkable. Although the Emperor Julius Nepos personified the place as a goddess on his coins, Sidonius declared that 'the movement of ships stirs up the filthy sediment in the canals, and the sluggish flow is fouled by the bargemen's poles, piercing the bottom slime'. Nevertheless, under the direction of Honorius' half-sister Placidia, a glittering capital was built, notable especially for the mosaic-filled interiors of its churches and mausoleums.

Many of the buildings we see today date from the period after the downfall of the Western Empire, when Germans and Byzantines ruled the city in turn. But there are also surviving constructions of great beauty which belong to the epoch of the last Western Emperors. One is a cruciform mausoleum, with its interior filled with blue mosaics, which was the burial place of either Placidia or her husband Constantius III. There is an octagonal edifice too, known as the Baptistry of the Orthodox, or sometimes described as the Baptistry of Neon owing to a tradition that it was decorated by an archbishop of that name in the middle of the fifth century; but it may be some decades earlier.

Wherever they were, Emperors tended to be cut off from the world by their scheming courts and elaborate pomp. At Constantinople, for example, in 400, Synesius upbraided its ruler for his pomp-encrusted remoteness. 'You hide in your apartments,' he declared, 'in case men should discover that you too are human!' And he went on to urge a clean break with the palace clique and all its stultifying ceremonials. His criticism applied even more strongly to Ravenna, where geography further encouraged the tendency to seclusion. The pagan historian Zosimus painted a vivid contrast between the rest of Italy, a defenceless prey to the Visigoths, and the court of Ravenna, which continued the pursuit of its rituals and intrigues as if it were playing some insubstantial, ghostly game.

Moreover, once Ravenna had become the capital, Western Emperors, with a few short-lived exceptions, never again went out and commanded the Roman army in wars. Honorius stayed behind in safe seclusion, and so did Valentinian III. The latter sometimes visited Rome, because he enjoyed its luxuries, and a few of his transient successors resided there for a time. But for the most part the rulers preferred to remain in the shadows of Ravenna, leading a sedentary life entirely separated from the hard realities of the waning Empire.

Their chief or only contact with the world came from their courtiers. The numerous speeches these men delivered in praise of their masters have left us many sickening examples of servility. Valentinian I, Valens and Gratian even found themselves compared with the Trinity. One of the worst offenders was the poet Ausonius, whose effusion in honour of Gratian's consulship presents the young Emperor's uninteresting personality in a ludicrously unrecognizable form.

. . . There is no place, I say, Most Gracious Emperor, but
stamps my consciousness with the wondrous image of your
most worshipful Majesty. Not the court, which was so
formidable when you came to the throne, and which you have
made so agreeable. Not the Forum and basilicas, which once
re-echoed with legal business, but now with the taking of vows
for your well-being – for under your rule who is there whose
property is not secure? Not the Senate-house, now as happy in
the business of passing resolutions in your honour as it was
formerly gloomy and troubled with complaints. Not the public
highways, where the sight of so many joyous faces suffers no
one to be alone in showing delight.

Not the universal privacy of the home – the very bed,
destined for our repose, is made more restful as we reflect upon
your benefits: slumber, which blots out everything,
nevertheless presents your picture to our gaze!

Another appalling flatterer is Claudian, who forecasts that the dim young sons of Theodosius I are going to equal the Scipios and Metelluses and Camilluses of old. His reiteration of the almost non-existent merits of the boy Honorius are painful indeed.

> While kindness and severity, combined
> With tranquil ease, pervade your lofty mind,
> No terrors swiftly round you spread affright,
> Nor novelties astonishment excite.
> Your knowledge and capacity are clear;
> In every word superior charms appear;
> Your answers raise ambassadors' surprise;
> And, wrapped in manners grave, youth hidden lies.
> In every feature is your father seen:
> Majestic ease conjoined with modest mien.
> Now on you is a parent's helmet placed;
> The lance your ancestors had often graced
> At once so dexterously by you is thrown
> The Romans fondly glow such powers to own.
> What noble elegance in every air
> Whene'er the shield, or armour gilt, you wear!

Such adulation overflowed all too easily into the business of the state. When the Code of Theodosius II was presented to his Senators in 438, they cried out in unison: 'Through you we hold our honours, our property, everything!' And they shouted it not once, but twenty-eight times. But that was nothing. Nine years earlier, when the edict ordering the Code had been read out in the Senate of Valentinian III at Rome, there were no less than three hundred and fifty-two repetitions of the cries acclaiming himself and his colleague. And at introspective Ravenna, the habitual obsequiousness around the bejewelled figures of the Emperors was more intensive still.

Yet at the same time, even at sequestered Ravenna, there did remain a persistent, uncomfortable, sometimes acute, awareness of the ruler's urgent need to make some impression upon the surrounding Roman world. And the government reached out to make contact with that world by the most readily available and traditional method – through the designs and inscriptions stamped on the coinage.

Ever since the beginning of the Roman Empire there had been an astonishing proliferation of official propaganda on these issues, which fulfilled the same purpose, from the viewpoint of official publicity, as modern newspapers, radio and television. A number of mints had been habitually used, but as the Empire finally dwindled the output was mainly from mints in Italy itself, especially Rome, Mediolanum (Milan) and Ravenna. The messages, however, that appear on the products of the different mints are at this epoch almost entirely uniform, proceeding from a single, universally valid directive which emanated from the Emperor's bureau itself, often in synchronized collusion with his Eastern colleague – at times when relations between the two capitals were good enough for this to be practicable.

These designs and inscriptions are fewer and less varied than those of earlier Roman times, so that at first sight they bear a somewhat stereotyped air. Yet the highly selective range of slogans and pictures upon which the government chose to concentrate, imprinting them on thousands and millions of coins that enjoyed an extensive circulation, is always revealing. For these, evidently, were the themes that the authorities had decided were most likely to gain support for their regime and for the defence of the Empire.

Every coin, just as hitherto, depicted on its obverse side the head of one of the Emperors themselves or of a prince or princess of his house. But in contrast with earlier epochs, these 'portraits', like the marble portrait-busts of the same rulers, lack all individuality, and have instead become generalized representations, not of a particular person any longer, but of a mighty symbolic monarchy. Often, too, the features are no longer in profile but frontal, like the blank and awe-inspiring faces on the Byzantine mosaics which were now inaugurating their long history.

The supreme priority of defence needs is reflected in an increasing number of coin-portraits of military type, displaying the ruler equipped with spear, shield, and gem-encrusted helmet. When these military emblems do not appear, the plain heads of an earlier tradition are very often replaced by busts adorned with the trappings of power–sceptre and orb, and the Imperial mantle heavily embroidered and studded with precious stones. Moreover, the laurel wreath of old Rome is replaced by a diadem of autocratic monarchy, intertwined with pearls and flowers. In the Imperial nomenclature on the coins, the venerable title 'Augustus' is retained, but the traditional 'Imperator' has been replaced by 'Our Lord', and traditional epithets alluding to the Emperor's piety and blessedness have become almost invariable. The designation 'Perpetual' is also employed. It was a term that seemed somewhat ironical when Emperors were succeeding each other at the rate of almost one a year; but at least it was a reminder of the hoped-for eternity of their office.

The reverse sides of the coins, too, are often devoted to the person of the monarch, in his various capacities. Many of these designs (when the Western and Eastern allies were sufficiently friendly) display him enthroned beside his Constantinopolitan colleague, sometimes with specific allusion to the alleged Harmony between them. Moreover, the same inscription is sometimes accompanied by seated personifications of Rome and Constantinople themselves. The Empress Flaccilla, the wife of Theodosius I, is acclaimed in terms of this Harmony, because she has given birth to the heirs to both thrones. An earlier heir, Gratian, on his accession to the purple, is called 'the Glory of the New Age'. The constant, inappropriate use of the word 'Glory' is a novel, strident, feature of the time.

It had always been customary for the government to seek

demonstrations of solidarity by organizing loyalty vows to the Emperor, especially as each five-year period of his reign drew to a close; and the coins meticulously continue to record these ceremonies. But above all, the references are to the ruler's supposed military triumphs. Although the habit of celebrating specific victories by explicit numismatic allusions has ceased, there are innumerable and incessant tributes, in general terms, to his victorious grandeur. Often – indeed, right up to the very last year of the Empire – these allusions are accompanied by a winged female figure of a type that had formerly stood for the pagan goddess Victory, but could now be interpreted instead as a Christian angel. There are also many representations of the Emperor wearing his military uniform.

These designs reveal a ferocity and brutality which had never been displayed with such emphasis until now. One ruler after another is shown as 'Triumphant over the Barbarian Nations', setting his foot on a cringing captive – who is sometimes replaced by a human-headed serpent, denoting the powers of evil. On coins inscribed 'the Glory of the Romans', Valentinian I is seen dragging a war prisoner along the ground by his hair.

There is also an obsessive increase in references to the Roman state – which the government was at such pains to preserve, at whatever cost to individuals. For example the coinage lavishly celebrates the Glory of the State and its Salvation and Security, Happiness and Peace. Valentinian I is the State's Restorer, and its Revival is illustrated by a scene in which Emperors are depicted raising the kneeling figure of Rome to her feet. Victor, son of the usurper Magnus Maximus, declares that he and his father were 'Born for the Good of the State'.

Unconquered, Eternal Rome is lyrically proclaimed. Moreover, even in the latest days of Imperial shrinkage, it is quite common to find the Empire equated with nothing less than the whole world itself, of which the 'Glory' and 'Salvation' are hailed on the coins. The latter conception (SALVS MVNDI), under the transient Emperor Olybrius (472), is represented by a cross; and this device, or a Christian monogram, is also seen in the grasp of Victory or an Emperor, and appears as the apex of military standards.

Such standards appear frequently, since the coinage never for a moment allows the population to forget the vital role of the soldiery. In addition to the constant eulogies of the Emperors as generals and conquerors, the Courage of the Army is emphatically honoured. The paramount needs of defence are symbolized by the picture of a fortified camp or city gate, defined by Magnus Maximus as the 'Hope of the Romans'. Nothing, of course, is said of the blacker side of the picture, since one rightly expects the messages on the coinage, like other propaganda, to concentrate on heartening uplift. Nevertheless, what is remarkable about the later Imperial issues is the unusually accentuated, indeed total, dissociation of their designs and inscriptions from what was really going on – from the truth.

To say this raises the general question of what the authorities were trying to achieve through these types and slogans. It is not quite satisfactory just to dismiss them all as lies. When, for example, the mint invokes the concept of the Security of the State at a time when security was non-existent, to suppose that the government was merely trying to deceive the population by telling them they were secure, when they were not, would be too simple an inference.

It was more a matter of *aspirations*. The administration wanted to tell the people that it regarded national security as its major concern, and that it was doing its best to revive this security and make it come true once again. There was ample precedent for this sort of hopeful thinking on the coins. For example, the Emperor Otho, during the Empire-wide civil wars of AD 69, had inscribed his coinage 'the Peace of the World', without surely expecting anyone to believe that this was actually the situation at the time.

But Otho's coinage also hints to us what was really wrong with these much later monetary slogans and designs that we are considering here. For the reason why his 'Peace of the World' so forcibly strikes the eye is that, at the time of its issue – *even* viewed as an aspiration for the future prospects of his regime – it was so totally divorced from reality that it became merely ridiculous: unlike the more customary numismatic publicity of the same period. Sometimes it had just dealt with plain facts, or, at worst, facts that were only slightly slanted. And when it published aspirations rather than facts, they had been of reasonable appearance, or carefully calculated to seem reasonable, and calculated also to strike some answering chord in the minds of the public, on the grounds that they would possibly or even probably be fulfilled.

In the later Empire, however, all that was changed. The message of the coinage was now as remote from reality as it was possible for it it be, utterly and obviously incapable of fulfilment. A new and appalling gulf had opened up between the credibility of the government on the one hand, and the hearts and minds of the people on the other. One instance has already been quoted: security. It was nonsensical even to talk about the 'Security of the State' when there were invaders in the fields and at the door, and when no-one had even the faintest hope that they could ever be ejected. And there are many other examples too.

Possibly there was some point in referring to the Concord between the Western and Eastern Empires – even when everyone knew they were in a state of cold war – because there was a certain chance of this situation ending. But the unceasingly reiterated term 'Glory' was singularly out of place. And even more misplaced and anachronistic was the imperialism that showed captive barbarians being dragged along by the hair. Indeed, many of the Emperors whom the coins display as military conquerors were well known never to have taken the field at all, and scarcely to have stirred outside the palace apartments of Ravenna.

The 'Victory' to which appeal was constantly made did not exist, and there was no possibility, even in the most sanguine view, that the Western regime would ever give the concept any real substance, much less that it would justify these fatuous identifications of the Empire with the entire world. To speak of the Safety or Salvation of the State, or to claim in an edict, like Valentinian III, that he was 'providing for the peace and tranquillity of the provinces', was merely inane and counter-productive at a time when their inhabitants were both invaded and taxed almost out of existence.

To talk of national Restoration, Reconstruction and Revival seemed equally beside the point, because it was so totally out of keeping with any detectable likelihood. And there was a breath-taking inapplicability, not to say impudence, about the 'Unconquered, Eternal Rome' of Priscus Attalus, the puppet of Alaric the Visigoth whose current contribution to Eternal Rome was to capture the city and loot it.

In these circumstances it is difficult to agree with Harold Mattingly's view that slogans of this kind offered 'bright encouragement'. True, a very large proportion of the coins were now gold, so that it was the upper class, more often than not, which had them in its hands, and not the destitute poor who would have found this sort of publicity particularly ludicrous.

Yet, although the sufferings of the rich were negligible in comparison, their superior knowledge made them all the more able to appreciate just what nonsense all such messages were. As for the rest of the population, if they had the good fortune to have any gold coins in their hands at all, and if they retained any inclination or leisure to look at them, they were so distracted and harassed that they must merely have found this sanctimonious, unfounded uplift an additional irritation – and proof, if further proof was needed, that the emperors at Ravenna were so hopelessly cut off from the thoughts and feelings and needs of their subjects that any nationwide movement of recovery was out of the question.

IV

THE
PARTNERSHIPS
THAT FAILED

8

Ally against Ally

Another very relevant and destructive disunity which helped to destroy the Roman Empire was of a political and geographical nature. For that Empire, disastrously as it turned out, was divided into two halves, each under a separate ruler – one in the West and one in the East.

The idea that Rome's Empire was too large to be ruled and defended by a single man was nothing new. Already in the second century, Marcus Aurelius had elevated a co-Emperor to share his power. A hundred years later, Valerian had divided the provinces on a geographical basis between himself and his son Gallienus, to whom he allotted the West. Next, Diocletian (284–305), while undertaking an elaborate reorganization of the Imperial system, gave the Western regions to a colleague, establishing his own Eastern residence at Nicomedia (Izmit) in Asia Minor. Constantine the Great reunited the Empire, governing it from his new capital at Constantinople. Then it was divided again between his sons, and subsequently for a brief period was reunited once more, from 353 to 364.

It was in the latter year that Valentinian I was hailed Emperor by the army. Immediately afterwards, the soldiers demanded that he should appoint a colleague to share his power. For whenever there was only a single Emperor, the troops felt that the risk of his death, and of consequent chaos, was too great, and indeed the death of the last monarch, Jovian, had resulted, like similar moments of transition throughout the past centuries, in a perilous emergency.

Valentinian I, in his inaugural address to the troops, expressed agreement that a joint Emperor should be nominàted: 'That, in order to meet all chances, necessity requires the choice of a colleague with equal powers, after much complex deliberation I am impelled neither to doubt nor to dispute! For I myself, too, am profoundly apprehensive of the masses of cares and varied changes of circumstance that lie ahead.'

He was thinking in particular of pressing external threats on many sectors of the frontier; and there were dangers of internal revolts as well. So he immediately raised his brother Valens to an equal share in the Empire. Valens was not the best man for the job, but in view of their blood relationship he was the man who could best be trusted. Granting him the Eastern provinces as his sphere, Valentinian himself took the West, because although this was the less wealthy of the two halves of the Empire its frontiers were in the greater peril. He chose, like some of his predecessors, to reside not at Rome but nearer to the danger zone at Mediolanum (Milan).

The domination of the Mediterranean by one single power, which had lasted for so many centuries, was now at an end. Henceforward, the Western realm consisted of the whole of Roman Europe except the Black Sea coast and its immediate hinterland. It also possessed North Africa as far as Tripolitania – the western part of modern Libya – inclusive. The remaining part of Libya fell to the Eastern Empire, which also comprised the European Black Sea fringe (extending down to the capital Constantinople) and Egypt, and the Asiatic territories that now belong to Turkey, Syria, Lebanon and Israel.

All the court services were duplicated at each of the two capitals; and we shall speak henceforward of Western and Eastern 'Empires'. But contemporaries did not do so, for ancients were convinced that there could be only a single Roman Empire. Admittedly it had two separate sovereigns, but they were both endowed with full legislative powers and a mutually inter-changeable coinage. Thus the two states, officially speaking, were ruled by Emperors not *of*, but *in*, 'the parts of the West and East'.

Nevertheless, this theory of unity became increasingly

fictitious. The harmonious alliance between Valentinian I and Valens was celebrated on their initial coinages, which displayed and acclaimed them together. But after Valentinian's death in 375, signs of a rift soon began to appear. For example, his son Gratian failed to come to the help of Valens, when the latter was about to fight the fatal battle of Adrianople against the Visigoths. Where the blame for this failure of cooperation lay is not quite clear, though Gratian's principal German general was suspected of sabotage.

However this may be, Gratian, after he had appointed Theodosius I to succeed Valens, very soon granted his new Eastern colleague a major concession which was to have serious effects in the years to come. For it was probably now that he ceded to Theodosius most of the former Western possessions in the Balkan peninsula. Henceforth, the frontier between the Western and Eastern Empires, while remaining unchanged in North Africa, ran in Europe from Belgrade due south to the Adriatic, where Albania is today.

In spite of overlappings, it was broadly true that the Western Empire spoke Latin and possessed a Latin culture, whereas the culture and language in the East were Greek. The difference between Latin West and Greek East was plain, longstanding and fundamental – and highly divisive. Roman and Greek had never got on very well, not surprisingly since one was the conqueror and the other the conquered. If, far back in 31 BC, Antony and Cleopatra had won the battle of Actium, and their enemy Octavian (Augustus) had lost, matters might have turned out differently. For Cleopatra was a Greek and Antony was pro-Greek, and had they been victorious, they might well have inaugurated, under Roman overlordship, a regime aiming at partnership between the two cultures. But Augustus, who defeated them, believed that the Romans should maintain political supremacy over the Greeks – the supremacy which his admirer Virgil openly proclaimed.

Ever since then, that was how it had been – until the time of Constantine the Great. For Constantine's foundation of Constantinople as his capital heralded a new era in which the East was to reassert the power of its Greek heritage. After Valentinian separated the two regions politically, this process accelerated. True, the official language of Constantinople was still, for the present, Latin, and so was the language of Eastern coinage and legislation. The time when the Eastern, or Byzantine, Empire would take a purely Greek appearance still lay far ahead. Antony and Cleopatra were still not wholly avenged. But meanwhile the goodwill between those who spoke Latin and those who spoke Greek was by no means extensive. The East, as Gibbon remarked, had always been 'less docile than the West to the voice of its victorious [Roman] preceptors'.

There were also recurrent practical reasons why the friendship between the two Empires was not as thoroughgoing as it ought to have been. The failure of Gratian to help his Eastern colleague Valens has been mentioned. And then in 383, for example, when the usurper Magnus Maximus rose against Gratian in Gaul, the preoccupations of the Eastern Emperor Theodosius I with his own frontier problems meant that he, too, did not send help in time to save his colleague's life. Indeed he even felt it necessary, for a time, to recognize the usurper's claims to the throne.

Later on, it is true, he succeeded in suppressing the upstart – briefly effecting the reunification of the entire Empire. But when, after his death in 395, it was divided in two parts once again, between his two sons Arcadius and Honorius, East and West were more sharply separated from each other than ever before.

Moreover, it was now that the relations between the two Empires began to become really bad, so bad that this must be regarded as a major factor in the debilitation of the weaker partner, the West. The worsening of relations was directly due to a Western leader, one of the most able men of the age. This was Stilicho, the German who was the Western Empire's Master of Soldiers, or commander-in-chief. We have a highly eulogistic account of Stilicho's doings from the poet Claudian. But there is also an opposite viewpoint that needs equally serious consideration.

Theodosius I, before his death, had appointed Stilicho, his nephew by marriage, to be the guardian of his younger son Honorius. But he had also chosen Stilicho's personal enemy, Rufinus, a cobbler's son from Elusa (Eauze) in Novempopulana (Aquitania, south-western Gaul), to be the guardian of his older boy, Arcadius, who became the Eastern Emperor. Stilicho, however, claimed that Theodosius I had solemnly charged him with the care of *both* his sons. In consequence, it became his determined ambition to reunite the whole Empire – with himself as its real controller. This would necessarily involve the suppression of Rufinus, against whom Stilicho's protégé Claudian, an Easterner who wrote in Latin and had become more Western-minded than any Roman, retrospectively launched the most savage attacks.

> Nor wife, nor husband, nor their children slain,
> Sufficed his savage hatred to restrain;
> Nor friends nor kindred from each other torn –
> These death to suffer; these to exile borne. . . .
> Nor would he doom to death at once his prey,
> But seek, with cruel torments, to delay,
> 'Mid chains, and dungeons dark and anguish dire,
> The blow with which their sufferings might expire. . . .

At a moment when the civilized world could only survive if West and East cooperated, the split between their governments had become almost total.

One of the worst results of this serious misunderstanding between Rufinus and Stilicho was that it enabled the Visigoth Alaric to penetrate into Greece. Claudian declared that Rufinus had treacherously withdrawn his troops, but in all probability it was Stilicho's deliberate plan that Alaric should be diverted against the Eastern Empire in order to keep him out of the West.

Next, Rufinus fell from power and was assassinated. This was almost certainly at the instigation of Stilicho. Indeed, Claudian openly congratulated him upon the murder. Then the eunuch Eutropius took over Rufinus' post as chief minister in the East. Initially, there may have been slight hopes that collaboration between the supposed allies would be restored. But if so, such hopes were very soon to prove without foundation.

First, Stilicho, after the East had invited him to intervene against Alaric in Greece, mysteriously let him escape from his clutches in 397 and depart. Noting this unhelpfulness, Eutropius, on behalf of the Eastern government, not only declared Stilicho a public enemy, but felt it necessary to appease the Visigoth by appointing him Master of Soldiers in the Balkans – a step which caused understandable consternation in the West.

At this juncture, fresh cause for mutual ill-will was provided by the vital provinces of North Africa – source of Rome's principal

117

grain supply – where a rebellion broke out in the same year. For its leader, Gildo, was encouraged by the bad relations between the two Empires to propose the transfer of these provinces to the East – a catastrophic prospect for the Westerners. Eutropius connived with the rebel to the extent of menacing anyone who should act against him, thus incurring fierce abuse from Claudian, who actually urged Stilicho to deliver a military attack upon the East. And Stilicho did probably make a hostile move, though by surreptitious means rather than openly, for he is likely to have had a hand in the overthrow of Eutropius that now followed in 399.

This violent dispute between West and East had given Claudian an opportunity to reach beyond it to the underlying issues, and to lay bare the fundamental rivalry between their two cultures. And so he proceeded to assail Constantinople as the sink of all the vices, and expressed true Roman hatred and scorn of its nobles, picturing the disgust of the war-god Mars at their unwarlike effeminacy. Stilicho, he declared, had restored Rome's rightful place as the true capital of the entire Roman world.

Meanwhile, however, that statesman's successive interferences, resulting in the removal first of Rufinus and then of Eutropius, had made the hostility between the two Empires, which was already exacerbated by savage ecclesiastical dispute, far more serious than it had been before. Already this tension had done a great deal to aid the ambitions of the Visigoths; and now, in 401, their king Alaric crossed the border from the Eastern into the Western Empire, and appeared inside the borders of Italy itself. Had the Constantinople authorities privately encouraged him to leave their territories, so that he could become a burden to its Western neighbours instead? Probably they had. If so, they had contributed materially to the downfall of the West.

Stilicho's reaction to Alaric's invasion was once again ambivalent. He defeated him in two successive years, but twice let him go when he could have finished him off. For both men were Germans, and Stilicho was so obsessed by his suicidal unfriendliness towards the Roman East that he preferred to keep his fellow-German in existence as a potential ally.

When Claudian pronounced it to be the treachery of the Eastern authorities, not of Stilicho, it is difficult to believe him. For Stilicho, for some time past, had nourished the intention of bringing the entire Balkans back from the Eastern into the Western Empire once again; and that was why he had allowed Alaric to escape, since the Visigoths could so effectively weaken the Eastern Empire's control over the Balkan peninsula.

In 405, however, Stilicho's plans were momentarily interrupted by the invasion of Italy by a new mass of Germans. And when, at the end of the following year, further German hordes broke across the frozen Rhine, he at first sent no troops to repel them. For hostility to the Eastern Romans still came uppermost in his mind. And their government, too, was similarly preoccupied, for it did nothing to assist the West against its invaders. If it had felt more friendly, and had managed to send substantial aid, it might once more have delayed the Western Empire's not too-far-distant collapse.

Pursuing his master plan undeterred by these disasters, Stilicho, in 407, actually prepared to launch an invasion of the Eastern provinces. Closing the harbours of Italy to all their ships, he instructed Alaric to occupy the Greek sea-coast on behalf of the Western Emperor. But again his plans had to be postponed, owing to the rebellion of a usurper in Britain. The death of Arcadius in 408 momentarily kindled his aggressive ambitions once again. But soon afterwards the Western Emperor, Honorius, persuaded by Senators that Stilicho was planning to place his own son on the throne, arranged for him to be murdered.

One of the very worst periods in the relations between the two Empires was now over. But meanwhile irreparable harm had been done – particularly in the more vulnerable West, the interests of which, paradoxically, Stilicho had been so passionately determined to serve. As a result of the tension and mutual ill-will, the frontiers had been gravely undermined, and the enemies of the Roman world were strengthened in every quarter.

Nor were all the troubles between the two sides by any means finished. True, when Alaric, now bereft of his supporter Stilicho, invaded Italy on three successive occasions, the regent of the new Eastern boy-Emperor Theodosius II (408–50) closed all his ports and check-points to prevent the infiltrations of Visigothic agents, and sent help to the West; and he later struck gold coins to celebrate his colleague Honorius with himself.

Nevertheless, owing to his own frontier difficulties, this assistance against Alaric only amounted to a few thousand men. And in the years that followed there were signs that relations between the two states were still far from satisfactory. In 414, for example, Eastern troops offered provocation by occupying Salonae (Solin) in Dalmatia, and thus establishing a base only just across the Adriatic from the new Western capital at Ravenna. In the same year, too, Honorius' sister Placidia, who had been carried off by Alaric after his raid on Rome, married his son Ataulf, the new occupant of the Visigothic throne. But the marriage was probably arranged on the advice of a leading Eastern politician, with the express intention of damaging Honorius.

After Ataulf's death, Placidia was compelled to marry the great Roman general Constantius. But when, in 421, Honorius elevated him to the throne as his own Western colleague – the Emperor Constantius III – a fresh source of tension arose with the Eastern authorities, since they refused to recognize Constantius as one of the Imperial team. This was probably because they were now behaving like Stilicho in reverse: looking ahead to Honorius' death, they hoped to reunite the entire Empire under their own control.

But to the Westerners Constantinople seemed to have behaved unforgivably, and Constantius III actually revived the idea of launching an attack on its territory – which was only prevented by his death. Once again, there had been serious disunity between the two states, at a time when only maximum unity could have prevented the West's continuing progress towards disintegration.

When Honorius died two years later, the Eastern Emperor Theodosius II, responding to Placidia's appeal to help her four-year-old son Valentinian III ascend the Western throne, struck a hard bargain; he would help, and would remove a usurper who had intervened, on the condition that a large strip of central Europe, bordering the middle Danube west of Belgrade, must be transferred to his territory. The bargain was kept, and the territory ceded – though perhaps not until 437, when Valentinian III married the daughter of Theodosius II. This event was celebrated by the last coinage of Constantinople ever to show one of its Emperors in the company of his Western colleague.

Theodosius II and his successors also assisted the West against the German invaders of North Africa – Gaiseric and his Vandals – on at least three occasions. But the expeditions were always defeated, for they were never on a substantial enough scale. It looks as though the East felt obliged to help for the sake of appearance, but preferred to keep its help down to a minimum level. Aiding the Western Empire probably appeared, at least to some Eastern statesmen, an unrewarding activity. It seemed better not to pour too many troops down the drain: and the opposing arguments did not, unfortunately for the West, prove to be successful.

The last important cooperative enterprise in which the two Roman Empires both had a share was the legal Code of Theodosius II, published in 438. At first sight the joint sponsorship of the Code by the Emperors of East and West could be hailed as an impressive symbol of the unity between them, reversing a recent tendency of the two capitals to strike out and legislate each on its own. Nevertheless, a degree of separation between the Empires was formally recognized by the provision that future Western laws would no longer be valid in the Eastern Empire unless they were formally communicated to its government, and vice versa. Moreover, this step was not, henceforward, regularly taken. Eastern edicts were rarely sent to the West, and the Western authorities did not dispatch their regulations to the East at all.

Indeed the prospects of cooperation scarcely existed any longer. For the dissolution of the West was under way, and the Easterners were almost powerless to stop the process. They could have stopped it once. But now, owing to faults on both sides, it was too late.

Meanwhile the failures of the two Empires to aid each other against the Huns continued to result in mutual recriminations. Other misunderstandings, too, did not fail to arise. When Marcian (450–57) was proclaimed the Eastern Emperor, the West showed an initial reluctance to recognize him. And he in return contrived, deliberately or otherwise, to divert the hostile Attila from East to West, by refusing to pay his annual subsidy. The Westerners could afford to pay it even less, but Attila moved against them because he expected to be able to seize what he wanted from their provinces. Nor would Marcian agree to become entangled with Gaiseric and his Vandals, who were the Western Empire's enemies in Africa. He had not forgotten the West's initial unwillingness to recognize his claim to the throne: and he refused in his turn to acknowledge either of the two transient successors of Valentinian III. The second of them, Avitus, retaliated in 455–6 by demanding back the recently ceded Danube strip.

The German general Ricimer, who controlled the Western Empire for the next sixteen years, largely maintained himself during that precarious period by his diplomatic handling of the Eastern ruler Leo I. Yet it was all to no avail, because now that the old Western dynasty had ended with Valentinian III, the East felt even less enthusiastic than before about offering support.

Moreover, Leo I refused to recognize the last competent Emperor the West ever produced. This was Majorian (457–61) who, after vainly waiting eight months for the approval of Constantinople, occupied the throne at Ravenna without it, and hopefully struck a coin on which he and Leo were depicted together. Soon afterwards, however, Leo confirmed his predecessor's policy of refusing the West further help against the Vandals, with whom instead, despite Ricimer's efforts to persuade him to the contrary, he concluded peace in 462.

However, in spite of the obvious decay of the West, Leo did finally and belatedly make an attempt to save it from destruction. For when its throne once again became vacant in 457, he nominated one of his own men, Anthemius, to be its occupant, and Ricimer, placated by the promise of marriage to the new ruler's daughter, agreed. Anthemius, more plausibly than his predecessor, celebrated his relations with Leo on a Western coin, and the poet Sidonius, delivering a panegyric of Anthemius, declared that, since the princes of the West had failed, it was right for Rome now to seek its fortune through an Emperor from the East. 'Farewell, division of Empire!' he hopefully cried: with united counsels, even at this late date, everything might turn out well, and the foes of the Empire, particularly the Vandals in Africa, could be defeated after all.

But the Vandals were not defeated because, although the East now launched against them the most ambitious of its expeditions to date, the onslaught, like all its predecessors, proved a failure.

And then Ricimer, when his Emperor Anthemius described him as a mere savage, concluded that a more docile puppet than this 'Greekling' was necessary, and killed him – only soon to die himself, in 472.

Next followed two extremely short Western reigns. One of them the Eastern ruler Leo entirely ignored: and then he sent his own relative by marriage, Julius Nepos, to take over the Ravenna throne. But at this juncture Leo died. His successor Zeno (474–91) was too involved in his own grave internal troubles to shore up the West any longer, and reverted permanently to peace with the Vandals.

Nepos, failing to establish himself, retired to Dalmatia, and in 476 the Western Empire came to an end, when its last titular Emperor Romulus Augustulus was forced to abdicate by the local German army commander Odoacer. And now Zeno, while formally continuing to urge Nepos' claims, acquiesced, in practice, in Odoacer's position – as one of the German kings like Gaiseric the Vandal and Euric the Visigoth, ruling over former Imperial territories.

The Western Empire had ceased to exist. The East survived but, without the West, its survival was on an altogether inferior scale. The ancient world of Rome had been cut to half its size: and one of the reasons for this great shrinkage of the historic classical culture, as Gibbon pointed out, was because its two former halves had lamentably failed to cooperate. The loser was the West, the weaker partner.

9

Race against Race

When the Germans entered the Empire, Rome was presented with an opportunity to assimilate them, and the opportunity was missed, with the gravest results. Instead of unity and partnership between the two peoples, there was acute friction, which contributed grievously to the break-up of the Roman world.

Already for a long time before that terminal century, many German tribesmen had been living inside the Imperial borders. From the very beginning of the Empire, one Roman ruler after another had imported them in large numbers, so that there should be less trouble-makers beyond the frontiers, and more soldiers and agricultural workers within. From the time of Constantine the Great onwards, entire regiments of the Imperial field force were made up of these Germans. Many of them obtained officer rank. Emperors were surrounded by German officers. Indeed a characteristic feature of the entire period is the German who became the Master of Soldiers or commander of the Imperial armies. For Emperors were often inclined to feel that they could rely on the loyalty of a foreigner.

On occasion, these men became the virtual controllers of the government. Such a potentate, for example, was Arbogast, under Gratian and Valentinian II; though his trustworthiness, as it turned out, could not be relied upon after all, since the mysterious death of Valentinian II in 392 was almost certainly this general's doing. But the most remarkable of all such German commanders and rulers behind the throne was Stilicho, who governed the Western Empire for the young Honorius.

So great was the veneration felt for the Imperial monarchy that even the most powerful German generals did not aspire to it themselves. Out of all the numerous military usurpers and would-be usurpers of the fourth and fifth centuries, only two quite exceptional figures, during the 350s, seem to have been Germans. Even towards the very end, the German Ricimer still preferred to rule behind the throne of docile Emperors rather than attempt, in the face of tradition, to reign himself.

Yet the internal balance of power between Romans and Germans in the Empire had already shifted irrevocably towards the Germans three-quarters of a century before Ricimer. The change became apparent when Valens let a host of Visigoths into the provinces. 'The most experienced statesman of [modern] Europe', it seemed to Gibbon in the eighteenth century, 'has never been summoned to consider the propriety or the danger of admitting or rejecting an innumerable multitude of barbarians, who are driven by despair and hunger to solicit a settlement on the territories of a civilized nation'. But that was Valens' problem, and he let them in; and the immigrants he had admitted overwhelmed him at Adrianople.

They stayed, and in 382 Theodosius I took the revolutionary step of allowing whole German tribes to reside in Imperial territory as separate, autonomous, allied or federate units, committed to serving in the Roman army, though under the command of their own chieftains. Thereafter the practice continued and increased, until such federates became a regular and widespread feature of the life of the Empire.

Early in the fifth century, when the Visigoths and Burgundians settled in Gaul, there were formal partitions of lands, in which the local Roman proprietors handed over a third of their arable territory to German immigrants. Later, the proportion rose to two-thirds, and included immovable possessions as well; woodland was perhaps divided half and half. The principle of these arrangements was derived from an old Roman formula for quartering soldiers on landowners. But now the quartering was permanent, and so was the transfer of property. The original system had been known as *hospitalitas*, and the name continued to be used, so that the proprietor and his partial German supplanter were somewhat euphemistically described as 'host' and 'guest'.

These arrangements formed an important part of the process by which the ancient world gradually developed the new national patterns characteristic of the Middle Ages. Yet the part played by the Visigothic and Burgundian settlers in this historic transformation is only apparent by hindsight. At the time when they were first setting up their homes on Imperial soil they felt no desire whatever to dismember Rome or spurn its institutions.

As archaeological evidence reveals, Germans hitherto outside the Empire but in contact with it – with the exception of savages such as the Angle, Saxon and Jute invaders of Britain – had already acquired a certain degree of Romanization themselves. Their nomadic days were over, and what they wanted was land to cultivate. Like their earlier compatriots who had been filtering through into the Empire for centuries, their strongest ambition was to establish themselves in one of the Imperial provinces, and obtain a share of its peaceful prosperity.

When they entered the provinces, therefore, the question of their seeking full independence from the Empire around them did not, in the first instance, arise. On the contrary, these German newcomers hoped to establish a form of co-existence. It was an extraordinary moment. There was a glimpse of a new order, in which Romans and Germans might settle down together as partners.

The Romans had not been able to keep the Germans out, and could not eject them now. Clearly the provincials could not be expected to like the land transfers. Nevertheless, Rome imperatively needed the services of the newcomers for the army, and as agricultural labourers as well. Moreover, the Germans, since they were a 'Third World' hankering after the benefits of Imperial civilization, were willing enough, in so far as they thought about the matter at all, to deal fairly with the Romans among whom they had settled. Indeed, they had little alternative, since the German element in the combined population was and remained relatively small. Perhaps there were not more than 100,000 Visigoths in their whole kingdom when it eventually extended from the Loire to Gibraltar. If so, they only amounted to about two per cent of the total inhabitants of the area.

The Visigoths turned against Rome in the end and put it to the sack. Yet their leader, Alaric, should not be remembered just as the captor of Rome. He had originally been something far more positive and remarkable, the man who, according to the sixth-century Gothic historian Jordanes, wanted a single German-Roman people. His son and successor Ataulf (410–15), who married Honorius' half-sister Placidia, formulated the same ideal in language which remains impressively relevant to our racial problems today. Orosius, writer of the *Histories against the Pagans*, was told by a citizen of Narbo (Narbonne) that Ataulf had spoken in these terms:

> . . . To begin with, I ardently desired to efface the very name of the Romans and to transform the Roman Empire into a Gothic Empire. Romania, as it is commonly called, would have become Gothia; Ataulf would have replaced Caesar Augustus. But long experience taught me that the unruly barbarism of the Goths was incompatible with the laws.
>
> Now, without laws there is no state. I therefore decided rather to aspire to the glory of restoring the fame of Rome in all its integrity, and of increasing it by means of the Gothic strength. I hope to go down to posterity as the restorer of Rome, since it is not possible I should be its supplanter.

That, then, was the exciting ideal which at least a few of the German leaders articulately pursued. The practical possibilities have been analysed by Joseph Vogt in his book *The Decline of Rome*, published in 1967:

> . . . The Visigoths and Burgundians were 'billeted guests' in the Roman provinces and as such wholly dependent on what the institutions rooted in the land could provide. The numerical inferiority of the foreigners was itself a reason for reaching a considerable measure of accommodation with the native population. It was very difficult for these German minorities to withstand the pressure of Roman influence.
>
> Moreover, the solidarity of the Germanic peoples was to some degree impaired by their own social organization. The Visigoths had an upper and lower stratum, each with its own law, while the Burgundians were divided into the three strata of nobility, medium-free and low-free.
>
> Upon this shaky foundation the two peoples proceeded to

errect a state which comprehended both Germans and Romans, two elements which were required to live side by side and yet preserve their identity.

The most important binding ligament was the [German] monarch. To his Roman subjects he was made acceptable by the offices and honorific titles conferred by the Emperor or a fictitious kinship with the Imperial house. The Assembly of Germanic warriors was rarely consulted before important decisions, and the Germanic aristocracy had to content themselves with serving the king.

From the beginning, Romans had access to high positions in the central government, and in the royal household with which it was closely associated. The chancery retained its Roman stamp, the structure of the provincial government was left untouched and there was no interference in economic affairs. Latin was adopted as the administrative language, the tax system remained in being, and the coinage followed the imperial pattern.

But the vital question was this. How were the Romans going to respond to this unprecedented experiment in co-existence, in which they were required to share their provinces and their lands with another race in a novel sort of partnership?

On a lofty plane, there was no absence of reassuring general statements. Augustine, pointing out that we all share the bond of descent from Adam and Eve, duly echoed the ecumenism of Paul's *Epistle to the Galatians:* 'There is no such thing as Jew and Greek, slave and freeman, male and female; for you are all one person in Christ Jesus.' Moreover, as in earlier centuries, there was still great stress on the universal, multi-racial unity of the Roman Empire. 'We may drink of the Rhine or the Orontes,' declared Claudian, 'we are all one people', and Rome's enduring service was to establish friendship among the nations:

> She is the only one who has received
> The conquered in her arms and cherished all
> The human race under a common name,
> Treating them as her children, not her slaves.
> She called these subjects Roman citizens
> And linked far worlds with ties of loyalty.

And the Christian lyricist Prudentius wrote at length in the same universal spirit.

> A common law made them equals and
> bound them by a single name. . . .
> We live in the most diverse countries,
> like fellow-citizens of the same blood dwelling
> within the single ramparts of their native city
> and all united in an ancestral home.

By the same token another poet, Rutilius Namatianus, declared that Rome ruled because she *deserved* to rule – because she had wisely brought all men together beneath the rule of one law, to live without fetters.

Nor were the signs altogether lacking that these high-minded sentiments might be brought down to earth and related to co-existence with the Germans. In particular, the Christian historian Orosius saw a great opportunity in the peace which Ataulf's successor, Wallia, wanted to sign with Honorius. Orosius was even prepared to speculate that the day might arrive when the German chiefs would become great kings. Moreover, although admitting current frictions and hostilities, he noted that the Germans were already beginning to live on friendly terms with their neighbours, and that the Burgundians, for example, were mild and modest enough to treat their Gallo-Roman subjects as brothers.

Orosius, like a number of other churchmen, was already willing to come to terms with the new forces, and envisaged the possibility of a future Christian order comprising some sort of union between the Roman and the German nations – which would solve this most pressing problem of the age. To his co-religionist Paulinus of Nola, also, it seemed that barbarians, once converted, might well become allies of law and order.

Salvian, too, supports the new co-existence. Admittedly he does so primarily for ethical and rhetorical reasons, because he is continually contrasting the corruption of Roman society with the allegedly superior morals, humanity, social solidarity and justice of the barbarians – uncouth and imperfectly organized though they may be. Nevertheless, this point of view did help Salvian to take an unusually constructive view of the Germanic peoples. Looking ahead, and moving beyond the all-too-elevated sentiments of his contemporaries, he succeeded in detecting what was novel and important about this new German phenome-non. Could a fresh start have been made with the racial interrelationship, if only the Roman upper class had heard his isolated voice?

A member of that class, writing some two decades later – only a decade before the final collapse of Roman rule – was a certain Paulinus: not the better-known poet of Nola, but Paulinus of Pella, the town in Macedonia that was his birthplace, though he went to reside in Gaul. In his poem *The Thanksgiving* he tells us how the facts of life appeared to the Gallo-Roman nobility under barbarian rule. He himself had suffered grave material losses at its hands. Nevertheless, he had formed, in his younger days, a friendly personal relationship with Ataulf, and it was his decision to acquiesce in the Visigothic peace.

> It was peace I sought
> From the Gothic masters. They themselves wanted peace
> And before long they gave to others, though
> For a price, the chance to live without annoyance.
> This we did not regret because we saw that they
> Now held power and in their favour we prospered.
> Still it was not an easy thing; many endured
> Great suffering. I was not the least of these because
> I had lost my goods and outlived my fatherland.

Another Gallo-Roman aristocrat, Sidonius, came to feel much the same. In 471–5, it is true, as bishop of Arverna, he had helped to fight against the Visigothic king Euric. But both before and after that warlike interlude, he wrote and spoke in favour of co-existence with these Germans, many of whom he knew well. This attitude emerges, for example, in his panegyric of Avitus, who had been elevated to the purple in 455 by his fellow Romans of Gaul, in collusion with the Visigoths. In support of this combined action, Sidonius observed that, since the Germans and Romans were now friends, they had a common interest in saving the Empire.

That was, by then, no longer true, and Sidonius knew it. But the Visigoths were protecting him and his friends from other and much fiercer tribes of Germans, such as the Saxons. So Sidonius dissembled, and during the year of mild imprisonment which his resistance to their dominion at Arverna had earned at their hands he wrote in exceedingly flattering terms of King Euric, 'our lord and master, to whom a conquered world pays suit'. The Frankish Count of Treveri (Trier), too, received Sidonius' assurances that his Latin style flowed as delightfully as the Tiber stream itself.

Yet these views expressing some measure of sympathetic acquiescence in the new position of the Germans have to be sought for and extracted with care from an enormous mass of totally unfavourable Roman references. Even so distinguished a historian as Ammianus was no exception. He appreciated, it is true, that cynical ill-treatment of German immigrants by Roman officials had precipitated the disaster of Adrianople: they had given dog-meat to the starving Visigoths in exchange for their sons, sold as slaves. Nevertheless, he seemed to think, quite unrealistically, that all the Germans settled in the Empire could somehow be spirited away, if only the effort was made, or if not that they could at least be forced to live in bondage to the Romans. And the Huns, who were playing a large and helpful part in the armies of Theodosius I, appeared to Ammianus as scarcely human: 'They are so monstrously ugly and misshapen that one might take them for two-legged beasts, or for the stumps, rough-hewn into images, that are used in putting sides to bridges. . . . Like unreasoning animals, they are utterly ignorant of the difference between right and wrong.'

It was out of the question, declared Bishop Optatus of Milevis (Mila) in Algeria in the same spirit, for any Christian virtue to exist among barbarians. And Synesius of Cyrene (Shahhat), too, displayed extreme hostility to the German settlers, deploring the policy of giving them land and demanding that they be sent back (which he did not see was quite impossible), or, if kept, degraded into serfdom.

. . . The title of Senator which, in ancient times, seemed to Romans the climax of all honours, has become because of the barbarians something abject . . . the same blond barbarians, who in private life fulfil the role of domestic servants, give us orders in public life.

Theodosius I, by excess of clemency, treated them with

gentleness and indulgence, gave them the title of allies, conferred upon them political rights and honours, generously made them gifts of lands. But they did not understand and appreciate the nobility of this treatment. They interpreted it as weakness on our part, and that inspired in them an insolent arrogance and an unheard-of boastfulness.

It is disappointing to find Prudentius also, who had so promisingly declared the peoples of the Empire 'equals and bound by a single name', nevertheless displaying the keenest distaste for all barbarians, lumping them together with pagan Romans as objects of contempt.

> As beasts from men, as dumb from those who speak,
> As from the good who God's commandments seek
> Differ the foolish heathen, so Rome stands,
> Alone in pride above barbarian lands.

Clearly, the universalism of St Paul had been replaced among Christians by the traditional Roman disdain for these outsiders. The same feelings, once again, were expressed by Ambrose, who recognized the Goths as the ferocious destroyers of Magog deplored by the prophet Ezekiel, and when a bishop seemed to be accepting barbarian ways, denounced his attitude as plain sacrilege. Ambrose noted the fierce wars *between* one barbarian nation and another, and this phenomenon inspired Claudian, like others, to assert hopefully that one of the advantages of Stilicho's enlistment of Germans is that they would now have to fight and kill each other.

Although Claudian's protector Stilicho was himself a German, the poet performed a notable feat of literary acrobatics by managing to denounce their Eastern enemy Rufinus for his secretly pro-German attitude:

> He, within the city's guarded space,
> Exulted in the crimes which spread disgrace. . . .
> The devastation gratified his sight,
> And savages he viewed with fond delight. . . .
> Nor blushed to see barbarian furs preside
> In courts, while Latium's laws were laid aside.

For in Claudian all the old traditional prejudices came out all over again. The barbarians, he declared, were nothing but savages, bent only on war and banditry. The Huns slew their own parents, and then took delight in swearing oaths over their dead bodies. And what a disgusting thing it was when a mixed marriage took place with an African, and 'a coloured bastard besmirched the cradle'! Jerome, too, denounced Rome's 'purchase of her life from the barbarians with gold and precious things', and repeated, with scriptural quotations, that they were just like wild beasts.

As for Symmachus, one of his highly cultured letters tells a story which shows his racial attitudes in a deplorable light. Gladiatorial games were still continuing at Rome, and Symmachus, as city prefect, imported a group of twenty-nine Saxons for these combats. But before the performance could take place, he complains, these men contrived to strangle themselves, or one another, in their cells. Greatly annoyed at this considerable waste of money, Symmachus spares no word of sympathy for the miserable captives, but merely regards them as uncooperative louts and outsiders who have played a dirty barbarian trick.

This contempt and hatred were deeply ingrained. Even Orosius, who took such an unusually enlightened view of the Germans as a political force, qualifies his verdict by a damping statement of his own personal feelings: 'I saw the barbarians, and I had to avoid them because they were harmful, flatter them because they were the masters, pray to them although they were infidels, flee them because they laid traps.'

Salvian, too, for all his insight into the future role of Germans in the Western world, does not fail to comment on the nauseating stink of their bodies and their clothing. And for all his favourable comparison of their simple, untutored virtues with the vicious corruption of the Romans, he also finds time to abuse each of their tribes in turn, describing the Goths as perfidious, the Alans as rapacious lechers, the Alamanni as alcoholics, and the Saxons, Franks and Herulians as wantonly cruel.

Another who had accepted the role of the Germans in contemporary life, Sidonius, likewise makes it clear that he only does so with extreme personal reluctance, since he, too, is disgusted by the coarse, ignorant, brutish habits of even the best among his German neighbours. He does not like the noisily gregarious skin-clad Goths, or the tattoos worn by the Herulians. Nor is he attracted by an unfragrant custom of the genial but

133

boorish Burgundians, men 'in body and mind as stiff as stocks, and very hard to form' who smear their hair with rancid butter. The way in which Germans mourn their dead by gouging their cheeks with bloody scars does not appeal to him either. He can no longer write six-foot verses, he says, while he lives in the midst of the ill-smelling seven-foot giants with tow hair.

In fact, Sidonius' apparently tolerant attitude to the Germans is only superficial, or diplomatic: he himself wants to have nothing to do with them at all. '*You* shun the barbarians', he wrote to his friend Philagrius, 'because they have a bad name. *I* shun them even if their name is good.' And to another friend Syagrius, who was unusual because he spoke good Burgundian, Sidonius can only express sarcastic mockery for that helpful talent. In other words even this cultured and intelligent man, who was so well aware of the political significance of the Germans, failed to see the slightest value in having social relations with them, and was only too glad to keep them at arm's length.

On the all-important psychological level, the vision of partnership had utterly failed. The upper-class leaders of Rome were too much the prisoners of their inherited cultural stereotypes to meet the Germans half-way with any positive cooperation or social acceptance.

The Romans' intellectual and emotional response to the challenge of barbarian co-existence was depressingly inadequate at every level. At best, they viewed the immigrants with a contemptuous and imperfectly concealed aversion, based partly on superficial characteristics that they found distasteful, and partly on traditional, ignorant prejudice. This blend of preconceptions provided a sterile and harmful picture of these Germans' faithless, lecherous, sub-human characters, wholly alienated from all that was civilized. The Romans deliberately imposed on their new and unwelcome neighbours a kind of spiritual apartheid, viewing them as an unabsorbable lump of marked men, encapsulated by a wall of eloquent or silent dislike.

Surviving records of these immigrants show their consciousness of this imposed inferiority. On a tombstone from southern Gaul, two Germans apologetically record that their racial origin is 'part of the stain that baptism has washed away'. In the same spirit an epitaph from Antwerp announces that the dead man, Murranus – who came from the Danube region – had composed it himself 'since mere wretchedness teaches even barbarians to write'.

Other Germans, however, inevitably reacted in a very different fashion to all this hostility around them by refusing to become Romanized after all. Since they were less articulate than the Romans, no literary expression of their feelings has come down to us. But the facts themselves loudly illustrate their reaction. For the scheme of enrolling German federate units in the army proved a failure: disliked and despised as they were, they retaliated by disliking Rome, whose glories they had once hoped to share.

Theodosius I's initial idea of enlisting these units had not been a bad one. It had offered a chance of ethnic partnership and it was the best practical remedy at his disposal. Germans were good fighters, and cost less than Roman soldiers. If their military operations could be limited to what was required of them, and if, the fighting once over, they could be persuaded to return quietly to their new homes, then all would be well. In due course, therefore, the employment of such federate units greatly increased. The immigrants enrolled in ever larger formations, which virtually became parts of the regular army.

Despite a widespread, determined Roman impression to the contrary, the individual German soldiers in *Roman* units generally remained loyal. But the sad fact was that the federate units, although performing good service in certain emergencies, on more numerous occasions could not be trusted to carry out orders and proved totally unreliable. Indeed, they were in an almost perpetual state of turbulence and revolt. This was partly owing to a natural indiscipline, and a greed for more and more land. But it was chiefly, one may suppose, because they knew themselves to be surrounded by the hatred of the Romans, to whom, therefore, they felt little fidelity. And they were also well aware that some of Rome's very best generals, even officers of the calibre of Constantius III, preferred, in their recurrent wars, to spend allied and German rather than Roman blood.

In consequence, acts of insubordination and downright disloyalty by federate units rapidly multiplied. In 409, for example, they culpably failed to prevent other German tribes from crossing into Spain. Thirteen years later, they abandoned their Roman commander in that country in favour of his Vandal enemies –

once again their fellow-Germans. Subsequently, the federate forces got completely out of hand and proved a grievous peril, doing Rome a lot more harm than good.

The great experiment, therefore, had turned out to be a disaster. Instead of leading the way to a new form of unity it had created deadly disharmony within the very heart of the Empire. The mass recruitment of Germans was not delaying Rome's collapse after all. Instead, it was helping to bring the edifice down. But in itself it had been a sensible plan. The trouble was that the Romans were not ready for it.

It has been maintained that Rome fell because the purity of its race was polluted. The opposite is rather the case. Although much changed by racial intermixture in the course of the centuries, the Roman ethnic character had not necessarily changed for the worse. Indeed, it was a pity it was not changed more, by symbiosis with the Germans. Rather than deploring genetic pollution, it would be nearer the truth to maintain that Rome's downfall was accelerated by its total failure, once the Germans had been admitted within the Empire, to assimilate them by blending the two races.

Of course, economic and technological borrowings, at an everyday level, were made by both sides. On the German side, these were the result of their eagerness, at least at first, to take over whatever advantages they could. And, conversely, a considerable list of Rome's technical debts (for example the long, slashing German sword) made the writer *On Matters of Warfare* conclude that 'the barbarian nations are by no means accounted strangers to invention'. Yet official policy took no heed of such things, and vigorously reinforced the general Roman desire to segregate these immigrants.

It was bad enough when the local governors and commanders brutally exploited the Visigoths before the battle of Adrianople. But at least they were not acting on Imperial orders. However, such orders, designed to keep Romans and Germans apart, had already been forthcoming elsewhere by that time. For a law of Valentinian I and Valens in 370 deliberately failed to tolerate intermarriage between Roman citizens and German immigrants, insisting, on the contrary, that this must be avoided by the most stringent methods.

And similar vetos were even extended to superficial matters, such as clothing. Among Rome's borrowings from the barbarians were specific forms of dress. Noblemen, for example, liked to wear woollen shirts of a Danubian pattern, Saxon trousers, and cloaks from northern Gaul fastened at the shoulders by German filigree brooches.

But the Imperial authorities took a remarkably grave view of these fashions. In 397 the wearing of trousers inside the city of Rome was forbidden under threat of perpetual exile and confiscation of all property. Then followed three further edicts, and in 416 the wearing of barbarian furs and skins in the capital and its environs was likewise declared illegal, even for slaves.

If Aetius, the greatest leader of the age, had not been struck down in 454, even at that late date something might still have been saved, at least for a time, out of the wreckage of Roman-German relations. For he showed exceptional skill and tact in dealing with the Germans, as Gibbon's deserved tribute points out. 'The barbarians, who had seated themselves in the Western provinces, were insensibly taught to respect the faith and valour of the patrician Aetius. He soothed their passions, consulted their prejudices, balanced their interests, and checked their ambitions.' But Aetius was murdered by his own incapable monarch Valentinian III. And so the divisive process speeded up and entered upon its ruinous phase.

Roman estrangement from the Germans, on the official and unofficial planes alike, was considerably enhanced by differences of religion. For whereas the tribes which remained outside the Empire were pagans, those which settled within its borders became Christian. But they were of the Arian persuasion, and between this sect and the Catholics, who controlled the Roman government, the doctrinal differences, as indicated in Appendix 1, ran wide and deep.

The Germans had originally become Arians because the fourth-century missionary who first worked with them, Ulfilas, was an Arian. He did not live to see the final conversion of the Visigoths, but his work bore such abundant fruit that, during their settlement in the Balkans, they underwent mass conversion to the Arian faith. Subsequently this Arian brand of Christianity became the religion of every German nation, and every German general, within the Empire.

Although Arianism, as they interpreted it, was a somewhat arid and static affair, imposed on the rank and file from the top downwards, Germans found it much easier to understand than the Catholic form of Christianity, because the Arian doctrine that the Son must be younger than the Father, and therefore in a sense inferior, corresponded with the paternal structure of their society.

This religious difference, between the Arian Germans on the one hand and the Catholic church of the Western Empire on the other, only served to widen and deepen the already profound gulf between Germans and Romans.

There were, certainly, a few voices raised to remind people that the Germans were at least Christians, of a sort. According to Augustine and Orosius, that was why the capture of Rome by Alaric, an Arian like his compatriots, was conducted with due respect for church property. And Salvian added the lesson that the Germans, in spite of their regrettable heresy, still behaved better, on the whole, than Catholic Romans did. Yet these viewpoints were exceptional, and indeed deliberately paradoxical. Far and away the more common view was that friendship with the Germans, already a most unattractive idea, was made impossible by their Arianism. Indeed, this condemned them to eternal damnation.

These powerful racial and religious attitudes, diffused through every level of the population, inevitably led from time to time to outbreaks of violence against the Germans. Theodosius I, who not only allowed Visigoths to settle *en bloc* within the Empire but actually found their chieftains personally likeable, was at pains to keep these hostile demonstrations in check. Yet he was not always successful. When for example, in 390, the crowd at Thessalonica in northern Greece lynched the local military commander, Butheric (because he had imprisoned a favourite charioteer for homosexuality), it was largely because he was a German that he suffered this fate.

Five years later, Stilicho found it easy to arrange the assassination of his Eastern counterpart Rufinus because of Rufinus' pro-German connexions; and in 399 the Goths at Constantinople were systematically slaughtered by the local population. Next, in 408, Honorius found it quite easy to remove Stilicho – because

Stilicho, too, was a German. Before his execution, the Roman troops – with the Emperor's approval – murdered the German chiefs in the Imperial entourage, and then, after Stilicho was dead, the families of barbarian federate soldiers throughout Italy were massacred as well.

The attacks upon the Empire by German invaders, and most of all Alaric's invasion, roused these anti-German feelings to fever heat. Moreover, it was inevitable that this hostility felt by the Romans, whether justified or merely founded on prejudice, should also be directed against the federate tribes and states already settled within the frontiers. Such feelings contributed largely to the events of the following years, during which the attitude of the German immigrant tribes, at first not too unfriendly to Rome, was replaced by a more and more aggressive drive towards virtual independence – culminating, under Gaiseric the Vandal in North Africa, in the attainment of a complete independence which was uncompromisingly and virulently hostile.

Gaiseric, who raised the Vandal monarchy to heights of authority unprecedented among the German nations, faced the Romans with a fearful problem. True, he firmly based his government on Roman models. Yet his powerful personality confronted all the old Roman hatreds and prejudices against the Germans with an even more relentless German retaliation against Rome. Although the Roman and Romano-African population of North Africa, which outnumbered his own Vandals by a hundred to one, was allowed to keep its existing legal privileges and its leading men were retained in administrative posts, their exclusion from any political influence was total.

Moreover, Gaiseric lost no time in making a concentrated attack on the great Romano-African landowners. He also extended his onslaught to include the Catholic clergy. Under the German regimes in Gaul and Spain, there had been, on the whole, surprisingly little friction between the Arian conquerors and the Catholic church. But now came a big change, when Gaiseric launched violent persecutions designed as a deliberate counterblast to the Catholic persecution of Arianism in other parts of the Western world.

Under a sixth century successor of Gaiseric, one of the Catholic bishops in North Africa, Victor of Vita, wrote most gloomily about the situation.

. . . You few who love the barbarians and are always singing
their praises, condemning yourselves out of your own mouths,
do but consider their name and reputation. Could any other
name but that of barbarian, which signifies savagery, cruelty
and terror, fit them so well? One may coddle them with
kindness, woo them with assiduous service, all they think of is
their envy of the Romans.

Their design is obvious – all the time they are trying to
besmirch the glory and honour of the Roman name. Their
desire is that no Romans shall survive. If they spare their
subjects in one or another case, it is to exploit them as slaves.

While Gaiseric was at work, King Euric of the Visigoths was
making his people in Gaul and Spain into another separate
nation, once again much expanded and once again wholly
independent; and he too displayed an equally intolerant hatred
of the Catholics, subjecting them to vigorous oppression.

Euric also regulated the relations between his German and
Gallo-Roman subjects by issuing, in 475, a new legal code, which
was to exercise strong influence upon medieval law. Although he
himself did not know Latin very well, his chancellor Leo was
compared to Tacitus and Horace, and the Codex Euricianus was
drawn up by Roman jurists and was heavily Romanized in
character. Nevertheless, it totally rejected any amalgamation
between the two main peoples in his realm, declaring them to be
irremediably separate and distinct. The Code of Euric was
published only one year before the Western Empire finally
collapsed: and the segregation between the Germans and
Romans which these laws enforced sums up excellently one
reason why the collapse was inevitable – because the idea of a
constructive union between the two races had failed.

To keep the Germans out of the Roman Empire had long since
ceased to be within the bounds of possibility. But instead there
had existed a unique, unrepeatable opportunity to create a
working partnership between Romans and Germans. At one
time, certain leading Germans had wanted it. But it was up to the
Romans to transform this co-existence into a positively cooperative union. Because of their traditional, ingrained attitudes, the
opportunity was tragically lost.

That is to say, ethnic disunity was a major cause of Rome's downfall. To retain in one's midst a substantial and disappointed racial minority, without taking effective steps either to integrate it or to treat it on psychologically equal terms, was to invite serious trouble; and the Romans failed to meet the challenge.

V

THE GROUPS
THAT OPTED OUT

10

Drop-outs against Society

Furthermore, considerable sections of the population of the later Roman Empire decided to opt out altogether. In the first place, a large number of people, finding the social system intolerable, went underground and became its enemies. But a second movement consisted of numerous men and women who merely abandoned the company of their fellow human beings and divorced themselves from the community.

They became hermits or monks and nuns. But the monks and nuns of ancient times are in some ways less comparable to modern monks and nuns than to modern drop-outs, supporters of gurus, or others – not necessarily with any religious motivation – who abandon the conventional world and sometimes leave their houses for the streets or the mountains or deserts. For the numerous monastic recluses of the Roman Empire, too, often shook the dust of the social, financial and political system off their feet as completely as it they had never belonged to it at all. And so, as the final political and military reckoning rapidly approached, this substantial number of men and women was no longer available to contribute either to the actual defence of the Empire or to the revenue needed to pay for the defenders.

For two centuries past, ascetic withdrawal and solitary contemplation had increasingly become regarded as a desirable ideal. There are many traces of this viewpoint in the *Meditations* of the second-century Emperor Marcus Aurelius, although his Imperial

145

and military responsibilities totally denied him the possibility of putting it into practice himself. Such tendencies were also prominent among Manichaeans and other dualists, who detached the evil world entirely from the divine creation and tried to slough off the material dross in their daily existence.

Extreme puritanism likewise dominated important sections of the Christian community. They justified this attitude by the contempt for the human flesh and condition displayed by John the Baptist in his chosen way of living, reiterated by St Paul, and ascribed by the Gospels to Jesus himself, who was said to have departed to a solitary place and gone up into the mountain where he devoted himself to prayer.

Then, in the third century AD, the monastic movement originated, in the depths of the wastes of Egypt. Its origins are shrouded in legends, centring upon the figure of Paul the Hermit of Thebes in Upper Egypt. Jerome, who wrote his biography, declared him to be the first of the Christian hermits; but that distinction is more often attributed to the better documented St Antony. Abandoning his worldly property in about 270, Antony entered, fifteen years later, upon a life of total isolation, dwelling in an empty grave upon a desert hill-top. Many people flocked to follow his example and join him, and before long he began to organize them into groups, which resided in separate and scattered cells and came together only for common worship. Another Egyptian, Pachomius, brought his followers into a fully communal existence by establishing monasteries at nine Egyptian centres, comprising 7,000 monks and nuns. Then the monastic life spread to Palestine. Before long, it was ripe for extension to the West.

The motives which caused monks and hermits to withdraw to this anti-social seclusion were varied. Many of Antony's recruits came to him during the last great persecutions of Christians at the start of the fourth century. Yet after the Empire had been converted to Christianity, the influx still did not diminish. Some came to get away from the oppressive demands of taxation, conscription, and regimentation in all its various forms. Others had purely private problems to flee from – lawsuits, for example, or family quarrels. Others, again, were prompted by a pious devotion which found the official church too worldly.

For self-denial was a potent motive, and so were feelings of guilt, and a sheer, total distaste for humanity and the flesh. Often these feelings assumed extreme forms, including acute physical mortification and even castration (forbidden by law at this time). For these were the self-disciplinary measures felt to be needed in order to escape the eternal punishment earned by those who succumbed to worldly temptations.

It came as a terrible shock to the cultured, classically minded poet Ausonius when his great friend Paulinus of Nola, a scholarly, middle-aged fellow-Senator and fellow-poet from Burdigala (Bordeaux), decided to make a complete break with the worldly and civilized life. Ausonius' anguished and perplexed complaints, symbolic of a clash between two mutually incomprehensible ways of life, have come down to us. But they were all uttered in vain, for Paulinus abandoned his political career and went with his wife to Spain, where they renounced all their possessions. Then later, after Paulinus had taken holy orders, they settled at Nola in south Italy to live lives of austerity.

Paulinus wrote to a friend defending the secluded existence.

. . . So, as your letter says, you visit cities infrequently, and have grown to love the intimate remoteness of the silent countryside. It is not that you put leisure before activity, and you do not withdraw yourself from what is useful to the church. But you avoid the noisy councils and the bustle of the churches which almost rival the crowds of the Forum.

And I think that you are laying the foundation of greater services to the church by wisely deciding to devote yourself wholly to religious instruction. By concentrating on spiritual studies, to which solitude is conducive, you are fashioning and strengthening Christ within you every day. . . .

Let us strive for the kingdom of God as we strove for position in the world. In short, let us attend to heavenly goods as carefully as we attend to earthly ones.

Paulinus himself, like the friend he was writing to, did not abandon the world completely, for he became a bishop and cared for his congregation and the sick. But public opinion lavished its greatest admiration on a more uncompromising puritanical sort of figure, the hermit in his desolate solitude.

Jerome wrote from personal knowledge about the hardships and hallucinations of the hermit life.

. . . My unkempt limbs were covered in shapeless sackcloth;
my skin through long neglect had become as rough and black
as an Ethiopian's. Tears and groans were every day my
portion. And if sleep ever overcame my resistance and fell
upon my eyes, I bruised my restless bones against the naked
earth. Of food and drink I will not speak. . . .

But though in fear of hell I had condemned myself to this
prison-house, where my only companions were scorpions and
wild beasts, I often found myself surrounded by bands of
dancing girls. My face was pale with fasting. But though my
limbs were cold as ice my mind was burning with desire, and
the fires of lust kept bubbling up before me when my flesh was
as good as dead.

Such were the tormented words that have prompted hundreds of
European painters to depict Jerome's experience – masterpieces
which reveal the hold this austere idealist has exercised upon the
imagination of the world. His passionate withdrawal seems
strangely incompatible with his anxieties about the disasters that
were befalling Rome, and his assertions that patriotism was a
normal instinct. However, 'the world, in its material sense', as he
declared in 412, 'belongs to the violent'. And so he abandoned it.
Such a course was utterly deplored by Gibbon in the rational
tones of the eighteenth-century Western world.

The Western world of ancient times was introduced to the
movement by Athanasius, bishop of Alexandria, who played a
dominant part in the theological disputes of his age. During the
second of five periods of exile from his diocese, in about 341, he
arrived in Rome, accompanied by two Egyptian monks, the first
to be seen in the West; and he was able to tell the Romans about
his devotion and respect for the way of life entailed by the
monastic vocation. Fourteen years later, during another period of
exile, he took refuge in Egyptian monasteries, and soon afterwards his *Life of Antony* appeared in Greek. Judiciously mingling
fact and fancy, it became a bestseller, and when translated into
Latin made a profound impression throughout the whole of the
Western Empire.

Nevertheless, the monastic way of life itself was slow to be
adopted in those regions. The first regular Western monastery
was at Ligugé, near Pictavi (formerly Limonum, now Poitiers) in

France, established in about 360 by a former peasant and soldier, St Martin, who came from Savaria (Szombathely) in Pannonia Prima (Hungary). Later, Martin established another monastic foundation Majus Monasterium (Marmoutier), to which he liked to withdraw from his bishopric of Turoni (formerly Caesarodunum, now Tours) as often as he was able to get away.

Martin followed the Antonian ideal of a life that was partly hermit-like and partly communal. His eighty monks at Marmoutier lived in caves and tents, met each other only for services and meals, and fasted with rigour. Work was discouraged, except the transcription of manuscripts – the monastic task which handed down so many of its greatest achievements to the modern world.

Sulpicius Severus, who came from south-western Gaul, wrote a skilful life of St Martin, describing his supposed miracles and his death. The biography was designed to show that the West could produce a saint superior to any Egyptian ascetic. Sulpicius, a wealthy Senator, who organized a sort of monkish life on his own estates, was writing for his own friends and equals, and the cult of St Martin among his class lent supernatural sanction to the dominance of the great landowner bishops.

It remained for Jerome, whose account of the hermit life was so dramatic, to complete the popularization of such ideals. In 370–73 he established his first society of ascetics at Aquileia in north-east Italy, and later he left for Palestine to found a monastery at Bethlehem in about 389. He also wrote extensively on the life the monks lived, and translated the rules that had been drawn up for their Eastern institutions. Meanwhile Augustine too, in North Africa, had gathered around himself a group of clergy, to live a regulated communal life. His treatise, *On the Works of Monks*, insisted that they should earn their own living by manual labour rather than begging. Yet he was also eager to develop the link between monasticism and learning.

Then, shortly after 400, it was on Gallic soil once again that these various endeavours bore significant fruit, when a more ambitious monastery was established by Honoratus on one of the Lérins Islands (S. Honorat), opposite Cannes, and the neighbouring islands were populated by monks shortly afterwards. Lérins served as a model for the future; and very shortly afterwards John Cassian, an ascetic from Scythia Minor (on the

Rumanian Black Sea Coast), founded a monastery and a nunnery at Massilia (Marseille) (*c.* 415). He also wrote the *Institutes* and *Conferences*, which dominated the monastic thought of medieval Europe. Meanwhile Cassian's guidance induced many a Senator, naturally inclined to devoutness or ruined by German invasions, to make the transition to monk and then bishop.

The former character of the monks as drop-outs had thus become considerably modified. In Ireland, it is true, the old semi-solitary Antonian tradition remained dominant. However, it was the more organized movement of Gaul which spread widely in the West during the fifth century AD. Captured by an articulate section of the aristocracy, it had become a highly respectable institution. It only remained for St Benedict, in the following century, to forge its peculiar, stable, permanent shape. But by that time the Western Roman world had fallen.

During the previous, decisive years of the Empire's gradual collapse, monasticism had *not* been a stabilizing but a disintegrating element. When society needed all the manpower and revenue that it could muster in order not to succumb to invasions, the monks had withdrawn both, and had encouraged others to withdraw them as well. That they had made this contribution to the disunities which brought the Empire down was widely appreciated by contemporaries. Some, admittedly, praised the monks for trying to better the lot of the local inhabitants, often by opposing the civil authorities. But their detractors were numerous and determined.

Jerome himself, though a determined pioneer of what he regarded as the right sort of monasticism, had the sharpest possible eye for the insincerity of many of its practitioners. His letters sparkle with onslaughts upon their conceit, lechery, gluttony and avarice. He can understand, he says, why many people prefer to live with wild beasts rather than with Christians of such a kind. But whereas he limited his criticism to bad monks, he was well aware that many others loathed them all indiscriminately, pointing out with a finger of scorn their black robes and shaven hair.

Non-Christians, too, found that monks provided much fuel for their attacks on the Christian faith. An Alexandrian epigrammatist, Palladas, could not understand why such well-organized pressure groups described themselves romantically as 'solitaries'; and Eunapius described how the pagan shrines were desecrated by these 'tyrants, who live like swine, accounting it piety'. They were also widely attacked for their idleness and begging, which Augustine, among others, greatly deplored.

The pagan historian Zosimus remarked that what they meant by 'sharing with the poor' was the reduction of everyone else to their own degraded level. But what was especially to the point was his emphasis on their uselessness to the state, to which they refused to make any contribution whatever.

Perhaps the general feeling was best summed up by Rutilius Namatianus, who, as his ship sailed up the west coast of Italy, passed a monastery on the island of Capraria, the modern Capraia:

. . . a dreary place, where
There are men who shun the light and call themselves monks . . .
They fear fortune, whether good or evil.
Would a man live in misery to escape it?
Because of their fear, they shun what is good.
Such reasoning is the raving of a madman;
Whatever their reasons, I find them strange.

The attitude of official churchmen towards monks and hermits was more ambivalent. Lip-service was often paid to the spiritual ideals of the monastic life, and bishops were sometimes ready enough to egg monks on to destroy pagan temples. Yet for a long time the church felt itself considerably weakened by their activities, since they deliberately defied its representatives, saw no reason to accept its universal claims, and deplored its alliance with the state.

In retaliation, an ecclesiastical synod of about 340, held in Asia Minor, deplored the infrequency of the monks' attendance at church services. Under Valens, Bishop Lucius of Alexandria even sent men to launch violent attacks on the monasteries, and a number of their occupants were put to death. Pope Siricius, likewise, declared roundly that numerous monks were impostors. Emperors, too, in their edicts, declared the inmates of the monasteries to be fanatical, unruly and rebellious, and only too ready to infiltrate the towns and exacerbate religious and social discontents.

These varying viewpoints were echoed by official pronouncements. A favourable attitude was apparent in 361, when Constantius II confirmed the exemption of monks from all public obligations. But then Julian compared them to his ragged itinerant fellow-pagans known as the Cynics, seeing both alike as 'troublesome, insolent, and vagabonds'.

Valentinian I and Valens were among the Christian rulers who similarly denounced monks for bad citizenship, and for hypocrisy into the bargain. Theodosius I, also, appealed to Ambrose in exasperation: 'What am I to do with those fanatical monks?' In 390 Theodosius still hoped to keep them away from the towns, commanding them to stay in 'desert places and vast solitudes'. But two years later, under pressure, he cancelled the order. Subsequently, Valentinian III forbade men to leave country estates to embrace monasticism, unless they had first obtained the landowner's permission. Yet none of these restrictive measures could keep the movement down.

On a long-term view, what was particularly perilous to the future of the Empire was the celibacy the monastic career involved, since it meant that the population, already scarcely large enough to provide the men and money needed for national defence, would diminish still further. Moreover, this urge towards the celibate life extended far outside the monastic movement, since the widespread fashion for chastity produced an enormous enthusiasm for abstinence from sexual relations.

This was declared to be a most desirable social ideal, because of the unworthiness of human beings and their bodies. For Jesus himself, according to the Gospel attributed to St Matthew, was said to have proposed celibacy as an example of superior virtue, and St Paul, writing to the Corinthians, had offered a similar recommendation. Thereafter, as the taste for self-denial rapidly increased, exhortations to total continence became increasingly numerous, and third-century puritans, like the fervent Tertullian, were tireless in their advocacy of this virtue. Treatises praising virginity soon began to appear in great abundance.

Augustine was one of the men who wrote vigorously and frequently in defence of such ideals. In his earlier days, he said that 'a whole frying-pan of abominable loves had crackled around him and on every side', and he had offered up the famous prayer,

'Give me chastity and continence – but not yet.' But he was utterly convinced that sex must be done away with: it was the punishment for Adam's sin.

Jerome strongly felt the same:

> . . . Our adversary the devil goeth about as a roaring lion seeking whom he may devour. . . . As long as we are held down by this frail body, as long as we keep our treasure in earthen vessels, and the flesh lusteth against the spirit, the spirit against the flesh: so long can there be no sure victory.

Sometimes Jerome descends from this lofty height to advise women not to marry on simple grounds of prudence, because of the troubled character of the times. But more often he was pursuing a principle, notably in a letter directing the upbringing of Paula, a girl of aristocratic family who had been dedicated to a nunnery from her birth – and now the most stringently rigorous education was prescribed for her by Jerome.

His insistence upon such views, while he was secretary to Pope Damasus, contributed largely to his expulsion from Rome in 385 after Damasus' death. For when Paula's aunt Blaesilla died, her end was believed to have been accelerated by the extreme asceticism urged on her by Jerome. At her funeral there were cries of 'The monks into the Tiber!', whereupon Jerome hastily left Rome, never to return. The new Pope, Siricius, who suspected him of aiming at the papacy for himself, was by no means sorry to see him go.

This episode reveals the extraordinary involvement of Jerome with Roman upper-class women – an interest he had shared with Damasus, who was known as 'the ladies' ear-tickler'. Such women, whatever the formal deficiencies of their status by modern standards – for example, their continued exclusion from all official and legal posts, and from public higher education – were far ahead of their menfolk in pressing forward towards Christian austerity. Jerome devotes a letter to the defence of his female friendships. 'Did I', he asked, 'ever enter the house of any woman who was inclined to wantonness? Was I ever attracted by silk dresses, flashing jewels, painted faces, display of gold? No other matron in Rome could win my approval but one who mourned and fasted, who was squalid with dirt, almost blinded with weeping!'

The further shrinkage of the already decreasing population to which this detestation of sexuality must lead was freely admitted by Christians. Their spokesman Eusebius explains that this aversion to sex made them reluctant to have children. For example, Saint Melania the elder – another of Jerome's friends – although she got married, felt no desire whatever to have children, and once they were born she left the last survivor without apparent remorse. Ambrose had been aware of ever-growing accusations that he and his co-religionists, by their praise of the pure unmarried state, were depriving Rome of the sons and daughters it needed. His reply was: 'Since when have men been complaining that they could not find a wife?'

Nevertheless, the opposite view had some right on its side, and the proliferation of monks and hermits and nuns, whatever their moral influence for good, tended to splinter a profoundly divided society still further, creating yet another disunity. So the assertion of Alexander Pope that 'the monks finished what the Goths began' contains a measure of truth. They had dropped out of the world, because they found society more than they could endure.

11

The State against Free Belief

In spite of its warning noises, the state did not take forcible steps
to bring back into society the men and women who had opted out
to become monks and nuns and hermits. But it practised violent
coercion on those who did not adhere to the same religion as itself
– and even to the same branch of the same religion. This coercion
was a major mistake. For instead of cementing the unity that had
been hoped for, it added a worse and more crippling disunity to
all the rest.

This ancient coercion proved possible because of a close
alliance between church and state. Until the early fourth century
AD, the official religion of the Roman world had been pagan. The
ancient paganism of the Roman state was willing to be all things
to all men. Being polytheistic, it was multiple and versatile. It was
very far from exclusive. Nor was it generally intolerant. True, it
had developed intolerance towards the Christians, because the
Christians, since they owed loyalty to a Higher Master, seemed to
be denying the sufficient minimum of loyalty to the Emperor and
the nation. But the Christians remained, for a long time, a small
and exceptional minority.

Then came the conversion of Constantine the Great to
Christianity, and his gradual conversion of the Empire to the
same faith. These events were astonishing because the Christians
were *still* a small minority, and not a very influential one at that.
Constantine's revolution, declared the English historian J. B.

155

Bury, was 'perhaps the most audacious act ever committed by an autocrat in disregard and defiance of the vast majority of his subjects'.

The Emperor took this surprising action because he felt an impulsive inner need for divine support; and the Christian faith, with its most satisfying of Redeemers, a Redeemer who had actually dwelt among mankind, gave a better promise of providing this aid than the various pagan saviours who had never been seen upon the earth. And so Constantine, looking around him, and noting all the grievous internal disharmonies which threatened to bring the Empire down, decided that the best possible unifying factor was Christianity. Under his guidance, it would bring everyone together, effectively counterbalancing all the many divisive trends. State and church, he planned, were to work together in the closest possible association. But the state was, at first, the controlling partner. Under Valentinian I, Bishop Optatus of Milevis (Mila) in Algeria admitted this, declaring 'The State is not in the Church, but the Church is in the State.'

Nevertheless Valentinian's policy of toleration could not fail to encourage the idea of ecclesiastical independence. He did not even prevent the scandal of the age, the papal election of 366 in which 137 corpses were left on the pavement of a Roman basilica. The successful candidate was Damasus, who thereafter worked for a Concordat in which the importance of the Pope would be enhanced. A leading pagan, Praetextatus, commented on his grandeur with the remark, 'Make me Bishop of Rome, and I will be a Christian at once.'

Yet it was a bishop not of Rome but of Mediolanum (Milan), now the Imperial residence, who raised the power of the church to a new peak. This was Ambrose, who occupied the bishopric from 374 until his death in 397. Ambrose declared, in contradiction to earlier doctrines, that 'the Emperor is not above the church, but *in* the church. . . . If one reads the Scriptures, one sees that it is bishops who judge Emperors. . . . A good Emperor does not spurn the assistance of the church: he seeks it.' These words were addressed to Valentinian II, who employed their author on important political missions.

Next, Ambrose had two immensely famous clashes with Theodosius I – from both of which the churchman emerged victorious. First, in 388, when an Eastern bishop had ordered a

Jewish synagogue at Nicephorium Callinicum (Raqqa) in Syria to be burnt, and Theodosius instructed that it should be rebuilt and its destroyers punished, Ambrose, speaking from the pulpit, ordered the Emperor to repent, and would not enact the Mass until the Imperial instruction had been revoked. Then, two years later, after the army commander at Thessalonica had been lynched for imprisoning a popular charioteer, and Theodosius, as a punishment, had 7,000 people massacred, Ambrose refused to admit him to Mass until he had done penance. These were moments of decision. By bowing to Ambrose's instruction on both occasions, Theodosius had deferred in spectacular fashion to the power of the church.

After Ambrose's death, the spiritual initiative returned from Milan to Rome, where Pope Innocent I (401–17) made it clear that this new ecclesiastical authority was going to be vested not in a Milanese bishop but in himself. When Alaric approached Rome with his Visigoths, Innocent was the only national leader with sufficient prestige to negotiate with him. Later Pope Leo I (440–61) likewise treated with Attila, scoring a triumphant success. It was Leo's view that collaboration between state and church was a bargain beneficial to both, like the contractual arrangements familiar to every Roman jurist.

Some contemporary thinkers, including Jerome and Salvian, deplored the tendencies of churchmen to join the comfortable establishment. But many others were delighted with this union of the spiritual and secular powers, declaring it to have been by no means fortuitous that the births of Jesus and of the Empire had coincided in date.

And indeed this union might well, as was its intention, have proved a factor cementing the disunited Roman world together. But it turned out to be exactly the opposite, because of the excessive zeal with which the civil authorities, carrying out the requests of their ecclesiastical partners, sought to enforce conformity upon all who did not agree with the doctrines of the official church. For by such means they transformed differences of opinion and doctrine into irremediable hostilities.

This willingness to use forcible methods was based on a disastrous interpretation of a text in the Gospel according to St Luke, in which Jesus was declared to have said, 'Go out into the highways and hedges, *and compel them to come in*, that my house may be filled.' In the later Roman world, this sentence, as well as utterances by St Paul, was used by church and state as an invitation to the fatal policy of coercion.

The problem arose in an acute form as early as the lifetime of Constantine himself. When he boldly converted the state to Christianity, the overwhelming majority of his subjects were still pagans. Although this was an obstacle to harmony which would, he believed, eventually be overcome, he initially announced that he was going to 'permit those who are in error to be free to enjoy the same peace and tranquillity as those who believe'. But, in the end, the strength of the opposition compelled him to sharpen this moderate attitude. Pagan temple treasures were confiscated, and finally pagan sacrifices were banned. Then his son Constantius II, whose personal devoutness was intensified by a terror of sorcery, stepped up this fight against paganism, passing laws in 346 and 356 of a strongly repressive nature.

His cousin and successor Julian the Apostate (361–3) reacted strongly against his Christian upbringing, and restored official paganism. At first he appeared to favour religious neutrality, and after the model of Constantine proclaimed a general willingness to permit any and every cult. However, after reinstituting pagan worship, he deprived the Christian churches and clergy of their privileges, and forbade Christian professors to teach the classics. But then he was killed in battle; and pagan historians declared this the most disastrous event in Roman history, an event which directly presaged the downfall of Rome. After his death Christianity was restored as the state religion.

Such was the situation which Valentinian I inherited – a situation in which the relationship between the two faiths, except among a few intellectuals, had become characterized by violent hostility and antipathy.

Although a Christian believer himself, Valentinian, in 371, decided to launch a policy of universal toleration. 'I do not', he said, 'consider *any* rite permitted by our ancestors to be criminal': and the pagan Ammianus, although willing enough to criticize Valentinian in other respects, hails this policy with proper admiration. The Pope of the time, Damasus, had connections with the pagan aristocracy, and this made it easier for Valentinian to damp down the growing intransigence of some of the other bishops.

Valentinian's liberal attitude was one of the few triumphs of the age. In opposition to the general feeling and practice, he felt that unity would better be achieved by tolerance, and this decision stands out as a beacon during a millennium and a half in which, for the most part, rulers of the leading nations continued to think and act otherwise.

Gratian at first adopted a similar policy, because he was initially under the influence of the poet Ausonius, whose Christianity was not obtrusive. But a new phase began when, in 397, Gratian appointed Theodosius I as his Eastern co-Emperor. First, Gratian abandoned the old traditional pagan chief priesthood, and his new colleague never assumed it. Then Gratian decided to remove the pagan statue of Victory from the Senate-house. Seized upon by influential pagans as a decisive menace to their tradition and faith, this action provoked, over a period of three years, a series of famous oratorical duels between Symmachus, the foremost pagan of the day, and the most outstanding Christian, Ambrose, bishop of Mediolanum (Milan).

The discussion was conducted with decorum. 'Everyone', declared Symmachus, 'has his own custom, his own religion. The love of habit is great. We ask for the restoration of the cult in its former condition, which has been beneficial to the Roman state for so long. One cannot reach so great a secret by one way alone.' This explicit denial of the Christian claim to universality was duly refuted by Ambrose, who insisted that the Emperor should 'do what he knew would be profitable to his salvation in the sight of God'. His view prevailed, and the statue was excluded from the Senate-house. It was the worst setback for paganism so far.

Ambrose also attacked marriages between Christians and pagans, citing the union of Samson and Delilah. And at the same time Symmachus had to contend with the lyrical Prudentius, whose forward-looking, rejuvenated, Christian Rome created a more vigorous impression than his own somewhat melancholy and nostalgic attitude. Besides, Prudentius ingeniously met his opponent's defence of traditionalism by arguing that change did *not* mean the negation of Rome's genius. It was a constructive approach, and Prudentius, a Christian with a profound appreciation of old Rome, sometimes seems nearer than anyone else to a genuine understanding between Christians and pagans. But no such understanding was allowed to develop. For the Christian regime did not feel that its vigilance could be allowed to drop for a single moment.

One danger that it had constantly in mind was apostasy from the faith, the subject of six severe enactments within fifteen years. The fiercest measures were the work of the intensely devout Theodosius I. In gratitude for his reconciliation with Ambrose, he forbade any pagan worship whatever, and in 381 even visits to temples were prohibited. Then, in the following year, on the death of Theodosius' fellow-Emperor Valentinian II, events occurred which intensified this severity. For a usurper, Eugenius, was set up in the West, and although nominally a Christian he was such a lukewarm believer that his accession put fresh heart into the pagans of Rome.

Theodosius I retaliated with drastic edicts. Every sort of pagan observance was even more emphatically forbidden, and judges, town councillors and chief citizens were made responsible for all evasions, under the threat of dire penalties. The Code of Theodosius II includes no less than twenty-five laws, drawn up by his predecessors and himself, directed against paganism in all its forms. The influence of Ambrose had indeed been effective –at least upon legislation, if not, perhaps, upon its enforcement, since even after this strongly anti-pagan law the Emperors still felt it necessary to issue thirteen more edicts to the same effect.

Theodosius I, in a spirit of deliberate vengeance, seems to have interpreted his role as the precise counterpart and reversal of the old pagan persecutions of the Christians. The opposing view was expressed by a pagan writer, Eunapius of Sardis (Sart), who declared, with the Christians in mind, that 'our age has risked being wholly kicked about by jackasses'. Meanwhile, in 394, the upstart Eugenius was suppressed, and, owing to the discomfiture of his pagan supporters, this was the time when the Christians first achieved a decided majority in the Senate. The age of ambivalence, of possible latitude of thought, was gone from the ancient Roman world for ever.

Nevertheless, when Theodosius I died in the following year, the regents of his sons Arcadius and Honorius at first adopted a moderate policy towards the pagans, seeking to assert the state's authority against the anti-pagan excesses of the clergy. But in North Africa religious riots broke out in 399 among the pagans because their shrines had been closed, and in consequence the bishops of the region, two years later, asked the Western government for new laws to 'extirpate the last remnants of idolatry'.

Augustine, bishop of Hippo Regius – now Annaba in Algeria – found himself actively caught up in this situation, and came out in favour of coercion of the pagans by the state. They must be compelled to change their ways. And apostates, too, must be forcibly returned to the fold as the Imperial edicts so rightly insisted, since Christ, like a general who brings back deserters recognized by the brand on the back of their hands, is entitled to use military methods to recall his own deserters to his army.

Augustine exulted over the destruction of pagan temples. A philosopher who belonged to the old religion, Nectarius, tried to bring home to him, in human terms, the hardships that these persecutions caused. But all such efforts to change his mind proved vain. And they became more useless still after Alaric had captured Rome. For this event frightened the Christians, since it gave paganism a new lease of life. Look, said the pagans, what has happened to Rome, now that it is Christian and has abandoned its ancestral gods! And that was the case Augustine's *City of God* sought to refute. Although this great work branched out in many directions, its immediate stimulus came from the need to stem this new pagan revival, made possible by the traumatic events of 410.

Until the death of Stilicho two years earlier, there had still been hopes of a more conciliatory official attitude towards the pagans. For he himself, during the period when he was virtually controlling the Empire, had urged a certain measure of religious toleration and balance. Nevertheless, even Stilicho had felt it necessary to burn the Sibylline books, the most sacred documents of paganism. For that, he was posthumously assailed, in 417, by the pagan poet Rutilius Namatianus, who reiterated firmly once again that it was because of the Romans' desertion of the gods that disaster had overtaken them; and he derided the Christian saints for failing to save the city.

Stilicho's death was immediately followed by a law excluding pagans from the army – since their loyalty was no longer regarded as secure. Thereafter, acts of repression against the pagans continued well on into the 430s. Then the beginning of the next decade witnessed the accession of Pope Leo I, who declared that 'Truth, which is simple and one, does not admit of variety'. In the same spirit, in 448, Theodosius II started to burn pagan books: 'all the volumes that move God to wrath and that harm the soul we do not want to come to men's hearing'. The pagan cult was evidently still active enough, even at that late date, to prompt such stringent precautions.

After that, it did little more than linger on. One of the last eminent pagans was the Greek historian Zosimus, who wrote his *New History* at about the turn of the sixth century. Like Rutilius Namatianus, he looked back upon Theodosius I's forced Christianization of the Empire as the direct cause of Rome's downfall – because it had obviously provoked divine retribution. Ironically enough, the results of that forcible official policy had been the disastrous reverse of what Constantine intended, when he saw Christianity as the potential unifying element of his Empire.

The men who originated and developed this idea, of which the Greco-Roman world had hitherto been free, that people should be coerced because of their opinions, bear a heavy load of responsibility for the persecutions that followed throughout medieval times, and subsequently. And meanwhile, these coercions had helped to destroy the Roman Empire, by intensifying the very disunities they were designed to eliminate.

Equally divisive and equally destructive were the conflicts within Christianity itself. When Constantine had made the Christian faith his state religion, he was no doubt prepared for objections from the pagan majority. But the savage enmities which rapidly developed among the Christians themselves took him by surprise. 'The very persons', he wrote to Bishop Chrestus of Syracuse in Sicily, 'who ought to display brotherly harmony and concord are estranged from one another in a way that is disgraceful if not positively sickening'.

Constantine's surprise did not, perhaps, sufficiently take into consideration the historical background. Greco-Roman paganism had never been monolithic; it consisted of a variety of different and separate cults, only loosely associated. So to most people it was not particularly surprising that, among the Christians too, there was a wide variety of different 'heresies' (from the Greek word *hairesis*, choice or sect). Yet the later Empire witnessed the growing official conviction that there ought to be a single orthodoxy – and the existence of numerous heresies became a source of ferocious dissatisfaction, not only to the established church but to the Emperors. It was their persistent ambition that the brand of Christianity favoured by themselves should become *Catholic*, in other words universal and unifying.

That was why Constantine, in 314, wrote to a functionary in North Africa that divine favour could only be secured by *united worship*, which must rise above disputes and quarrels, since these were distasteful to the Highest God. For nothing, declared his ecclesiastical supporter Eusebius, so greatly infuriates God as the division of the church: it is like cutting the body of Christ into pieces.

Yet all Constantine's hopes were doomed to frustration. He spent the greater part of his reign striving to establish cooperation among the Christians he had elevated so abruptly – and he strove in vain. It was not very long before his patience was exhausted; whereupon the adherents to heresies found their churches confiscated and their bishops sent into exile. Five years afterwards, Constantine declared it better, after all, to leave their punishment to God. But it was too late: the damage had already been done, and the hateful precedent set. Christians, almost as soon as they became a power in the land, had begun to persecute other Christians.

From this time onwards, in less than a century and a quarter, successive Emperors passed no less than sixty-six decrees against heretics. In his *Panarion* or Medicine Chest, written in 378, Bishop Epiphanius of Constantia (Salamis) in Cyprus, listing as many as eighty heresies, prescribed remedies for their adherents just as if they had been bitten by poisonous snakes; and a characteristic coin design shows Emperors stamping upon human-headed snakes representing these dissidents.

When Julian came to the throne in 361, his reaction against the Christian faith was largely prompted by these violent quarrels within its ranks, 'since he knew from experience', as Ammianus puts it, 'that no wild beasts are such enemies to mankind as are most of the Christians in their deadly hatred of one another'. However, Valentinian I, although official Christianity had been restored, remained as tolerant to 'heretics' as to pagans. But Gratian and Theodosius I, under the influence of Ambrose, reversed both policies alike.

In 380 Theodosius I suddenly published a very strong regulation denouncing heresies. A year later he ordained that all the church buildings of such sects were to be surrendered to Catholic bishops as defined by himself. Then, during the remaining fourteen years of his life, he issued as many as seventeen other laws against all such dissidents. From now on, laws against heresy outnumbered laws against paganism by five to one. Most remarkable of all, because of the feelings of insecurity to which it bore witness, was an edict which actually forbade the discussion of any religious question whatever – thus attempting, with complete futility, to deprive contemporaries of one of their favourite occupations.

In 407–8, heresy was once again declared a public crime, 'because offences against the divine religion are injuries to the whole of the community'. At the same time, all non-Catholics were excluded from court: though in the following year Honorius was compelled to relax these regulations, because it proved impossible to exclude or coerce every Arian German. But then in 410 and 415 came further edicts, denouncing the heretics all over again. For bishops who could boast co-religionists of the calibre of Ambrose, Jerome and Augustine were in no mood to allow the government to tolerate deviators, and all three of these outstandingly influential thinkers continued to thunder vigorously against such criminals.

We have seen how Augustine, after long and careful deliberation, came to the conclusion that it was right to request the secular authorities to suppress the pagans by force. But he spent an even greater part of his life urging similar action against heresies. For their adherents, in his belief, would be tormented for ever in hell-fire. For him, as for the Emperors, there could only be one single church. And those who stayed outside it, however eloquently they might call themselves Christians, were outside the Body of Christ.

Initially, Augustine had rejected the use of force against heretics, as he rejected it in the first place against pagans as well. But later, after prolonged thought, he changed his mind, because 'he had learnt their potential wickedness, and how they could benefit from discipline'. So he came round to a belief in coercion, convincing himself, as he had convinced himself about the pagans, that the state must be called in to compel them to conform. For this forcible method, he now explained, was really just like giving medicine to an unwilling patient – and could therefore even be described as a true work of love: 'loving with severity' was better than 'deceiving with indulgence', and Emperors, with all their array of repressive resources, could serve God in a way which private citizens could not emulate. In a letter to Vincentius, bishop of Cartennae (Ténès) in Mauretania Caesariensis (Algeria), he enlarged on the reasons for this altered attitude.

> . . . For originally my opinion was that no one should be coerced into the unity of Christ, that we must act only by words, fight only by arguments, and prevail by force of reason, lest we should have those whom we knew to be avowed heretics feigning themselves to be Catholics.
> . . . But this opinion of mine was overcome not by the words of those who controverted it, but by the conclusive instance to which they could point. For in the first place, there was set over against my opinion my own town which, although it was once wholly on the side of Donatism, was brought over to Catholic unity by the fear of the imperial edicts. I was made to own that to this matter the word of Scripture might be understood as applying: 'Give opportunity to a wise man and he will become wiser.'

But 'opportunity' was nothing better than a euphemism for violent suppression (Appendix 1).

Later, in the *City of God*, Augustine added the paradoxical justification that those who could *really* claim to be victimized were not the heretics at all but the faithful who were their persecutors – because the very existence of such evil-doers caused loyal Christians to 'suffer persecution, not in their bodies but in their hearts'. Hence the psalmist says, 'According to the multitude of sorrows in my heart' – not 'in my body'. But that did not help the heretics, whom the government, agreeing on political grounds with Augustine's theological arguments for compulsion, was now using force to bring into line.

This systematic, active intolerance was something hitherto unknown in the Mediterranean world. It reflected the growth of dogma, which in turn reflected a decline of rational intellectual activity. And now Augustine had placed himself in the forefront of this intolerant movement. Because of his eloquence and influence, he has been declared the Prince and Patriarch of Persecutors. He has also been denounced as the forerunner and first theorist of the Spanish Inquisition. It is only fortunate that, since he lived across the sea in North Africa, he was not in a central enough position to make himself the Grand Inquisitor of the whole Roman world. But even so, the damage done by the coercion he favoured and encouraged was great. Voltaire and Gibbon were right to blame the hostility between Christian and Christian, as well as between Christian and pagan, for helping to bring down the Empire.

It remains to discuss the rifts between the Christian authorities and members of two other religions which they oppressed, religions that were neither pagan nor Christian: the Manichaeans and the Jews.

Manichaeanism is still today the faith of millions of ordinary people, if they only knew it. This forceful doctrine survived from the third to the fifteenth centuries, demanding from its adherents an absolute belief in the distinction between good and evil. Both were eternally co-existent, and therefore it upheld the widespread instinct that, since we cannot admit God's responsibility for the evil things of this world, they must have been created by some other agency. This dualism, known as Gnostic (from *gnosis*, knowledge), was reputed to go back to Simon Magus, who is denounced in the Acts of the Apostles. In the second century AD, dualist places of worship were set up over extensive areas of the Roman provinces, declaring that the creator of the world and its evil was not God but an Independent Maker (Demiurge).

But most of these sects eventually became merged in Manichaeanism, the creed Mani began to preach in *c.*240 in Mesopotamia. Identifying the eternal contrasts of good and evil with Light and Darkness, Mani established an elaborate, well-organized church, and his religious ambitions exceeded even the Empire-wide universalism of Constantine and his ecclesiastics, since he planned to found a spiritual community that would conquer the entire world. Within less than a century, his doctrines had spread throughout vast regions of the Roman world; and successive Imperial governments, first pagan and then Christian, treated this growth of Manichaeanism as a major threat.

Diocletian, who persecuted the Christians, introduced savage sanctions against the Manichaeans as well, apparently regarding them as potential instruments of Rome's Persian foes. Nevertheless, their devotees were now arriving in the capital itself, and before long they spread to southern Gaul and Spain. The Christian Emperors, who treated them as severely as their predecessors had, felt anxiety, in the words of the Theodosian Code, because the Manichaeans proselytized among 'persons of the lower classes'.

They must indeed have appeared to represent some quite special threat, since even the unbigoted Valentinian I felt unable to include them in his general programme of toleration, and sent out orders that their property should be confiscated. Yet this was the very time when the Manichaeans obtained their most distinguished convert, Augustine, whose nine years of adherence to their views left their distaste for the world permanently in his heart – but added zest, after he had left Manichaeanism, to his endeavours to convert to true Christianity all who had once strayed to false and heretical doctrines, as he himself had earlier done.

In 383 Gratian, Theodosius I and Valentinian II reinforced previous anti-Manichaean legislation in savage terms. And this sort of hostile attitude was soon the cause of a tragedy. For it resulted in the first Christian execution of a man for his religious views. The victim was Priscillian, a Hispano-Roman who had attracted a substantial spiritual following. Although he was elected bishop of Avela (Avila) in Spain, his extreme ascetic contempt for our sordid physical existence caused the hierarchy to suspect he was a Manichaean. In 384 therefore, with the approval of the usurper Magnus Maximus, he suffered condemnation by a church synod at Burdigala (Bordeaux), and in the following year, after being judged guilty of sorcery and immorality, he was executed.

The court that passed the death sentence was a secular one. Nevertheless, it was for his religious opinions that Priscillian was sentenced, and the precedent was deeply ominous. Disunity in the Empire had indeed reached a destructive height when the authorities, secular and ecclesiastical alike, could take the decision to kill someone for such a reason. St Martin of Tours objected strongly to the execution, declaring that church and state should each be content to occupy itself with its own affairs. Even Ambrose, who generally favoured rough treatment of heretics and schismatics, was appalled, and he and Pope Siricius excommunicated the men who had brought the fatal charges.

The persecution of the Manichaeans by Theodosius I drove them underground for a time, yet proved so ineffective, in the long run, that during the fifth century they still greatly prospered, especially in Spain and in Gaul. Pope Leo I (440–61) was alarmed to find Manichaean infiltrators in his own congregation; and another two harsh laws against them were published by Valentinian III shortly afterwards. No other sect was so severely attacked, or was rejected with such extravagant emphasis.

The Manichaeans, however, continued to live on in the East for many centuries. And in the West, too, dualism proved ineradicable, and Manichaeanism had many spiritual heirs under various different designations. A full eight hundred years after the fall of Rome, St Louis IX of France was misusing the name of 'Crusade' to try to suppress similar faiths all over again.

The Jews, too, received unfavourable treatment from the Christian rulers of West and East alike. It was now a matter of centuries since the First and Second Roman Wars or Jewish Revolts had ended in terrible failure and the suppression of the national homeland. Yet the millions of Jews of the Dispersion, throughout the Roman Empire and Persian Mesopotamia, survived and maintained their faith. In Israel itself, too, although the old Jerusalem had been obliterated and replaced by a Roman settlement, life revived among Jewish communities in other parts of the country, and these were soon granted Roman recognition once again, under their own autonomous Patriarchate and Council.

Relations with Rome flourished under the Patriarch Judah I ha-Nasi ('the Prince') (135–219), who is also traditionally regarded as the principal organiser of the Mishnah, that massive repository of Jewish tradition and belief. But then paganism ceased to be the official religion of the Empire. Why was it that Christianity, and not Judaism, took its place? They had so very much in common, including nine-tenths of their ethical background. But once again, like the pagan religions, Judaism could never win over the bulk of the population, because the world hankered after a saviour: and the Jews had no historical Messiah to offer.

Ever since the life and deeds of Jesus had first been recorded, relations between the two communities had been hostile. The Gospels contained much anti-Semitic material, designed to show to the Roman authorities that Christians had nothing to do with the First Jewish Revolt. On the Jewish side, the *Toledoth Yeshu* described Jesus as a sorcerer, the Son of Uncleanness.

Jews had feared the rise of Christianity as one of the ultimate plagues announcing the end of the world. And when it became the official church of the Empire, their situation duly worsened. They were attacked for having caused the death of Jesus: Bishop Severus of Antioch told his colleague at Beroea (Aleppo) that 'the whole community should be penalized for participating in that sin'. Yet it could also not be forgotten that Jesus himself had been a member of their race, and had fulfilled many of their prophecies, so that they were the witnesses, however involuntarily, to the glory of his mission.

That being so, there could be no question of suppressing the Jews by force, like pagans or Manichaeans or heretics. Nevertheless, their treatment by the Christian Emperors remained equivocal and grudging. Because they had prepared the way for Jesus and had given him human birth, they could not be forcibly stamped out. Yet since, on the other hand, they had repudiated and killed him, their lives ought to be made as miserable as possible. So the bishops demanded; and so the Emperors ordained. True, the Sabbath was legally tolerated, Jewish sacred property was declared inviolate, and rabbis enjoyed the privileges of the Christian clergy. But at the same time measure after measure was taken by Roman officialdom to lower the status of synagogues, to forbid conversions or reconversions to Judaism, to prevent intermarriage between the two communities, and to eliminate any conceivable defiance of Christian ecclesiastical domination.

Jewish hopes momentarily rose when Julian, in his attempt to depose Christianity, authorized the rebuilding of the Temple at Jerusalem, nearly three hundred years after its destruction following the First Revolt. But Julian died before his plans came to fruition. There was another comparatively favourable moment when Theodosius I endeavoured to treat the Jews with greater liberalism than he showed in the handling of pagans and heretics; and after his death his Eastern minister Eutropius maintained the same policy. Yet it was not long before the Jewish situation deteriorated again. In 415, the Patriarch Gamaliel VII was subjected to penal measures, and when he died four years later the office of the Patriarchate itself was soon abolished, and its finances annexed by the government. Then the Code of Theodosius II systematized all the numerous recent sanctions directed against the Jewish faith. Their constant references to its foul, abominable, outrageous, lethal, sacrilegious perversity makes gloomy reading.

No doubt the Imperial bark was somewhat worse than its bite, being intended to placate the more fanatical Christian clergy. But it was perilous that such clerics were continually inciting their congregations to hold similar views. Ambrose, for example, informed Theodosius I that the reason why the usurper Magnus Maximus had fallen was because he had impiously commanded the reconstruction of a synagogue which had been burnt down at Rome – and that was why Theodosius must cancel his order to reconstruct a similar building that had been destroyed in the East.

Augustine, too, no less than twenty times in his surviving writings, strikes the old sour balance once again, declaring these obstinate people 'witnesses of their own iniquity and the Christian truth'. The fifth-century Bishop Theodoret of Cyrrhus (Kurus in southern Turkey) complained that the Jews still felt superior to the Christians; and Jerome implausibly accused them of hoping to gain supreme political control. The poet Rutilius Namatianus, in a passage full of brutal contempt for Judaism, even declared that this had already happened, and that the conquered race had subdued its conquerors – 'their belief is a plague that creeps back again after it has been rooted out'. Sidonius, on the other hand, happens to have a good opinion of a Jew, Gozolas – 'he is a man whom I should like as a person, if I did not despise his religious faith'. Yet even that grudging word of appreciation, anticipatory of the notorious saying 'some of my best friends are Jews', was exceptional. On the whole, we have a mournfully divisive picture.

It has recently been asserted that the final split and separation between Christians and Jews 'is going to be seen by many scholars, both Christian and Jewish, as a greater disaster by far than any subsequent schism within the Christian church itself'. If not a full union, then at least an alliance between the Christians and the very numerous Jews throughout the Empire could have provided a united front against which internal Christian dis- unities might have seemed less significant. It would thus have strengthened the declining Roman world: whereas the exact opposite occurred, and the bitter hostility between Christians and Jews became just one more of the many disharmonies which weakened the Western Empire's will to defend itself and thereby contributed to its collapse.

'It seems to me impossible to deny', concluded Arnaldo Momigliano, 'that the prosperity of the church was both a consequence and a cause of the decline of the state.' And what contributed above all to this decline was the application of religious coercion; for it achieved precisely the opposite of its unifying aims, powerfully accelerating the forces of disintegra- tion and dissolution.

VI

THE UNDERMINING OF EFFORT

12

Complacency against Self-Help

We must now turn from official divisive actions to the ways of
thinking that lay behind them. And it will be found that neither
pagan nor Christian habits of thought helped the government
very much in its unsuccessful struggle to ensure national
survival.

For the pagans, on the whole, relied too complacently on the
glories of the past, and the theologians preached doctrines that
minimized the importance of serving the state. Each of these two
philosophies in its turn, therefore, increased the massive national
disunities by setting up its own characteristic attitude *against* the
attitudes that were needed if the Empire was to be saved.

First, the pagans. Their ancient educational habits still
flourished. Indeed their purveyance of the classical tradition kept
the field to itself, since the Christians had no rival educational
theory or practice to offer. And the teachers of the time adhered
to the old pattern of the Seven Liberal Arts – Grammar, Rhetoric,
Dialectic, Arithmetic, Geometry, Astronomy, and Music; though
the last four were now scarcely taught.

Within the limited field required, academic merit was excep-
tionally well rewarded. But promotions were strictly controlled.
Julian asserted the Emperor's right to revise professorial appointments made by local authorities. Salary grades were fixed by
Gratian. An edict of 425 asserted the sole control of the state over

education, and penalized the opening of institutions of learning by unauthorized persons.

Rome was still the greatest of the state universities. Valentinian I took vigorous measures to keep its students in order. If freshmen came from outside the city, they must have permits from the governors of their provinces, declaring them to be fit and proper persons to attend the university. Details of their qualifications were requested, and they were expected to outline a proposed course of study, for which the approval of the city prefect was required. On reporting for work, they must communicate their addresses to the functionaries known as the Censuales, whose business it was to note these residences on their files.

It was also the duty of the Censuales to give warnings of the dangers of dissolute behaviour and excessive addiction to public shows; and students who were recalcitrant could be sent away or flogged. No doubt also, more boldly than their modern successors, the university authorities echoed the admonition of John Chrysostom, the bishop of Constantinople: 'Do not let your son's hair grow long – Nature disallows it, God has not sanctioned it, the thing is forbidden.'

The other leading universities of the West were at Mediolanum (Milan) and Carthage. Carthage, however, had serious student troubles, about which Augustine reminisces, though he himself seems to have played a somewhat unhelpful role among the silent majority.

> . . . I was at the top of the school of rhetoric. I was pleased with my superior status and swollen with conceit. All the same, as you well know, Lord, I behaved far more quietly than the 'Wreckers', a title of ferocious devilry which the fashionable set chose for themselves. I had nothing whatever to do with their outbursts of violence, but I lived among them, feeling a perverse sense of shame because I was not like them.
>
> I kept company with them and there were times when they lived up to their name. Without provocation they would set upon some timid freshman, gratuitously affronting his sense of decency for their own amusement and using it as fodder for their spiteful jests. . . . 'Wreckers' was a fit name for them, for they were already adrift and total wrecks themselves.

Nevertheless, the university of Carthage maintained a higher academic standard than almost any other institution.

Gaul possessed famous municipal schools of grammar and rhetoric, among which those at Lugdunum (Lyon), Vienna (Vienne), Burdigala (Bordeaux) and Arverna (Clermont-Ferrand) were outstanding. During the Constantinian epoch Gallic education enjoyed a considerable. renaissance, and an edict of 376 propounded an elaborate system of state-controlled education throughout the country. In the following century, which was the great age of Gaul's poets, its schools still continued to exist, although the political disturbances of the time caused them to show signs of decay, so that teaching tended to become conventional and superficial.

Indeed, a barren worship of convention was now all too frequent in colleges of every sort. Nor had anything whatever been done to remedy the characteristic failing of Roman education, which was its narrowly literary and oratorical character. The neglect of science and technology to which this curriculum testified was singularly incapable of meeting the continually recurrent crises of the age. Empty, pedantic classicism was the order of the day, and the system went on turning out cultured graduates who possessed a talent for verbal felicity and valued superficial expression but were totally lacking in practical constructive ideas.

Constantine, far from adjusting educational institutions to meet the new attitudes of a Christianized Empire, gave a vigorous stimulus to the old outworn system by deliberately assuming its patronage. Although not a highly literate man himself, he spoke fervently in support of the classics, without feeling the smallest obligation to broaden their scope. And even Valentinian I, who came from a non-Roman milieu and disliked the upper class, did nothing to reverse this conservative trend.

On the contrary, throughout the entire fourth century, there was a significant resurgence of the historic literature and oratory. 'If we lose eloquence,' declared the rhetorician Libanius, 'what then will there be left to distinguish us from the barbarians?' Yet the circle of people who maintained this civilization had shrunk considerably, as the middle class, which had hitherto played a prominent part in it, gradually faded away. In consequence, the basically aristocratic nature of the traditional Roman culture reasserted itself, and its pursuit became limited to a comparatively small number of pagan noblemen and Senators, whose cultural and literary attitudes remained singularly uniform.

The letters they wrote to one another, couched in a language meaningful only to a few persons of refinement like themselves, display elegance and nostalgic charm, but have been justly pronounced to be as accomplished and as jejune as the visiting cards of the mandarins of Imperial China. Sadly memorable examples of this sterility are provided by the epistles of Symmachus. Ausonius' *Mosella* is a charming poem of natural description, but his remaining works mostly justify the poet's own admission, 'I know that my readers will yawn over my poor verses. Such is their usual fate, and they deserve it.' Claudian's poems, which greatly influenced medieval Latin verse, attain a higher level, displaying a competent fluency of diction and versification. But the inscription on his statue in the Forum of Trajan at Rome, dedicated 'to one who has combined a Homer's music with a Virgil's mind', is wildly overstated.

Typical products of the period were thirty-page summaries of Roman history, for people who did not have the time or patience for more. The fifth-century writer Martianus Capella, on the other hand, wrote a lengthy allegorical treatise, which was once again employed as a model in the Middle Ages. Its dry-as-dust, though quaint, pedantry is adequately suggested by its title *On the Wedding of Mercury and Philology*, and by the choice of the Seven Liberal Arts as Philology's bridesmaids.

Macrobius' academic symposium the *Saturnalia*, perhaps written at about the same time, includes a mass of varied and obscure material, which throws much light upon the current antiquarian revival. But although the *Saturnalia* possesses a melancholy interest as the determined bulwark of dying academic classicism, it is by no means a literary masterpiece.

Sidonius, again, is equally informative about the Roman Empire. His letters and poems, however, are woolly, bombastic, artificial and turgid – as the English historian Thomas Hodgkin remarked, he is a conceited member of a foolish mutual flattery society. But Sidonius was at least a powerful believer in the dignity of the literary profession, and at the end of his life he wrote rather impressively: 'Now that the old degrees of official rank are swept away – those degrees by which the highest in the land used to be distinguished from the lowest – the only token of nobility will henceforth be a knowledge of letters.'

Sidonius and many other leading cultural figures lived outside Rome, and outside Italy. Although the Emperors of the time rarely visited the ancient capital, residing instead at Mediolanum (Milan) and then Ravenna, the influence of the Eternal City, where the Senate was still located, remained gigantic, and even increased. It had already been called eternal by the poet Tibullus, half a millennium earlier, and the coins of rulers of many epochs repeated the same glorious epithet. Even the transient Priscus Attalus, protégé of Alaric the Visigoth, depicted the goddess Roma seated in traditional martial guise, with the proud, romantic, unconsciously ironical, inscription 'Unconquered, eternal Rome' – 'INVICTA ROMA AETERNA'.

When Attila, confronted by Pope Leo I, decided to withdraw from Italy, the motives that deterred the Huns from attacking Rome may have included not only practical considerations but the superstitious fear the city still inspired. And even after the German Odoacer had seized control of Italy, and the Western Empire was no more, the vacuum of sovereignty was filled by the romantic ideology of eternal Rome. No longer the governmental centre of the world which had taken its name, it had become, nevertheless, the symbol of that world in a new and significant manner, denoted by the use of the term 'Romania'.

When first used in the fourth century, this designation stood for the Roman Empire in the political sense, and then it came to denote the whole heritage of Roman culture in the Latin West, in distinction from Gothia, Francia, Alamannia. Emperors who had originated in far distant provinces, and who had scarcely even set foot in Rome, nevertheless passionately stressed their authentic Romanism, and even humbler provincials at last came to speak of themselves as 'Romans', although they, too, may never have been near the place at all.

At higher levels of culture and society, the city's appeal received fanatical literary expression. Ammianus, who left the Greek East and went to Rome to write a Latin history, described the fascination of the *urbs venerabilis* in solemn terms. Claudian, too, hailed the antique capital with heartfelt praise, admiring, above all, the universality which had been its greatest gift to history. In 416–17 another poet, Rutilius Namatianus, offered a further striking eulogy. The real Rome, only lately, had succumbed to the barbarian captor Alaric. But Rutilius discerned a Rome of a higher reality, which could never fail.

> No man will ever be safe if he forgets you;
> May I praise you still when the sun is dark.
> To count up the glories of Rome is like counting
> The stars in the sky. . . .

Sidonius, who came from a part of Gaul which prided itself on its Latin civilization, saw Rome as the 'apex of the universe, fatherland of liberty, sole commonwealth of the entire world'. And in his panegyric of the Emperor Majorian, he personified the city-goddess in the following fulsome and imposing terms:

> Rome, the warrior-goddess, had taken her seat.
> Her breast was uncovered, on her plumed head was a
> crown of towers . . . She had a sternness ready to
> rebuke exaltation, her modest mien only makes her
> more terrible.

Sidonius and his fellow-Christians were still quite at ease with this pagan personification, and indeed Leo I, traditionally believed to have been the first Pope who came from the old Italian countryside, praised the see of St Peter in the sort of language pagans were accustomed to use about the Capitoline Gods.

And yet there was endless argument among Christians about the extent to which they were entitled to dwell upon this classical heritage. Tertullian had taken the extreme view that it was sinful for a Christian to teach the pagan authors at all. That was not official; nevertheless, there was a considerable awareness that one must not give in too completely to the allurements of the pagan classics. Jerome dreamt that God upbraided him for being a Ciceronian (wherein the Almighty paid his literary background a somewhat excessive compliment). Augustine, too, contrasted *your* Virgil with *our* Scriptures. Nevertheless, he felt it appropriate to recall that even the ancient Israelites had been allowed to 'spoil the Egyptians' and take captive women as concubines: so he too was entitled to take what he could from the pagan writers. Paulinus of Nola felt the same. You should not be too greatly bemused by the classics, he advised, but nevertheless it was permissible for you to exploit them for your own Christian advantage.

These same writers who venerated Rome – pagans and Christians alike – display a strong tendency to see every contemporary event in terms of *previous* Roman happenings. In order to ram these comparisons home, they call continually upon a wide range of precedents, taken from the entire gallery of the glorious past. When, for example, the Romans are defeated by the Visigoths at Adrianople, Ammianus at once compares the disaster to German invasions nearly five hundred years earlier. The events of past and present are continually juxtaposed and juggled together.

Claudian plays just the same game, persistently and elaborately relating his contemporary heroes to their alleged historical forerunners – Horatius on the Bridge, the Scipios, Cato, Brutus, and so on downwards into Imperial times. Sidonius is another writer who pours forth a veritable torrent of antique precedents. Indeed, even Salvian, in spite of all his distaste for the conservative establishment, nevertheless remains a tremendous eulogist of times gone by.

Contemporary Emperors, too, employ just the same sort of language in their edicts. The legislation of Majorian, for example, specifically invokes the praises of the laws of ancient times. And, indeed, the nomenclature of these rulers still retains its ancient ring. Majorian himself was called 'Julius' after Caesar who had died exactly five hundred years before his accession: and the very last Emperor of all was both Romulus and Augustus. 'These names', remarked J. B. Bury, 'meet us like ghosts rearisen from the past days of Roman history.'

Such was the atmosphere in which the scholars of the period spent their time actively unearthing and preserving the ancient masterpieces of Latin literature. 'If we have any discernment,' advised Macrobius, 'we must always venerate antiquity.' His advice was scarcely needed. No age had ever looked backwards with such passion.

Yet this admiration for the past led directly to catastrophes, since it conspired to prevent anything being done to avert them. For when Ammianus compared the Visigoths to the German invaders of half a millennium before, his whole point was that those former Germans, perilous though they seemed at the time, had nevertheless been successfully driven from the Empire. Moreover, he explicitly attacked anyone who maintained that such parallels with present times were not perfectly satisfactory.

> . . . Those who are unacquainted with ancient records say that the state was never before overspread by such a dark cloud of misfortune, but they are deceived by the horror of the recent ills which have overwhelmed them. For if they study earlier times or those which have recently passed, these will show that such dire disturbances have often happened.

So the battle of Adrianople, which had resulted in a crushing Visigothic victory, was nothing really serious to worry about. And other writers, too, speak in almost exactly the same terms.

Now, to interpret this as praiseworthy courage in the face of adversity is inadequate. For such an interpretation would ignore the fallacy inherent in Ammianus' view. The fallacy lay in the real difference that existed between the ancient events and the recent disaster. For the German invasions defeated by Marius had not been fatal to Rome, and had never threatened to be fatal. The degree of magnitude had altogether changed: the blow represented by the battle of Adrianople was a peril of quite a different order, and the symptom of a plight far more desperate than had ever been threatened before.

The current situation, as described by Ammianus himself without the benefit of hindsight, would have seemed to make it clear that this was so. He reveals the Emperors constantly engaged in checking German breakthroughs at one point after another along the frontier: Adrianople had surely made it clear that, unless some novel, large-scale remedies could be found, the collapse of Roman control in many provinces was close at hand. That is to say, Ammianus' optimism could only be in the slightest degree justified if he were able to point to some plan for averting this collapse. But this was not within his powers.

Enmeshed in classical history and classical education, all he can do is to lapse into vague sermonizing, telling the Romans, as many a moralist had told them throughout the centuries, that they must undergo an ethical regeneration and return to the simplicities and self-sacrifices of their ancestors. Indeed, that is the one plan that can be expected of him, since he was only able to conceive the present in terms of Rome's splendid past, when each successive obstacle had been triumphantly overcome. There was just no room at all, in these ways of thinking, for the novel, apocalyptic situation which had now arisen, a situation which needed solutions as radical as itself.

The Romans reached exactly the opposite conclusion. The self-satisfaction with which they reacted to current events displayed a sluggish insensitivity to current developments. Ausonius, although a political adviser of Emperors, is a conspicuous example. His whole attitude is a complacent acceptance of things as they are, without a single new idea.

And above all this acceptance was accompanied by greatly excessive optimism about the present and future. North-African inscriptions of the turbulent later fourth century refer with an utterly misplaced hopefulness to 'the youthful vigour of the Roman name' and 'golden times everywhere'. And the same inane spirit is found in writer after writer. For example, Claudian spoils his moving praise of the universality of the Empire by gross exaggerations of the theme that there will never be a limit to Roman power. Rome only has to threaten, he cries, and the Rhine is pacified. Yet these traditional assertions by the poets that countries even as far afield as India will bow beneath the Roman Imperial yoke were little less than ludicrous in the circumstances of decline.

> Now, to my sight, is Babylon subdued;
> The Parthians take to flight, as if pursued;
> To Roman laws, submission Bactria shows;
> The Ganges pale 'mid captive borders flows;
> And Persia, at our foot, with humble air,
> Spreads costly ornaments and jewels rare.
> Your course to Bacchus' utmost limits bend;
> From pole to pole your Empire shall extend.
> The Ruddy Sea will you with pearls supply;
> On Indus' stream for ivory rely; . . .

Symmachus, too, with equal fatuity, pronounces the conquest of new territories to be the Empire's continued aim. Moreover his Christian opponent Prudentius holds just as firmly to the same belief that the Eternal City has been granted a wholly new lease of life under its new Christian management. As he makes the goddess Rome declare,

> My grey hairs become gold again. Let all that is mortal
> Age according to the law; for me time has ushered
> in another century
> And a long life taught me scorn of death.

Even when the end was only sixty years away, and the Empire was already crumbling fast, Rutilius Namatianus continued to address the spirit of Rome with the same supreme assurance:

> Your power is felt wherever the sun's light shines,
> Even to the farthest edge of the world. . . .
>   Let your
> Bright armour flash the light of perpetual fire. . . .
> Let your law extend to all the known world;
> It will not die. You have lived a millennium
> Plus sixteen decades and now nine more years.
> You need not fear the Furies; the years that remain
> Have no limit but the earth's firmness and
> The strength of Heaven supporting the stars. Your strength
> Is the weakness of other Empires:
> You are strong because you can learn from misfortune.

That is nobly said. But it entirely diverts attention from the need to take the most vigorous imaginable steps to ward off the collapse of his beloved Rome, which was, in fact, so urgently imminent.

Sidonius paid his second visit to the city as late as 467, only nine years before the Western world ceased to exist. And what did he find? He found that everything was in excellent order. As he gazed at the Romans enjoying their holiday celebrations, the ancient institutions seemed to him wholly unshaken. He neither saw nor felt the slightest indication of the portentous changes under way.

Once again, that was not the spirit in which anything was likely to be done to save the declining Empire: or even to see that there was anything more than usually wrong with it. This blind adherence to the ideas of the past ranks high among the principal causes of the downfall of Rome. If you were sufficiently lulled by these traditionalist fictions, there was no call to take any practical first-aid measures at all.

13

The Other World against This World

If the pagans, and the products of their educational system, failed to meet the challenge of the crisis owing to excessively traditional attitudes, the great churchmen and theologians, men of superior brains and character who in earlier times would have been public servants, were guilty, too often, of a different but equally serious fault: that of discouraging other people from serving the state, either in a peaceful or a warlike capacity.

This had been a natural enough attitude in the old days when the state was engaged in persecuting Christianity. Their feelings at that period were summed up by Origen: 'We Christians defend the Empire by praying for it, soldiers in a spiritual welfare much more vital than any in which a Roman legionary serves.' In the same spirit, his more radical contemporary Tertullian argued that a Christian soldier in the Roman army who had refused to put a garland on his head during a pagan festival was entirely justified, even though his refusal might be followed by his own imprisonment, and by the persecution of his co-religionists. Indeed, the command to 'turn the other cheek', attributed to Jesus, made it difficult for a Christian to be a Roman soldier at all; and there were numerous specific instances of men who, after embracing Christianity, felt unable to serve in the army any longer.

Nor was the Christian attitude to civilian public service any more favourable. For the scriptural saying 'You cannot serve two masters, God and Mammon', was interpreted by identifying

Mammon with the Emperor. 'Nothing, then, is more foreign to us than the state,' felt Tertullian. And the church Council held in about 306 at Illiberis (Elvira) in Spain declared that no member of the faith who had been appointed to an official post could be allowed to come to church throughout his entire period of office.

But it may seem somewhat surprising that, after the Empire became Christian, the church and its leaders, although they were now the partners of the Emperor, still persisted in their old conviction that Christianity was incompatible with state service. In 313, for example, the Council of Arelate (Arles) in Gaul pronounced that those who wished to take up political life were excluded from communion. For, in the words of an early papal letter to the Gauls, 'those who have acquired secular power and administered secular justice cannot be free from sin'. In consequence, a series of Popes, including Siricius and Innocent I, debarred those who had held administrative jobs from holy orders, explaining that this was because such government posts, even if not actually sinful in themselves, were gravely perilous to a man's soul all the same.

Moreover, this veto was still specifically extended, as in earlier days, to those who had served in the army. Indeed, the Christian leaders of the time, in spite of their new and intimate associations with the government, still continued to speak out frequently and openly against military service. Athanasius explicitly praised Christianity because it alone implanted a truly pacifist disposition, since the *only* foe it battled against was Evil. Basil of Caesarea related this attitude very rigorously to practical life, declaring that a solider who killed a man in the course of his duties was guilty of murder and must be excommunicated. Even Pope Damasus, from his position of close alliance with the state, still praised Christian soldiers who courted martyrdom by throwing away their arms. St Martin of Tours asked to be released from the army because 'I am Christ's soldier: I am not allowed to fight'. And when taxed with cowardice, he was said to have offered to stand in front of the battle line armed only with a cross. But then, according to the legend, the enemy surrendered immediately, so that no such gesture proved necessary.

Paulinus, bishop of Nola, supported these arguments against the profession of arms in explicit detail, contrasting it with the wearing of armour for God.

. . . Do not any longer love this world or its military service, for Scripture's authority attests that whoever is a friend of this world is an enemy of God. He who is a soldier with the sword is the servant of death, and when he sheds his own blood or that of another, this is the reward for his service.

He will be regarded as guilty of death either because of his own death or because of his sin, because a soldier in war, fighting not so much for himself as for another, is either conquered and killed, or conquers and wins a pretext for death – for he cannot be a victor unless he first sheds blood.

For those who were defenders of the tottering fabric of society, there is not much sign of any encouragement here. It remained for the unknown fifth-century writer *On the Calling of all Nations* to express, not merely the common belief that barbarians were the instruments of divine punishment, but the actual hope that Roman arms would *fail* against the enemy whose 'weapons which destroy the world do but promote the grace of Christianity'.

When such views were being expressed by bishops and theologians, it was hardly to be expected that their congregations would show any greater enthusiasm for the army and its tasks, however pressing these might be; and so the power of the Empire to resist its foes was sapped. Pacifism can only be pursued when no potential external enemies exist – and that was not the situation of ancient Rome.

Another menace to the loyal defence of the state was something more subtle. It came from Augustine, who possessed one of the best intellects of his own or any other age, and composed very numerous and abundant writings. Now Augustine could not accurately be described as a pacifist at all. The saying 'turn the other cheek', he pointed out, can only be regarded as metaphorical, since to take it literally would be fatal to the welfare of the state. Wars were sometimes, he believed, a grim necessity, and might even be just, and in any case Jesus never told soldiers not to serve and fight. Yet Augustine discouraged national service by more insidious means. Just as the monks undermined the Empire by physical withdrawal, so he undermined it, too, by a sort of spiritual withdrawal: the state we most urgently need to serve is not the Roman Empire, but an ideal, heavenly state.

His work the *Civitas Dei*, rendered as the 'City of God' though the word rather means 'community' or 'society', is not primarily a political treatise, but a work of theology. Nevertheless, its abundant pages yield important evidence of Augustine's influence on the political events of his time. Plato had described an ideal city which was the forerunner of Augustine's. It was 'laid up somewhere in heaven', to be a model for actual communities upon earth. In later Greek times the Stoic philosophers had envisaged the world as a single unit, a cosmopolis, which is itself a potential City of God on earth, since all men possess a share of the divine spark. Then another philosophical thinker, Posidonius, turned this doctrine to the advantage of the Roman Empire. which he saw as the only realizable cosmopolis.

St Paul, too, wrote that the minds of the enemies of Christ are set on earthly things, whereas Christian believers on earth 'by contrast are citizens of heaven'. Yet he held that earthly governments had to be obeyed, for they are instituted by God and are in the service of God, so that those who rebel against them are flouting divine authority. And in the same spirit the Gospels record a much-discussed saying of Jesus, 'Render to Caesar the things that are Caesar's, and to God the things that are God's'.

After the accession of Constantine, it was believed by his supporters that the words of Jesus and Paul enjoining obedience to the earthly power had become peculiarly relevant, since the unity between the heavenly and earthly communities detected by Posidonius had actually begun, under the reigning Emperor's auspices, to come about. Subsequently Theodosius I, by his total union between state and church, seemed to have completed the process, and the official doctrine was now insistent that by serving the Christian government a man was also serving heaven.

But when Alaric sacked Rome in 410, a wave of pessimism came over the relations between church and state, and it finds expression in the thought of Ambrose, Jerome and Augustine. This gloom was based on certain antique attitudes. In particular there had always been a widespread pagan doctrine that the world, so far from exhibiting modern concepts of progress, was steadily declining from the Golden Age of the past down to the

Iron Age of the present, with catastrophe to come in the future. Such doctrines, which conveniently coincided with Christian views of the Day of Doom and the Last Judgment, enabled Ambrose, for example, to take a most unfavourable view of the condition and prospects of the Roman Empire. After the battle of Adrianople, he announced 'the massacre of all humanity, the end of the world', and then again in 386 he recorded 'diseases spreading, time nearing its end. We are indeed in the twilight of the world'. Christianity he saw as the crop coming just before the frosts of the winter: and the approaching world's end, as one of his followers explicitly declared, was to be preceded by the collapse of Rome.

Since the Romans, when they expressed over-optimism, were speaking foolishly, it seems hypercritical to denounce them when they were pessimistic as well. And, indeed, there was one thing to be said in favour of this gloomier attitude. It did at least appreciate that there was something terribly wrong. But useful plans to put it right were scarcely more apparent among Christians than among pagans.

Upon this world of unconstructive thinking burst Alaric in 410. Almost a century earlier, the Christian writer Lactantius had said that the fall of the city of Rome would mean the end of the world, and now, with Alaric's onslaught, both these events seemed to have come at one and the same time. Although, in fact, the Visigoths only stayed for three days, and did not do as much damage as might have been expected, this blow that felled the Eternal City seemed an appalling horror to optimists and pessimists alike.

Jerome, although far away in Bethlehem, took it as hard as anyone else. Alaric's earlier invasions had already filled him with the gloomiest forebodings, and now, after the sack of the city, he wrote to other friends in desperation, almost believing that the blackest prophecies had been right, and that the last days of the world were truly come.

> . . . I dare hardly speak until I receive more definite news. For I am torn between hope and despair, tormented by the terrible things that have befallen our friends. But now that this glorious Light of the World has been tampered with – defiled; and now that, with this city, the whole world, so to speak, is faced with

annihilation, 'I am dumb, and am humbled, and kept silent from good things.'

Three years later, he was still reverting to the same theme.

> . . . Terrifying news comes to us from the West. Rome has been taken by assault. Men are ransoming their lives with gold. Though despoiled, they are still hounded, so that after their goods they may pay with their very lives.
>
> My voice is still, and sobs disturb my every utterance. The city has been conquered which had once subjugated an entire world.

Nevertheless, the Christian view remained equivocal since Alaric, in his work of destruction, seemed to be acting as the human instrument of God, and imposing a divine visitation, punishment, and test. 'God's providence', wrote Augustine, 'constantly uses war to correct and chasten the corrupt morals of mankind, as it also uses such afflictions to train men in a righteous and laudable way of life, removing to a better state those whose life is approved, or else keeping them in this world for further service.'

Yet on hearing for the first time of the capture of Rome Augustine's first reaction, like Jerome's, had been one of deep shock. 'Tidings of terror are reaching us,' he declared to his African congregation. 'There has been a massacre: also great fires, looting, murder, torture.' Later he realized that these first reports were overstated. Acting with relative restraint, Alaric, himself a Christian, had spared the personnel and property of the church.

However, many people, and not only pagans, were asking why, since the Imperial government was Christian and allegedly enjoyed God's backing, had God allowed such a thing to happen. Nothing so frightful had ever occurred under pagan rule. It was in order to meet this challenge that Augustine began to write the twenty-two books of the *City of God*. 'The first five', explains its author, 'refute those who attribute prosperity and adversity to the cult of pagan gods or to the prohibition of this cult. The next five are against those who hold that ills are never wanting to men, but that worship of the pagan gods helps towards the future life after death.' The second part of the work contains twelve books. The first four describe the birth of the two cities, one of God, the other of the world. The second four continue their story, and the third four depict their final destiny. These last twelve books contain a far-reaching philosophy of history which does not depend solely on Alaric's capture of Rome but possesses a universal application.

Augustine had read Plato's *Republic* in Latin translations, and had studied commentaries on the work. But he borrowed the concept of the two cities from certain contemporary North-African Christians, the Donatists (see Appendix 1), who held that one city served God and his loyal angels, while the other worked for the Devil and his rebel angels and demons. At present, it was true, the two cities seemed inextricably mixed together within the church as in the rest of the world, but at the Last Judgment they would appear in manifest separation, one on God's left and the other on his right, like the captor city Babylon and its liberated captive Jerusalem.

This vision of captivity and liberation excited Augustine and inspired him. And in consequence, during the year following 410, he began to develop this whole theme for his readers and congregations, elaborating it with the passion of a masterly and persuasive artist. Two loves, he says, have created two cities: love of God the heavenly city, to the contempt of self; love of self the earthly city, to the contempt of God. The city of God is the city of the righteous, which contains God and his angels and saints in heaven, and all men and women who lead good lives on earth. The earthly city contains all unrighteous men and women wherever they be in the universe – fallen angels, the souls of the unrighteous, the unrighteous in the world. Although, therefore, marginal points of contact exist, the earthly city is *not the same* as the Roman Empire.

What, then, does Augustine think of that Empire? His answer is founded on his doctrine of Grace. Without this god-given help to human beings, he feels that we who are lumps of perdition – sinful ever since Adam's Fall – can never attain eternal salvation. Augustine's own recurrent struggles between the flesh and the spirit caused him to share St Paul's poor opinion of what a person can achieve by his own unaided will, and made him break with the more optimistic, classical, humanist view that we can achieve great things by our own endeavours.

Augustine's attitude incurred the intense disapproval and

anger of another Christian theologian of the day. This was Pelagius. Of British or Irish extraction, he came to Rome as a monk about 400. Like others, he was horrified by Alaric's sack of Rome, when 'the mistress of the world shivered, crushed with fear, at the sound of the blaring trumpets and the howling of the Goths'.

But Pelagius' reaction to such disasters was by no means limited to fatalistic gloom and despair. Both before and after the capture of the city, he found himself deeply dissatisfied with the moral sluggishness of many prosperous people of Rome. In an attempt to raise their easygoing standards, he insisted on a strenuous individual endeavour to attain salvation. He was convinced that the barrier of corruption which keeps original innocence and goodness out of our reach is insubstantial, and can be overcome by a bracing effort: we sin by a *voluntary* imitation of Adam, and an equally voluntary decision can cast our sins behind us.

The salvation to which Pelagius primarily referred was not of this world. Yet his doctrine was obviously applicable to worldly salvation as well – to the rehabilitation of the failing Roman Empire. If people bestirred themselves more and tried harder, it could be deduced from Pelagius, they would be better men. And that also meant, though he did not put it in such a way, that they would be better able to come to the rescue of their country.

This earnest belief in self-help caused him to abhor the tenth book of Augustine's *Confessions*, in which the writer repeatedly emphasized his dependence not on his own will but on the Grace of God. Pelagius himself, on the other hand, while not disbelieving in God's Grace, failed to see it as an overriding necessity. To him it was rather a form of divine assistance which can derive from moral exhortation and from a study of the supreme example of Christ: Grace, in this sense, will help us to fulfil and express the noble natures that have been bestowed on us by God. Like the earlier sort of modern existentialists before they became closely aligned with Marxism, Pelagius believed that man makes his own history on his own account.

Learning of this insistence upon the basic soundness and effectiveness of the human will, Augustine revolted against Pelagius even more violently than Pelagius had revolted against Augustine. He accused Pelagius of teaching, 'like the philosophers of the pagans', that man by his own unassisted free will could achieve goodness without any help from God at all. Probably the criticism was unjustified, since what Pelagius really wanted to say was that heaven helps those who help themselves. But Augustine persisted in his censures for many years and wrote a treatise, *On Free Will*, endeavouring to strike what he felt to be a more pious balance between men's limited capacity for autonomous enterprise and his dependence on the divine power. In effect, however, the 'higher freedom' which emerged, while professing to admit the liberty of the will, tended towards its annihilation as a well-spring of action.

Although Augustine's diffidence in his own powers (reflected in his formulation) displays an engaging humility, the doctrine of Pelagius was of greater value – on the practical plane of daily events and emergencies – to the later Roman Empire. It is true that he disliked the current spiritual inertia, and perhaps the whole social system that lay behind it, so much that he even spoke warmly in favour of monasticism. Nevertheless, his doctrine of the will at least wanted people to *try*. Augustine's philosophy, on the other hand, led to fatalism. Yet his incomparable eloquence, ably supported by many other preachers, ensured that it was his view which ultimately prevailed.

So Pelagius was doomed to failure. Jerome called him a fat hound weighed down by Scotch porridge, and he twice suffered excommunication. When and where he died is unknown. But after his death, the controversy continued with unabated vigour, and the Gallic monks and theologians felt considerable sympathy with his views, for Augustine's increasingly vehement assertions of Grace as man's only hope seemed to undermine human effort.

Indeed, his pronouncements also carried more fundamental political implications, affecting the whole concept of the Roman Empire. For since man, he concluded, is so totally corrupted by the fall of Adam that he is bound at some time to sin, and even Grace cannot prevent this inevitable outcome; since, that is to say, for as long as he lives, he can never cease to be flawed, then all his institutions are flawed as well. Even the church, though it provides the only bridge to the heavenly city, remains a mixture of good wheat and bad weeds. How much more imperfect, then, must be the state, the Roman Empire itself!

True, although often perverted by evil wills, it is a natural and a divine necessity which God granted to the Romans. By his ordinance, continued Augustine, there is a king for temporal life, as there is a king for eternal life. Earthly rulers have special services they can render to God, just because they are rulers. And although Constantine was by no means perfect – for Augustine was one of those who believed that Christianity had lost virtue as it gained wealth and power – he paid honour to Theodosius I, as a prince whose devotion to the faith was exemplary.

When such men rule, one can see 'a faint shadowy resemblance between the Roman Empire and the heavenly city'. The state, in fact, has its uses. Love of our neighbour, felt Augustine, makes our patriotic and civic duties obligatory. Soldiers, rulers, and judges alike have to stay at their posts. And yet, all the same, we are reading the thoughts of a man in whom national feeling is so strictly and totally subordinated to religious considerations that it can hardly, in any meaningful sense, be said to exist.

From the nationalist sentiments which had defended the frontiers of ancient Rome for so many centuries we have travelled a vast distance. For example, while granting that wars can be just and even necessary, Augustine concludes that their 'victories bring death with them or are doomed to death', and the vast extent of Rome's Empire, he adds, has given rise to every sort of detestable foreign and civil war. Augustine even says he would have preferred a number of small nations living in peace to the monolithic Empire of the Romans. 'Without justice', he declares, 'governments are merely great bands of brigands' – gangsterism on a massive scale. But 'without justice' is precisely what, in the very nature of things, these states inevitably were: and what Rome could not fail to be.

And so he preached, as others had preached before him, that 'we do not want to have dealings with the powers that be'. That is frank: it is a call to withhold service from the government. Equally frank is his reminder that the Empire is bound to collapse anyway. 'If heaven and earth are to pass away, why is it surprising if at some time the state is going to come to a stop? – if what God has made will one day vanish, then surely what Romulus made will disappear much sooner.' Even the current identification of church and state will not, cannot, suffice to stop the rot.

Where does all this leave the individual citizen? Rome, for his benefit, has been firmly cut down to size. Our *real*, permanent fatherland, he is told – the only true kingdom, according to the strictest idea of what is right – is elsewhere altogether. 'What we want', states Augustine, 'is a way to help us to return to *that* kingdom: that is how we shall bring our sorrows to an end.' As for all the earthly crises and catastrophes, they can just be ignored – or even welcomed, seeing that God has sent them as a discipline. The calamities of a country in which you are merely a foreigner do not really affect your interests at all. When, therefore, such calamities appear, just treat them as an invitation to concentrate your desires on things eternal: and rejoice that your treasure is in a place where no enemy has the power to approach. To a patriotic pagan, disturbed by the disasters that have befallen Rome, Augustine spells out the message: 'Please pardon us if *our* country, up above, has to cause trouble to yours . . . you would acquire still greater merit if you served a higher fatherland.'

Those are not words that will impel a man to the defence of the falling Roman Empire. Augustine has shifted the centre of gravity so that the state is now a good deal less than half of what matters: far from helping his country to survive, his attitude contributed to its downfall. But his implied suggestion that, since it was up to Providence whether the Roman world should collapse or not, human endeavour could do nothing about it in any case, met with the strong disapproval of thinkers such as Pelagius. 'Man is not trapped by history', as David P. Jordan expressed it in his book *Gibbon and his Roman Empire*: 'he does not live in a haunted house, he can emancipate himself through reason'.

Although Augustine's full influence was not exerted for generations to come, subsequent writers during the last years of the Western Roman Empire were already echoing his fatalistic attitude. For example, it was perhaps now that the poet Commodianus positively gloated over the downfall of the city: 'She who bragged that she was eternal now weeps to eternity.' And in the words of Orientius, bishop of Ausci (formerly Elimberris, now Auch) in south-west France, 'why go over the funeral ceremonies of a world falling into ruins, in accordance with the common law of all that passes away?' Moreover, Orosius, whom Augustine commissioned to write a history of

Rome, not only reminds us once again that Rome deserved the German onslaughts – because in earlier days it had persecuted the Christians – but that these attacks will actually be beneficial, 'although this may involve the crumbling of our Empire'. Presbyter Salvian, who believed the same, added two realistic comments. First, the Empire was *already* dead, or breathing its last. Secondly, most Romans lacked the imagination to realize the supreme peril they were in: and if they did happen to possess such discernment, they lacked the nerve to do anything about it.

For the existence of this inertia – which is a very accurate diagnosis – the suggestion of Augustine that human endeavour could be of no consequence, either in this situation or any other, bore a share of the blame; or at least he very accurately represented a prevailing feeling which fell all too readily into line with the numerous other tendencies conspiring to bring about Rome's fall.

Appendix 1

Some Religious Disunities

CATHOLIC AGAINST ORTHODOX

The separation and friction between the Western and Eastern Empires, described in Chapter 8, helped to bring about the most important internal division in the history of Christianity: the split between the Catholic and Orthodox churches.

The bishopric of Rome, described subsequently as the papacy, had enjoyed particular respect from the earliest beginnings of the faith. Christians in the Eastern provinces admitted the special prestige of the Roman church, yet were reluctant to agree that it had the right to dictate to them or legislate on their behalf. They also maintained that ecclesiastical authority was not vested in any one person, but (with the reservations that certain sees were entitled to precedence of honour) was assigned by the Scriptures to all bishops, who expressed this authority corporately through their general councils. For the Greeks of the East did not share the legal, centralized, autocratic approach which the Romans of the West owed to their legal tradition and metropolitan location; while the Romans, for their part, felt little sympathy for the Hellenizing, philosophical tendencies with which Eastern Christianity had become imbued.

Another factor that perpetuated these failures of mutual comprehension was the continuing, widening, cultural gulf between the Latin and Greek-speaking peoples of the Empire. Bilingualism was becoming increasingly rare in either region:

after the 230s AD, spokesmen for the Greek point of view were no longer to be found in the church at Rome, while few Eastern ecclesiastics possessed any knowledge of Latin. Nor did they feel any inclination to acquire any, since the language of the New Testament was Greek. Moreover, the continual absences of successive third-century Emperors from Rome gave its bishops, especially in times of persecution, ever greater opportunities for accepting independent responsibility on their own account and thus enhancing their own status.

But after Constantine had founded his new capital at Constantinople, a fresh situation arose. For although previously the Roman bishops or Popes had hitherto felt more independent when the Emperor was away, it now became clear that his decision to reside permanently at Constantinople was going to elevate the bishop of that city (known as the Patriarch, as elsewhere in the East) to a powerful position which might eventually rival Rome. For Constantine, desirous that Christianity should create a universal bond linking the whole Empire together, hoped that his foundation of Constantinople would play a special part in this process. In the words of St Gregory of Nazianzus in Cappadocia (eastern Asia Minor), the new capital was to be 'a bond of union between East and West to which the most distant extremes from all sides were to come together, and to which they look up as the common centre and emporium of their faith'.

However, what happened was exactly the opposite. Far from contributing to the union of the two parts of the Empire, the new capital led to their increasing religious polarization. This became apparent at the Council of Serdica (Sofia, 343), when a vigorous dispute on theological matters rapidly turned into a split between the Eastern and Western governments. Then, after the political division between the two territories in 364, the difficulties affecting their relations soon extended to the ecclesiastical sphere. For one thing, the growing power of the Roman Popes inspired those dignitaries to make increasingly far-reaching claims for their own universal authority. And Western Emperors were naturally not averse to these claims – though they caused tension with the Eastern Patriarchs.

Meanwhile, Latin religious scholarship was flourishing. Hitherto Latin Christian literature had been far inferior to Greek, but an immense step towards remedying this was Jerome's translation of the Bible from Greek into Latin, the Vulgate, originating from a commission by Pope Damasus to revise the old Latin texts of the Gospels. Augustine's treatise *On the Trinity*, too, showed that at last Latin theological skill had reached a level unrivalled by any contemporary Greek. These achievements increased the ecclesiastical prestige of the West.

Before long the relations between the churches of Rome and Constantinople had deteriorated further, with ill effects on the general political relationship between West and East. In 404 an Eastern church council, jealous of the popular, progressive John Chrysostom, Patriarch of Constantinople, ordered his deposition and sent him into exile. This angered the Western administration of Honorius, who twice wrote to deplore that this hasty sentence had been passed without awaiting any decision from the head of the Roman church, Pope Innocent I, who, according to Honorius, should have been consulted. Further friction occurred over the religious control of the Balkan provinces, after most of these had been transferred from the West to the East. For Pope Siricius, in spite of this change, declared that the bishop of Thessalonica (Salonica), the capital of the area, remained dependent upon himself. Subsequently the Eastern Emperor Theodosius II issued the counter-claim that all ecclesiastical disputes in the transferred territory should be judged by the bishop of Constantinople, 'which rejoices in the prerogatives of the old Rome'. But when Honorius protested, he gave way.

In 451, the Council of Calchedon (Kadiköy) in Bithynia (western Asia Minor) further embroiled the Western and Eastern churches. The Council voted to confirm the precedence of the Patriarch of Constantinople over other Eastern bishops, and added three dioceses to his jurisdiction. The papal envoys, however, who had played a prominent role at the Council, protested, and Pope Leo I himself, in subsequent letters, objected categorically to this explicit promotion of Constantinople to the second place in the hierarchy. But what he probably disliked most was the allocation of the three additional dioceses to the bishop of Constantinople, whose residence in the Eastern capital, where he could easily obtain the support of its Emperors, seemed to make him a serious rival to Rome. Leo was also worried because the offending clause made no specific mention of the

Apostolic, Petrine character of the Roman see, which his delegates had stressed on every occasion. In consequence, Leo delayed his acquiescence for two years, and even thereafter, although Constantinople effectively controlled its three new dioceses, the clause was not officially accepted at Rome until the sixth century.

Although it was not apparent at the time, much the most far-reaching and long-lasting feature of the rift between the Western and Eastern Empires was taking substantial shape. Later stages of this growing breach between Catholic and Orthodox can be identified in one subsequent century after another. But the estrangement had already begun during the concluding period of the ancient Roman Empire.

The initial divergences which set them apart were largely theological. But these differences were enhanced by the general political tensions between the Western and Eastern Empires – tensions which they in their turn made even more acute.

STATE AND CHURCH AGAINST TWO HERESIES

In Chapter 11 it was explained how the government of the later Western Empire allied itself with the ecclesiastical authorities, and, with the approval of Augustine, persecuted those who failed to conform, including the deviant Christian sects. These sects, however, although denounced comprehensively as heresies, differed greatly in character. One, Pelagianism, was discussed in Chapter 13. Two others of special importance, Arianism and Donatism, will be briefly described here.

The earliest of the important heretics of the Christian Empire was Arius, probably a Libyan by birth, who became a religious teacher at Alexandria. Like Unitarians in recent times, he was accused of stressing the humanity of Jesus at the expense of his divinity. Among Alexandrian Christians brought up in the classical tradition, such opinions already had a long and complex past. These philosophically minded men could not tolerate the *duality* of God the Father and God the Son, for it seemed to them that only one God was possible. Their views culminated in Arius, who concluded that Jesus could not be God, since, being the Son, he derived his being from the Father, and was therefore both younger and inferior.

After the death of Arius in 336, some Emperors supported his followers, but most did not, deploring their depreciation of Jesus' Godhead: and finally, in 381 and 388, their sect was proscribed and all its office-holders banished. Though it continued to prevail in the German tribes and nations, as far as Romans and provincials were concerned it came to an end. However, the damage was done, since this relentless controversy had plagued the Imperial church during its critical, formative, period – dooming Constantine's hopes of a united Christendom to failure.

The second major heresy which Constantine immediately encountered was longer-lived, and even more destructive and divisive – although limited to North Africa. This was the Donatist sect. It was named after Donatus who, in 313, had been set up as a rival candidate for the bishopric of Carthage, since the official appointee, Caecilian, was accused of softness to those members of the clergy who, during the recent pagan persecutions, had surrendered sacred scriptures and vessels and otherwise betrayed their flocks. But this protest stood for a much more deeply rooted disharmony. For the Donatists completely spurned traditional, classical, urban culture, and rejected the sovereignty of Constantine's official church which they identified with this sort of hated background. After prolonged discussions, Constantine imposed confiscations and banishment upon them. These coercive measures, it is true, were soon called off. But meanwhile the sect had already begun to draw up its own proud list of martyrs.

Their founder, with his chief supporters, was exiled to Gaul in 347, and died there some eight years later. Yet the Donatists in North Africa continued to flourish. Moreover, it was becoming ominously apparent that they could command an underground army. Such African fighters, known as *circumcelliones* ('those who wander about from shrine to shrine'), were seasonal labourers on the local olive plantations; and they were rapidly joined by debtors and other fugitives. Taking advantage of the religious tension, these desperate men, dressed in the costume of monks, moved around in bands, intimidating the local populations with their olive-staffs, and from time to time breaking into Catholic churches, and beating up money-lenders and others whom they had reason to dislike. 'None', declared Bishop Optatus of Milevis

(Mila), 'could be safe on his estates. . . . What landowner was not compelled to fear his own slaves?' Certain proprietors, indeed, felt it more prudent to turn a blind eye to these terrorist activities.

Some of the adherents of Donatism, who were mainly poor but came from every social class, found this sort of violence frightening. But on the whole those thugs served them effectively enough as the shock troops of their faith. Indeed, Augustine complained that a Donatist bishop could whistle them up any time he felt inclined.

Under Julian, surviving Donatist exiles returned home in triumph, and the neutrality of Valentinian I likewise operated in their favour; their cathedrals were some of the largest in Roman Africa. Yet before long they found themselves accused of supporting a local rebellion, led by the Mauretanian chieftain Gildo in 397. This gave Augustine a plausible reason to attack them, and a series of punitive official edicts against the sect was greeted by him as an act of Providence.

The outcome of a congress summoned at Carthage in 411 was utterly unfavourable to the Donatists, and the denial of all their rights was confirmed. In the following years, several further laws followed, while Augustine returned again and again to the assault, accusing them of currying favour with Rome's external enemies.

Yet these tough puritans still survived, and even flourished. At the time of the Vandal invasions of North Africa, their attitude once again caused grave anxiety. There is no evidence that they supported the invaders, although *circumcelliones* certainly joined their cause. Nevertheless the Donatists, in whose movement theological, egalitarian and even to some extent nationalist sentiments were perilously combined, had already made their contributions to the disunities which were shattering the Western Empire. This was not altogether their own fault. For it was persecution by the authorities that had blown up a doctrinal difference into an uncontrollable resistance movement.

Appendix 2

Why Did the Eastern and Not the Western Empire Survive?

It is no use claiming to detect a complete explanation of the fall of the Western Empire in any factor which applied to the Eastern Byzantine Empire as well, since the latter did not collapse in the fifth century AD, but instead remained in existence for a much greater length of time, until 1453 (with only a short interlude between 1204 and 1261). It is therefore necessary to speculate on the reasons why the two Empires had these quite separate and different experiences and fates.

Above all else, the Western Empire was far more vulnerable to external attack owing to its geographical location. In the words of A. H. M. Jones:

> . . . The Western Empire had to guard the long fronts of the Rhine and the upper [and middle] Danube, the Eastern Emperor only the lower Danube. For on the Eastern front his neighbour was the Persian Empire, a civilized power which was not on the whole aggressive and kept its treaties.
>
> Moreover, if the Western Emperor failed to hold any part of the Rhine and Danube fronts, he had no second line of defence; the invaders could penetrate straight into Italy and Gaul, and even into Spain . . . [whereas] no enemy could force the Bosphorus and the Hellespont, guarded by Constantinople itself.

For the same reasons the East, after its first admission of the Visigoths in 382–95, did not have to let nearly so many Germans into its provinces as settlers and federates.

Secondly, the Eastern Empire possessed a sounder social and economic structure than the West, embodying fewer glaring disunities. The American historian Glanville Downey explained why this was:

> . . . The structure of the government differed significantly in the East and West. In the West, the land-owning aristocrats, some of them fantastically wealthy, contributed much less money than they should have to the cost of the army and the government. The Eastern Empire, in contrast, possessed a civil service composed largely of middle-class professionals, and while graft unavoidably existed, the Eastern government received in taxes a higher proportion of the national income than the Western government could enjoy.

The government of the East, as a result, possessed much greater resources than the government of the West; it was therefore much more capable of maintaining its defences. It was also both more populous and better cultivated (in sharp contrast to the relative situation of the two areas in modern times); and its provinces had ridden the economic storm of the third-century invasions far more easily than the Western regions.

Downey's favourable reference to the Eastern bureaucracy also reminds us that the middle classes, which formed its traditional nucleus, possessed much more ancient and firmer roots in the Eastern regions – going back to Greek times – and continued to enjoy much better economic conditions.

Furthermore, the internal political stability of the Eastern Empire was far greater. In the whole period 364–476 its internal peace was only broken by two usurpers – Procopius at the very beginning, and Basiliscus at the very end – and both were suppressed quite easily: a remarkable contrast to the extensive and costly proliferation of such rebels in the West.

These were the main reasons why the Eastern Empire survived, and the Western Empire did not. That is to say, the Easterners suffered much less from barbarian invasions, and they were also less gravely affected by the disunities described in the first eleven chapters of this book. From some of the other rifts which rent the Western Empire they suffered as badly as the Westerners, or worse. For example they had many more monastic drop-outs, and their ecclesiastical divisions were even sharper. But these problems they could surmount, because the other disharmonies that destroyed the West affected them so much less acutely.

Lists of Emperors and Popes

WESTERN EMPERORS

AD 364–75	Valentinian I
375–83	Gratian
383–92	Valentinian II
387–95	Theodosius I
395–423	Honorius
421	Constantius III
425–55	Valentinian III
455	Petronius Maximus
455–6	Avitus
457–61	Majorian
461–5	Libius Severus
467–72	Anthemius
472	Olybrius
473–4	Glycerius
474–5	Julius Nepos
475–6	Romulus Augustus (Augustulus)

EASTERN EMPERORS

364–78	Valens
379–95	Theodosius I
395–408	Arcadius
408–50	Theodosius II
450–57	Marcian
457–74	Leo I
474	Leo II
474–91	Zeno

POPES

AD 352–66	Liberius
366–85	Damasus
385–99	Siricius
399–401	Anastasius
401–17	Innocent I
417–18	Zosimus
418–22	Boniface I
422–32	Celestine I
432–40	Sixtus III
440–61	Leo I
461–68	Hilary
468–83	Simplicius

A Who's Who of
Ancient Writers

Latin

AMBROSE (ST) *c.* 339–97. Born at
Treveri (Trier, west Germany).
Bishop of Mediolanum (Milan).
Works include sermons, hymns,
and 91 epistles (literary letters).

AMMIANUS MARCELLINUS *c.* 330–
95. Born at Antioch (Antakya,
south-east Turkey). Pagan. Wrote
history of years AD 96–378 (Books
14–31, about AD 353–78, survive).

AUGUSTINE (ST) 354–430. Born at
Thagaste (Souk Ahras, Algeria).
Bishop of Hippo Regius (Annaba,
formerly Bône, Algeria). Ninety-
three writings include *Confessions*
(*c.* 397–400), *On the Trinity* (399–
419), *The City of God* (413–426),
and attacks on eight sets of
heretics.

AUSONIUS *c.* 310–*c.* 395. Born at
Burdigala (Bordeaux, south-west
France). Consul in 379. Poems
including the *Mosella* (Moselle),
and 25 letters.

BENEDICT (ST) *c.* 480–*c.* 547. Born
at Nursia (Norcia, central Italy).
Abbot of Casinum (Monte
Cassino). Wrote *Rule* of monastic
life.

CASSIAN *see* **JOHN CASSIAN**.

CLAUDIAN died *c.* 404. Born at
Alexandria (Egypt). Pagan.
Poems include *Panegyrics*,
Invectives, and *Rape of Proserpine*.

Codes see **EURIC, JUSTINIAN,**
THEODOSIUS II.

COMMODIAN, variously assigned
to 3rd, 4th and 5th centuries AD,
and to Gaul, Palestine and North
Africa. Wrote metrical exposition
of Christian doctrine (*Carmen
Apologeticum*) and 80 short
poems.

DE REBUS BELLICIS *see* **ON MATTERS**
OF WARFARE.

ENNODIUS *c.* 473–521. Born at
Arelate (Arles, southern France).
Bishop of Ticinum (Pavia, north
Italy). Wrote poems and various
prose works.

EUGIPPIUS late 5th century.
Biographer of St Severinus of
Noricum (Austria, Bavaria).

EURIC King of the Visigoths in
Gaul and Spain, 466–84. Gave his
name to collection of laws, Codex
Euricianus, largely extant.

FRIGERIDUS *see* RENATUS.

HISTORIA AUGUSTA. Collection of biographies of Roman Emperors and princes from AD 117 to 284 (lacuna for years 244–59). The six names of alleged authors appear to be fictitious. Date of writing much disputed: perhaps end of 4th century AD.

JEROME (HIERONYMUS, ST) *c.* 348–420. Born at Stridon (north-west Yugoslavia). Secretary to Pope Damasus, 382–4; founder of monastery at Bethlehem. Numerous writings include translation of Bible into Latin (the Vulgate) and attacks on Pelagian heresy.

JOHN CASSIAN *c.* 360–435. Born in Dobrogea (Rumania). Founder of monastery and nunnery at Massilia (Marseille, southern France). Writings include *Collations*, dialogues of the Desert Fathers.

JORDANES mid-6th century. A Goth. Wrote one-volume summary (*Gotica*) of History of Goths by Cassiodorus (died 583).

JUSTINIAN I East Roman (Byzantine) Emperor, 527–65. Conquered large portions of former Western Empire. Gave his name to collection of laws (Codex [two editions], Digest, Institutes, 'Novels') under direction of Tribonian.

LACTANTIUS *c.* 240–*c.* 320. Born in North Africa. Works in defence of Christianity include *Divine Institution* and *On the Deaths of the Persecutors*.

LEO I the Great (ST) Pope 440–61. Born in Etruria (Tuscany) (?). 432 letters and 96 sermons are extant.

MACROBIUS. Perhaps wrote *c.* 430. Born in North Africa (?). Probably pagan. Works include *Saturnalia*, academic symposium in seven books.

MARTIANUS CAPELLA Wrote between 410 and 439. Born in North Africa. Pagan. Treatise in mixed prose and verse, *On the Marriage of Mercury and Philology*.

NAMATIANUS *see* RUTILIUS.

NOTITIA DIGNITATUM *see* RECORD OF OFFICIAL POSTS.

ON MATTERS OF WARFARE (DE REBUS BELLICIS). Anonymous treatise apparently addressed to Emperors Valentinian I and Valens, 364–75, explaining plans for the reform of the administration and the army.

OPTATIANUS *see* PORPHYRIUS.

OPTATUS (ST) Time of Valentinian I, 364–75. Born in North Africa. Bishop of Milevis or Mileum (Mila in Algeria). Writer of work denouncing the Donatist heresy.

ORIENTIUS Died soon after 439. A Gaul. Bishop of Ausci (Auch in south-west France). Writer of poem *Commonitorium* recommending the Christian way of life.

OROSIUS Wrote 414–17. Probably born at Bracara Augusta (Braga in north Portugal). Christian presbyter (church officer). His works included attacks on heresy and Chronicle attacking paganism (*Historiae adversus Paganos*).

PAULINUS OF NOLA *c.* 353–431. Born at Burdigala (Bordeaux, south-west France). Bishop of Nola (south-west Italy). Wrote more than 30 poems and more than 50 letters.

PAULINUS OF PELLA Wrote *c*. 457. Grandson of Ausonius. Born at Pella (north Greece), lived in south-west France. Wrote *Eucharisticus (Thanksgiving)*.

PELAGIUS Died after 419. From Britain or Ireland. Wrote commentary on 13 Pauline epistles. Seventy tracts supporting his theological viewpoint are the work not of himself but of his followers.

PORPHYRIUS OPTATIANUS Wrote 324–5. Author of verse panegyric of Constantine the Great and his eldest son Crispus.

PRUDENTIUS 348–after 405. Born in Spain, perhaps at Caesaraugusta (Zaragoza). Writer of Christian hymns and other poetry, including an attack on paganism.

QUEROLUS ('Protester'). Verse drama, apparently of 5th century AD, reflecting the viewpoint of the underground movement of the Bagaudae in Gaul.

RECORD OF OFFICIAL POSTS (**NOTITIA DIGNITATUM**). List of senior offices of state (with their staffs) in the Western and Eastern Empires (AD 395), including military posts and indicating the units under their command.

RENATUS PROFUTURUS FRIGERIDUS 5th century. Of German origin. Surviving prose writings include description of Alaric's capture of Rome (410) and eulogy of Aetius.

RUTILIUS NAMATIANUS Wrote in early 4th century. Gallo-Roman, probably from Tolosa (Toulouse,

south-west France). Pagan. Wrote poetical itinerary of journey in 416 or 417, *On his Return (De Reditu Suo)*.

SALVIAN *c*. 400–*c*. 480. Probably born at Treveri (Trier, west Germany). Presbyter at Massilia (Marseille, southern France). Writings include *On the Governance of God (De Gubernatione Dei)*.

SIDONIUS APOLLINARIS *c*. 430–*c*. 488. Born in Lugdunum (Lyon, France). Bishop of Arverna (Clermont-Ferrand), 469. Wrote panegyrics and other poems, and nine books of letters.

SULPICIUS SEVERUS *c*. 360–*c*. 420. Born in Aquitania (south-west France). Writer of Life of St Martin of Tours and historical summary.

SYMMACHUS *c*. 340–*c*. 402. Roman nobleman, consul 391. Leading pagan and orator. Fragments of speeches survive, also ten books of letters.

TERTULLIAN *c*. 160–*c*. 240. Born at Carthage (Tunisia). Writer of many militant Christian works.

THEODOSIUS II East Roman Emperor, 408–50. Gave his name to collection of laws (Codex Theodosianus, 438).

TRIBONIAN *see* JUSTINIAN I.

VEGETIUS Wrote after 383. Civilian official and author of manual on Roman military institutions (*De Re Militari*).

VICTOR OF VITA Wrote after 484. Bishop of Vita in Byzacena (southern Tunisia). Author of *History of African Persecution* (by the Vandals).

Greek

ARIUS c. 260–336. Probably Libyan by birth. Christian teacher at Alexandria (Egypt), founder of Arian heresy. Three letters and fragments of *Thalia* (verse and prose exposition) survive.

ATHANASIUS (ST) c. 295–373. Born in Egypt, probably at Alexandria. Bishop of Alexandria. Numerous writings include hostile *History of the Arian Heresy* and doctrinal letters.

BASIL the Great (ST) c. 330–79. Born at Caesarea (Kayseri, Turkey). Bishop of Caesarea. Writer of *Longer* and *Shorter Rules* of monastic life, and letters, tracts and sermons.

CHRYSOSTOM *see* JOHN CHRYSOSTOM.

EPIPHANIUS (ST) c. 315–403. Born at Bezanduca near Eleutheropolis (Beit Jibrin, Israel). Bishop of Constantia (Salamis, near Trikomo, Cyprus). Wrote *Panarion (Medicine Chest)*, an attack on 80 heresies.

EUNAPIUS c. 345–after 414. Born at Sardis (Sart, western Turkey). Pagan philosopher and priest. Wrote *Lives of the Philosophers and Sophists* and *Chronology* from 270 to 404.

EUSEBIUS c. 260–c. 340. Bishop of Caesarea Maritima (near Zikhron Jaakov, Israel). Works include *Ecclesiastical History* and *Life of Constantine the Great*.

GREGORY OF NAZIANZUS c. 329–89. Son of bishop of Nazianzus in Cappadocia (Turkey). Briefly Patriarch of Constantinople (381). Numerous works include *Five*

Theological Orations and long autobiographical poem.

JOHN CHRYSOSTOM ('Golden-mouthed') (ST), c. 354–407. Born at Antioch (Antakya, south-east Turkey). Patriarch of Constantinople (398). Works include many treatises (e.g. *On the Priesthood*), sermons, commentaries, and over 200 letters.

JULIAN 'the Apostate', Emperor 361–3. Pagan. Surviving writings include eight speeches, the *Misopogon* ('beard-hater', a satirical defence of his policy), the humorous *Caesars*, and 80 letters.

LIBANIUS 314–c. 393. Born at Antioch (Antakya, south-east Turkey). Pagan professor of rhetoric. Surviving works include 64 speeches and 1,600 letters.

MARCELLINUS 6th century. From Illyricum (Yugoslavia). Priest. Wrote *Chronicle* to 534.

OLYMPIODORUS before 380 – after 425. Born at Thebes (Luxor, Egypt). Pagan. Wrote history of memoirs (surviving only in summaries) from 407 to 425.

ORIGEN c. 185–254. Born at Alexandria (Egypt). Only a small proportion of his voluminous theological works has survived, including *Exhortation to Martyrdom*.

PALLADAS 4th century. Lived at Alexandria (Egypt). 150 epigrammatic poems survive in the Greek Anthology.

PRISCUS 5th century. Born at Panium-Theodosiopolis (European Turkey). Visited court of Attila the Hun in 449. Wrote *Byzantine History* from at least 433–72 (long excerpts preserved).

PROCOPIUS *c.* 500 – after 562. Born at Caesarea Maritima (near Zikhron Jaakov, Israel). Prefect of Constantinople (562). Wrote *History of the Wars of Justinian* and *Secret History*.

SYNESIUS *c.* 370–413. Born at Cyrene (near Shahhat in Eastern Libya). Philosopher and Bishop of Ptolemais (Tolmeta, 410). 9 hymns, rhetorical discourses, and 156 letters.

THEMISTIUS *c.* 317–88. Born in Paphlagonia (north Turkey). Pagan philosopher and rhetorician. 34 speeches, mainly official addresses, survive, and paraphrases of Aristotle.

THEODORET *c.* 393–466. Born at Antioch (Antakya, south-east Turkey). Bishop of Cyrrhus (Kurus). Numerous works include *Church History* to 428 and 30 ascetic biographies of *Religious History*.

ZOSIMUS wrote *c.* 500. Tentatively identified with sophist of Ascalon (Ashkelon, southern Israel) or Gaza. Pagan. Writer of *New History* from Augustus to AD 410.

Some Books on the Decline & Fall

A. ALFÖLDI
A Conflict of Ideas in the later Roman Empire: The Clash between the Senate and Valentinian I, Oxford University Press, 1952.

F. ALTHEIM
Niedergang der Alten Welt, Frankfurt-am-Main, 1952.

M. T. W. ARNHEIM
The Senatorial Aristocracy of the Later Roman Empire, Oxford University Press, 1972.

W. C. BARK
Origins of the Medieval World, Stanford University Press, 1958; Doubleday Anchor, 1960.

R. H. BARROW (ed.)
Prefect and Emperor: The Relationes of Symmachus (AD 384), Oxford University Press, 1973.

R. BIANCHI BANDINELLI
The Late Empire: Roman Art AD 200–400, Thames and Hudson, 1971.

G. W. BOWERSOCK, J. CLIVE, S. R. GRAUBARD (eds.)
Edward Gibbon and the Decline and Fall of the Roman Empire, Harvard University Press, 1977.

P. BROWN
Augustine of Hippo, Faber 1967.

P. BROWN
The World of Late Antiquity, Thames and Hudson, 1971

J. W. BURROW
Gibbon, Oxford University Press, 1985.

J. B. BURY
History of the Later Roman Empire, 1923; Dover, 1958.

A. CAMERON
Claudian: Poetry and Propaganda at the Court of Honorius, Oxford University Press, 1970.

R. A. G. CARSON
Principal Coins of the Romans, Vol. III, The Dominate AD 294–498, British Museum Publications Ltd., 1981.

R. A. G. CARSON and J. P. C. KENT
Part II (AD 346–98), Spink, 1960.

M. CHAMBERS (ed.)
The Fall of Rome: Can it be Explained? Holt Rinehart and Winston, 1963.

A. CHASTAGNOL
Recherches sur l'Histoire Auguste

(Antiquitas, Reihe 4), Habelt, Bonn, 1970.

K. CHRIST (ed.)
Der Untergang des römischen Reiches (Wege der Forschung), 1971

C. N. COCHRANE
Christianity and Classical Culture, Oxford University Press, 1940; Galaxy, 1957.

C. H. COSTER
Late Roman Studies, Harvard University Press, 1968.

P. COURCELLE
Histoire littéraire des grandes invasions germaniques, Paris, 1948; 3rd ed., 1965.

B. CUNLIFFE
Romans and the Barbarian West: Spheres of Interaction 600 BC–AD 400, 1988.

P. B. CRADDOCK
Edward Gibbon, Luminous Historian, John Hopkins University Press, 1988.

C. DAWSON
The Making of Europe, 1932; Meridian, 1956.

A. DEMANDT
Der Fall Roms, Munich, 1984.

E. DEMOUGEOT
La formation de l'Europe et les invasions barbares, Paris, 1969.

H.-J. DIESNER
Die Völkerwanderung, Leipzig, 1976, Gutersloh, 1980 (translated as *The Great Migration: The Movement of Peoples across Europe AD 300–700*, Orbis, London, 1982).

S. DILL
Roman Society in the Last Century of the Western Empire, 1898; Meridian, 1958.

E. R. DODDS
Pagan and Christian in an Age of Anxiety, Cambridge University Press, 1965.

G. DOWNEY
The Late Roman Empire, Holt Rinehart and Winston, 1969.

F. H. DUDDEN
Life and Times of St Ambrose, 1935.

V. DURUY
Histoire des Romains depuis les temps les plus reculés jusqu'à la mort de Constantin, Paris , 1879–85.

F. DVORNIK
Byzance et la primauté romaine, Cerf, Paris, 1964 (translated as *Byzantium and the Roman Primacy*, Fordham University Press, 1966).

D. EARL
The Moral and Political Tradition of Rome, Thames and Hudson, 1967.

W. ENSSLIN
Die Religionspolitik des Kaisers Theodosius des Grosses, Munich, 1953.

A. FERRILL
The Fall of the Roman Empire: The Military Explanation, Thames and Hudson, 1983, 1988.

S. FISCHER-FABIAN
Die Ersten Deutschen, Knaur Nachfolger, Munich and Zurich, 1975.

E. GIBBON
The Decline and Fall of the Roman Empire, London, 1776–88 (abridged by D. M. Low, Chatto and Windus, 1960, Washington Square, 1962).

213

W. GOFFART
Barbarians and Romans, AD 418–584: The Techniques of Accommodation, 1987.

W. GOFFART
The Narrators of Barbarian History (AD 550–800), 1987.

C. D. GORDON
The Age of Attila, University of Michigan Press, 1960.

M. GRANT
'The Fall of the Roman Empire: Is it Relevant to Us?' in O. Molden (ed.), *Evolution und die Zukunft der Menschheit*, Vienna, 1985.

M. GRANT
The Dawn of the Middle Ages, McGraw Hill and Weidenfeld and Nicolson, 1981.

L. HAMBLEN
Attila et les Huns, Presses Universitaires de France, Paris, 1972.

R. M. HAYWOOD
The Myth of Rome's Fall, Alvin Redman, 1960.

H. HOMEYER
Attila der Hunnenkönig von seinen Zeitgenossen dargestellt, de Gruyter, Berlin, 1951.

H. ISBELL (ed.)
The Last Poets of Imperial Rome, Penguin, 1971.

A. H. M. JONES
The Decline of the Ancient World, Longmans, 1966.

A. H. M. JONES
The Later Roman Empire, Blackwell, 1964.

D. P. JORDAN
Gibbon and his Roman Empire, University of Illinois Press, 1971.

W. E. KAEGI
Byzantium and the Decline of Rome, Princeton University Press, 1968.

D. KAGAN (ed.)
The End of the Roman Empire: Decline or Transformation, 2nd ed., Lexington Massachusetts, 1978.

J. N. D. KELLY
Jerome: His Life, Writings and Controversies, Duckworth, 1974.

M. MCCORMICK
Eternal Victory, Cambridge University Press, 1986.

H. P. L'ORANGE
Art Forms and Civic Life in the Late Roman Empire, Princeton 1965.

F. LOT
La fin du monde antique et le début du Moyen-Age, Paris, 1927 (translated as *The End of the Ancient World and the Beginning of the Middle Ages*, Routledge and Kegan Paul, 1931; reprint 1966).

R. MACMULLEN
Corruption and the Decline of Rome, Yale University Press, 1988.

O. J. MAENCHEN-HELFEN
The World of the Huns, University of California Press, Berkeley, 1973.

H. I. MARROU
S. Augustin et la fin de la culture antique, 4th ed., Paris, 1958 (translated as *St Augustine and his Influence* [Men of Wisdom series], 1957).

J. MATTHEWS
Western Aristocracies and Imperial Court AD 364–425, Clarendon Press, Oxford, 1975.

H. MATTINGLY
Roman Coins, Methuen, 1928; 2nd ed., 1960.

S. MAZZARINO
La fine del mondo antico, Garzanti,

Milan, 1959 (translated as *The End of the Ancient World*, Faber and Faber, London, and Knopf, New York, 1966).

S. MAZZARINO
Stilicone: La crisi imperiale dopo Teodosio, Rome, 1942.

A. MOMIGLIANO (ed.)
The Conflict between Paganism and Christianity in the Fourth Century, Oxford University Press, 1963.

C. L. DE S. MONTESQUIEU
Considérations sur les causes de la grandeur des Romains et de leur décadence, Paris, 1734 (translated as *Considerations on the Causes of the Greatness of the Romans and their Decline*, Cornell, 1969).

L. MUSSET
The German Invasions, University Park, Pennsylvania, 1975.

K. L. NOETHLICHS
Die gesetzgeberischen Massnahmen der christlichen Kaiser des vierten Jahrhunderts, Köln University, 1971.

H. O. OSBORN
The Emergence of Christian Culture in the West, Harper, 1958.

J. R. PALANQUE
Le bas-empire, Presses Universitaires de France, Paris, 1971.

A. PAREDI
S. Ambrogio, Milan, 1960 (translated as *St Ambrose*, 1964).

A. PARRY (ed.)
Studies in Fifth-Century Thought and Literature (Yale Classical Studies, Vol. 22), 1972.

F. PASCHOUD
Roma Aeterna (Bibliotheca Helvetica Romana, Vol. 7), Institut Suisse, Rome 1967.

S. PEROWNE
The End of the Roman World, Hodder and Stoughton, 1966.

C. PHARR
The Theodosian Code and Novels and Sirmondian Constitutions, Princeton University Press, 1952.

A. PIGANIOL
L'empire chrétien, Presses Universitaires de France, Paris, 1947; 2nd ed., 1972.

J. D. RANDERS-PEHRSON
Barbarians and Romans: The Birth Struggle of Europe AD 400–700, University of Oklahoma Press, Norman, 1983.

W. REHM
Der Untergang Roms in abendländischen Denken (Das Erbe der Alten, Vol. 18), Leipzig, 1930.

R. REMONDON
La crise de l'empire romain, Presses Universitaires de France, Paris, 1964.

R. SEAGER
Ammianus Marcellinus: Seven Studies in his Language and Thought, University of Missouri Press, 1986.

O. SEECK
Geschichte des Untergangs der antiken Welt, Stuttgart, 1910–19.

E. STEIN
Geschichte des spätrömischen Reichs, I: Vom römischen zum byzantinischen Staate (284–476 n. Chr.), Vienna, 1928 (translated and revised as *Histoire du bas-empire*, Paris, 1959).

R. SYME
Ammianus and the Historia Augusta, Oxford University Press, 1968.

215

R. SYME
Emperors and Biography: Studies in the Historia Augusta, Oxford University Press, 1971.

M. TESTARD
S. Jérome, Les Belles Lettres, Paris, 1969.

E. A. THOMPSON
The Early Germans, Clarendon Press, Oxford, 1965.

E. A. THOMPSON
A History of Attila and the Huns, Oxford University Press, 1948, Greenwood Press, Westport, 1975.

E. A. THOMPSON
Romans and Barbarians: The Decline of the Western Empire, University of Wisconsin Press, Madison, 1982.

M. TODD
The Northern Barbarians 100 BC–AD 300, London, 1978.

J. VOGT
Der Niedergang Roms, Kindler, Zurich, 1965 (translated as *The Decline of Rome*, Weidenfeld and Nicolson, London, 1967).

J. VOGT
Kulturwelt und Barbaren: zum Menschheitsbild der spätantiken Gesellschaft (Akademie der Wissenschaften in Mainz), Steiner, Wiesbaden, 1967.

F. W. WALBANK
The Awful Revolution, Liverpool University Press, 1969.

J. M. WALLACE-HADRILL
The Barbarian West AD 400–1000, 3rd ed., London 1967.

M. A. WES
Das Ende des Kaisertums im Westen des römischen Reichs (translated from Dutch; Nederlands Historisch Instituut te Rome), Ministerie van Cultuur, Rijswijk, 1967.

L. WHITE (ed.)
The Transformation of the Roman World: Gibbon's Problem after Two Centuries (UCLA), University of California Press, 1966.

D. WOMERSLEY
The Transformation or the Decline and Fall of the Roman Empire, Cambridge University Press, 1989.

N. YOFFEE and G. L. COWGILL (eds.)
The Collapse of Ancient States and Civilizations, University of Arizona Press, 1988.

MAPS

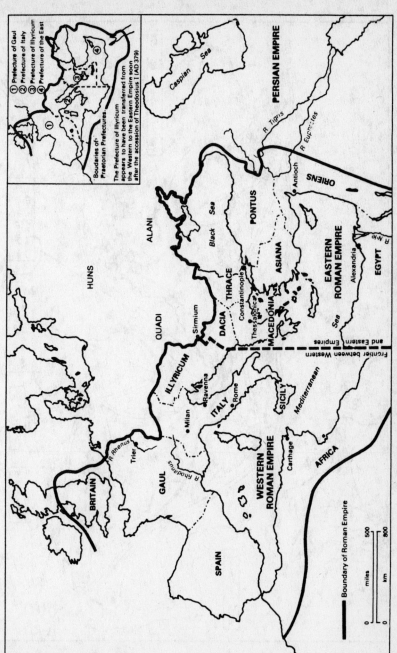

1. The Western and Eastern Empires AD 395

'Boundaries of Praetorian Prefectures

① Prefecture of Gaul
② Prefecture of Italy
③ Prefecture of Illyricum
④ Prefecture of the East

The Prefecture of Illyricum appears to have been transferred from the Western to the Eastern Empire soon after the accession of Theodosius I (AD 379)

Caspian Sea

PERSIAN EMPIRE

R. Tigris

R. Euphrates

Antioch

ORIENS

ALANI

Black Sea

PONTUS

HUNS

THRACE

DACIA

Constantinople

ASIANA

EASTERN ROMAN EMPIRE

QUADI

Sirmium

Thessalonica

MACEDONIA

Alexandria

EGYPT

R. Nile

Frontier between Western and Eastern Empires

ILLYRICUM

Ravenna

Rome

Sea

Milan

ITALY

SICILY

Mediterranean

R. Rhenus

Trier

GAUL

R. Rhodanus

BRITAIN

WESTERN ROMAN EMPIRE

Carthage

AFRICA

SPAIN

Boundary of Roman Empire

miles   0   500

km   0   800

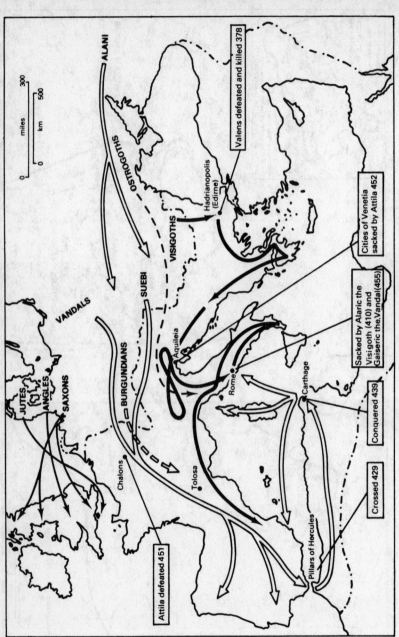

2. The Barbarian Invasions of the Fifth Century AD

ALANI

OSTROGOTHS

VISIGOTHS

SUEBI

VANDALS

BURGUNDIANS

JUTES

ANGLES

SAXONS

Chalons

Tolosa

Aquileia

Hadrianopolis (Edirne)

Rome

Carthage

Pillars of Hercules

Valens defeated and killed 378

Cities of Venetia sacked by Attila 452

Sacked by Alaric the Visigoth (410) and Gaiseric the Vandal (455)

Conquered 439

Crossed 429

Attila defeated 451

miles 300
0

km 500
0

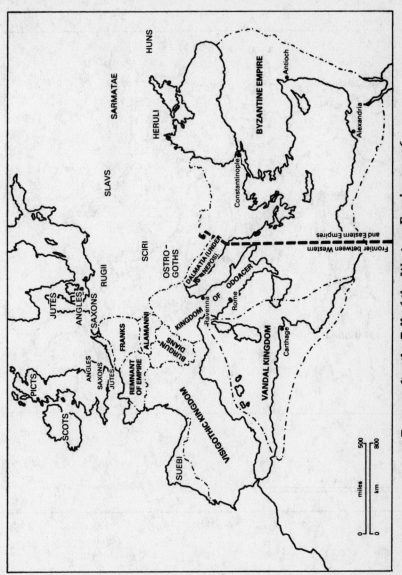

3. Europe after the Fall of the Western Empire AD 476

PICTS

SCOTS

JUTES
ANGLES
SAXONS

ANGLES
SAXONS
JUTES

REMNANT
OF EMPIRE

FRANKS

ALAMANNI

BURGUN-
DIANS

KINGDOM OF ODOACER

VISIGOTHIC KINGDOM

SUEBI

VANDAL KINGDOM

Carthage

Rome

Ravenna

DALMATIA (UNDER NEPOS)

OSTRO-GOTHS

SCIRI

RUGII

SLAVS

SARMATAE

HUNS

HERULI

Constantinople

BYZANTINE EMPIRE

Antioch

Alexandria

Frontier between Western and Eastern Empires

miles 0 500
km 0 800

4. Italy

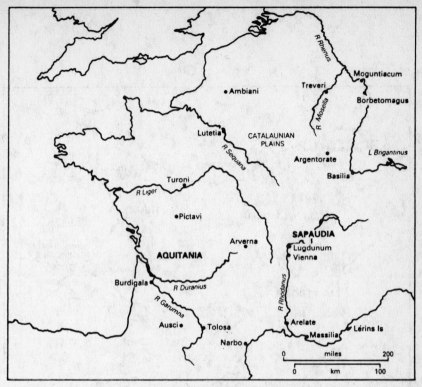

5. Gaul and the Rhine.

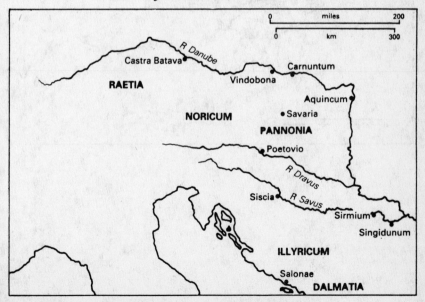

6. The Upper and Middle Danube.

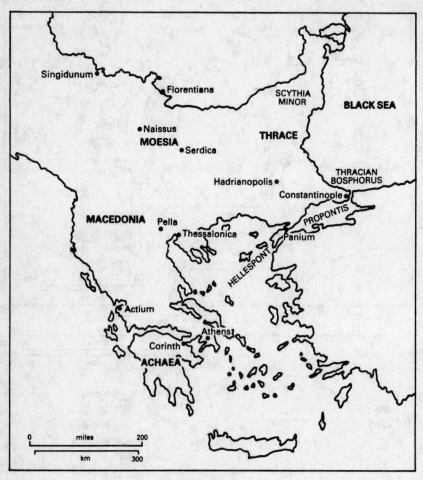

7. **The Balkans**

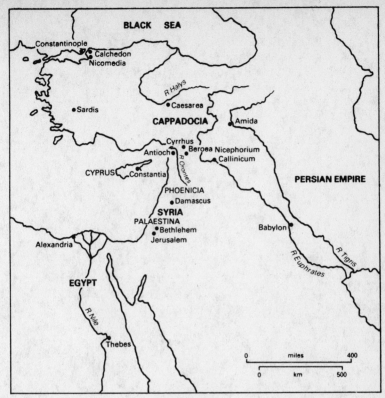

8. The East

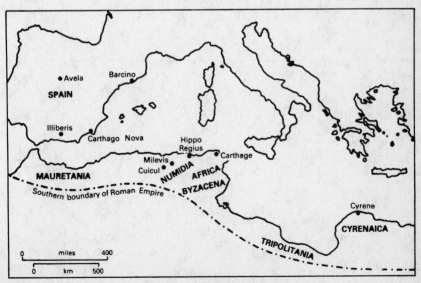

9. North Africa and Spain

Index